London,
Metropolis of
the Slave Trade

SHADES OF BLUE AND GRAY SERIES

Edited by Herman Hattaway and Jon L. Wakelyn

The Shades of Blue and Gray Series offers Civil War studies for the modern reader—Civil War buff and scholar alike. Military history today addresses the relationship between society and warfare. Thus biographies and thematic studies that deal with civilians, soldiers, and political leaders are increasingly important to a larger public. This series includes books that will appeal to Civil War Roundtable groups, individuals, libraries, and academics with a special interest in this era of American history.

Also by James A. Rawley

Edwin D. Morgan, 1811–1823: Merchant in Politics
*The American Civil War: An English View; The Writings of Field
    Marshal Viscount Wolseley* (editor)
Turning Points of the Civil War
*Race and Politics: "Bleeding Kansas" and the Coming of the
    Civil War*
Lincoln and Civil War Politics (editor)
The Politics of Union: Northern Politics during the Civil War
The Transatlantic Slave Trade: A History
Secession: The Disruption of the American Republic, 1844–1861
Abraham Lincoln and a Nation Worth Fighting For

London,
Metropolis of
the Slave Trade

James A. Rawley

UNIVERSITY OF MISSOURI PRESS
COLUMBIA AND LONDON

Copyright © 2003 by James A. Rawley
University of Missouri Press, Columbia, Missouri 65201
Printed and bound in the United States of America
All rights reserved
5 4 3 2 1   07 06 05 04 03

Library of Congress Cataloging-in-Publication Data

Rawley, James A.
   London, metropolis of the slave trade / James A. Rawley.
      p. cm — (Shades of blue and gray series)
Includes bibliographical references.
  ISBN 0-8262-1483-5 (alk. paper)
  1. Slave trade—England—London—History.
2. Slave traders—England—London—History.
3. London (England)—History—18th century.
4. London (England)—History—19th century.
I. Title. II. Series.
  HT1164.L7 R39 2003
  380.1'44'09421—dc21

                        2003010944

∞™ This paper meets the requirements of the
American National Standard for Permanence of Paper
for Printed Library Materials, Z39.48, 1984.

Designer: Stephanie Foley
Typesetter: The Composing Room of Michigan, Inc.
Printer and binder: The Maple-Vail Book Manufacturing Group
Typeface: Sabon

*To the History Department
University of Nebraska–Lincoln
faculty and staff,
with warm appreciation*

Contents

Foreword

BY DAVID ELTIS

The only substantial work on the London slave trade about the time that James Rawley began to explore the topic in the 1970s was Kenneth Davies's book on the Royal African Company. The RAC, as is well known, dominated the traffic from London in the late seventeenth century, just as the port of London dominated the slave trade from England, but thereafter, as Professor Rawley points out, scholars had assumed that patterns existed in the London slave trade that bore little relation to the reality that quickly emerged from his own work. The sheer size of London—it was the largest port in Europe long before it became involved in the slave trade—may have been one reason for popular and scholarly misconceptions. The slave trade was just one very small part of a vast number of overseas mercantile activities that were rooted in the capital. Bristol and Liverpool and several other ports on the continent rose to preeminence as the slave trade expanded, and for many researchers such a correlation seems to provide a dramatic and easy cause-and-effect story—though even this view fails to take into account what else was going on in these ports. By contrast, no one could argue that London's rise to preeminence was based on the slave trade. Not only was the slave trade a tiny fraction of all long-distance trade moving in and out of the Thames estuary in the eighteenth century, but the traffic to Africa had the largest non-slave-trade (or, in other words, produce) component of any port in the world that traded with Africa in the early modern period. Moreover, the major slaving ports of northwestern Europe, such as Nantes and Liverpool, got into the trade much later than did London, and the documentary evidence was therefore somewhat better than for

London. In particular, port books had survived for Bristol and Liverpool, but had been mostly destroyed for late-seventeenth- and eighteenth-century London.

Fortunately, none of this deterred James Rawley. Working without the incentive of direct competition, ferreting out private papers as well as the better-known public records, he has single-handedly revealed the extent and nature of slave trading in the British capital. He built his findings from the ground up using both official records and surviving business correspondence of leading merchants, as the present collection makes plain, but never forgetting the larger picture. He accumulated a database of voyages leaving London for Africa and then went out of his way to make such data available to others. When a group of us began to work on what became the Cambridge University Press CD-ROM transatlantic slave-trade database in 1992, he was one of the first to come forward with his own set of index cards, which he offered to us unconditionally. Most impressively, while working on the London slave trade, he published three books on nineteenth-century U.S. military and political history, as well as a survey of the transatlantic slave trade that has been updated and is shortly to be reissued.

How significant is the research encapsulated in the essays that follow? More recent work, which was greatly facilitated by Rawley's pioneering research, makes it possible to point to the London trade as not only the second largest among British ports, but also among the largest in the world. In terms of slaves carried from Africa by vessels leaving major ports of organization in Europe or the Americas, the London traffic is now estimated at almost twice the size of its Bristol counterpart, half again as large as that of the largest French port, Nantes, and greater than all slaving ports in the Netherlands combined. Only vessels leaving from Liverpool and Rio de Janeiro carried more slaves than London vessels, and possibly, too, those operating out of Bahia de Todos os Santos (now Salvador), if we include an allowance for the illegal slave trade after 1830. But both Brazilian ports, of course, were active in the slave trade for a much longer time span than was the port of London. No one could have had an inkling of this thirty years ago.

As well as charting the scale of these activities, Rawley's work also allows us to see the slave trade in all its complexity. Day-to-day decisions point to activities that have had little place in popular treatments of the slave trade. Thus, Humphry Morice's ships traded in Amsterdam before sailing to Africa, and their owner instructed his captains to try to sell slaves to the Portuguese for gold rather than carry their human purchases to the Americas. The merchants and captains that form the subject of this study, like the port of London itself, had financial interests that ranged far beyond the slave trade. Indeed, the direct, bilateral produce trade with Africa was far greater from London than it was from anywhere else in Europe. The subjects are captured in these essays as ordinary men wrestling with issues of making a living as well as the daily tensions between expediency and principle that we all face. Appalling as the slave trade was, they do not emerge as villains, and as for the most part they lived and died prior to the abolitionist era with its reshaping of the economic and moral context of society, this is entirely appropriate. To present them as such is to offer a major insight into an era that most of the general public and, increasingly, many historians have great difficulty understanding. The recognition that ordinary people could and did trade in slaves, as well as the fact that ordinary people became slaves, is, indeed, the beginning of comprehending the enormity of the forced migration of eleven million people and the attendant deaths of many more.

But the sweep of the essays over nearly two centuries also allows the perceptive reader to chart the shift in attitudes toward the slave trade. Two of the case studies are set in a period when there is no hint of the slave trade being regarded as a business different from any other. Three more involve careers that reach into the abolitionist era, and, fascinatingly, yield three very different outcomes in response to the new pressures. One slave trader, John Newton, becomes an abolitionist and equates his earlier slaving voyages as evidence of a profoundly sinful life. Another, Henry Laurens, also comes to reject the trade, but from the perspective of Charleston in the Revolutionary War period. He comes to see the traffic as having been imposed by the British. A third, Archibald Dalzel, is certainly aware of the new environment at the end of his long life, but fights to maintain both the slave trade and his own interest in it. The final case involves Nathaniel Gordon, who, like Dalzel, persisted in a trade that was by then illegal, but who paid for it with his life. Although he was the only individual in the Atlantic world to be executed for slave trading, his story is a highly appropriate conclusion to the collection. Gordon's case carries us into an era that, in its attitudes toward the slave trade, at least, is almost familiar.

A further theme that emerges is the complexity of the ties that linked London with the Atlantic slave trade. London's connections with Senegambia and the Gold Coast have received insufficient attention. The city's financial role is obviously rather better known, but the Henry Laurens connections described here give a nice microscopic view of how the credit the city supplied undergirded the slave trade. Moreover, while London's role as a center of abolitionism is well known, the fact that London was perhaps even more important than Liverpool as a center of the defense of the slave trade has remained largely hidden. As with all of the best historical writing, Rawley's essays show that the reality of eras other than our own is much more complicated and interesting than most of the better-known conceptions of that reality, and more important, that there are no easy interpretations possible once one moves beyond recognition of the moral enormity of Europeans carrying so many unwilling Africans to the Americas.

The publication of these essays, three of which have not previously appeared in print, thus provides insight not only into one of the world's largest slave-trading operations, but also into the environment in which slave-trading expeditions were organized, and, most of all, into how that environment changed rather suddenly. Most of the works published on slavery and the slave trade today, many with much larger pretensions than these essays project, do not achieve half as much.

Preface

Over a score of years I have written a number of essays and given talks on the Atlantic slave trade. The University of Missouri Press has invited me to bring these together to form a book. The contents complement my book *The Transatlantic Slave Trade: A History* published by W. W. Norton in 1981 and soon to be reissued by the University of Nebraska Press.

The sweep of the material extends through the years from 1700 into the American Civil War. The chapters explore the role of London in the slave trade, its activity as a port of departure for ships bound for Africa, its continuing large volume after the trade shifted to Bristol and Liverpool, and as a port whose parliamentary representatives, in sharp opposition to the abolitionist movement quartered there, defended the trade.

Four Londoners figure in the book: Humphry Morice, slave merchant, governor of the Bank of England, and owner of no less than fifty-three slave ships during his career; Richard Harris, slave merchant and spokesman for the London slaving community, who plied a brisk trade in slaves to Jamaica and elsewhere; Archibald Dalzel, slave-ship captain, owner of slave ships, and historian of Dahomey, an African source of slaves; and John Newton, slave-ship captain, Anglican priest, composer of the hymn "Amazing Grace," and, late in his career, a vigorous opponent of the trade. London also appears as home port of the slave ship *Henrietta Marie,* which in 1700 sank off the coast of Key West, Florida.

On the American side of the Atlantic, two very different figures are examined. Henry Laurens, an eighteenth-century Charleston slave merchant, was closely tied to the London slaving community, especially to Richard Oswald. The two men sat at the peace talks that preceded the end of the American Revolution. The other

American is Captain Nathaniel Gordon, who was caught by a U.S. naval vessel in 1860 while plying an illegal slave trade, becoming the first and only American to be executed under a law enacted four decades earlier. Despite pleas to President Lincoln for clemency, he was hanged in public in New York in 1862.

The book includes chapters on the London and American slave trades, and concludes with a chapter from my book *The Transatlantic Slave Trade* that sums up the book's contents.

This work offers the perspective that history does change, as facts accumulate, historians' interests alter, and new generations' eyes view the materials and their relevance to the times and to the needs of historians. A typical textbook on British history would mention Sir John Hawkins, the *asiento* (trading privileges exacted from Spain, of little actual consequence to the volume of the trade), and abolition of the trade in 1807, while neglecting Great Britain's role in transporting huge numbers of Africans to the Americas. A typical textbook on U.S. history, at least until recently, would recognize the first importation of Africans from a Dutch trader in 1619, the Constitution's compromise assuring federal restraint from abolition for twenty years, the law of 1807 making the trade illegal, and the actual closing of the trade in 1862 by diplomacy, signaled by the execution of the slave-ship captain Nathaniel Gordon.

The Atlantic slave trade in fact was a crucial element in the history of Britain, the United States, and the Western Hemisphere. For the British it provided an outlet for textiles, liquor, guns, and other exports. It expanded British manufacturing and shipping and offered an early example of free trade. For the people of the United States it added the black race to the white population; provided a labor force that in early years produced cotton, rice, and tobacco; occasioned a constitutional crisis; separated the North and South; challenged American values; and shaped the course of the nation's history. Elsewhere in the Western Hemisphere it swelled the population by millions and provided labor for producing sugar, mining gold, and other work.

The present book is more than a collection of previously published writings. The chapters on Laurens and Newton have not been published elsewhere. The chapter on the *Henrietta Marie* is my contribution to a volume about that vessel that is yet to be published. Further, this collection contains new and significant material drawn from the recently released *Trans-Atlantic Slave Trade: A Database on CD-ROM* (Cambridge University Press, 1999). Edited by the eminent slave-trade scholars David Eltis, Stephen D. Behrendt, and others, it provides documents on 27,233 slaving voyages. The editors estimate that 12 million Africans suffered a forced migration between 1519 and 1867. Their database is the most important contribution to the history of the trade in three decades, and illuminates the activity of the merchants and voyages presented here.

London,
Metropolis of
the Slave Trade

I

The Transatlantic Slave Trade

A SURVEY

This chapter was written for a book not yet published, a work on the London slave vessel *Henrietta Marie,* which sank off Key West, Florida, in 1700. The chapter explains the development in the early eighteenth century of the Atlantic system framed by Europe, Africa, and the Americas. It was an economic system that importantly produced sugar and tobacco, as well as gold and other commodities, by means of a massive migration of Africans from their homelands to the New World, where they were sold into slavery and forced to perform hard labor.

Portugal pioneered in the trade, France followed, and England soon entered. London, the political capital, was the site of a government monopoly, the Royal African Company, which saw investors prosper and perish. London also witnessed a struggle over the principles of monopoly versus free enterprise. Breaking the royal monopoly heralded a change in the British economic outlook.

The *Henrietta Marie* was probably owned by a group of investors, a common way of pooling capital and sharing risk. Thomas Starke, wealthy owner of five Virginia tobacco plantations, presumably was the largest investor. In September 1699, the vessel sailed from London to the Bight of Biafra. In that region it acquired 235 slaves. In May 1700 it disembarked 190 slaves in Jamaica. Forty-five more slaves disembarked before the vessel sailed the next month and was shipwrecked off Key West. Not until the twentieth century was the wreck discovered and placed, along with recovered artifacts, in the Mel Fisher Maritime Museum, Key West.

≈

This chapter is published with the very kind permission of Dr. Madeleine Burnside, executive director of the Mel Fisher Maritime Heritage Society, Inc.

I

When in 1620 the English trader Richard Jobson went up the Gambia River in West Africa, a native merchant named Buckor Sano offered to sell him slaves. Jobson indignantly replied, he later wrote, that "[w]e were a people, who did not deale in any such commodities, neither did we buy or sell one another, or any that had our own shapes."[1]

Only three decades later the English were briskly buying and selling Africans, supplying labor to their newly founded American empire. By the eighteenth century the English had come to dominate the transatlantic slave trade, and not until 1807, after a bitter twenty-year struggle, did the members of the English Parliament abolish the nefarious traffic in their own shapes. By that time the Western world had dramatically changed, with many millions of Africans toiling in servitude in the Americas, in a plantation regime made by white masters. Africa was undergoing changes that are still not fully understood by historians; Europe was consuming sugar, tobacco, and other commodities; and white men in Europe and America were accumulating wealth as a result of a new economic system.

This system, which in turn encouraged the growth of democracy for white people in the United Kingdom and the colonies that became the United States, was made possible by slave labor. Forced African labor, especially when applied to the cultivation of sugar, wrought vast changes in the Atlantic world made up of Europe, Africa, and the Americas. Europe's sweet tooth craved sugar, which was almost unknown to most Europeans before the transatlantic trade. England was the major consumer, and as early as 1660, only decades after acquiring islands in the Caribbean, sugar was England's most valuable import from her American colonies.[2]

Slavery itself was not new. Mentioned in the Bible, practiced by ancient Greeks and Romans, functioning in the Mediterranean basin as well as in Africa, it had a long history. Slavery in the Americas, however, differed from earlier forms of slavery: it was derived from a single source, Africa; it was racial, exclusively black; and it was more harsh than the institution known by most earlier unfree peoples.

1. Elizabeth Donnan, ed., *Documents Illustrative of the History of the Slave Trade to America*, 4 vols. (Washington: Carnegie Institution, 1930–1935), 1:79.
2. D. A. Farnie, "The Commercial Empire of the Atlantic, 1607–1783," *Economic History Review*, 2d ser., 15 (1962): 210.

Europeans long tried to satisfy their craving for sweetness with honey and rarely tasted sugar imported from the Middle East or North Africa. Toward the close of the Middle Ages the Mediterranean island of Cyprus became a large grower of sugar for the European market. Mediterranean sugar growing was characterized by both the plantation unit of production, in which laborers worked in gangs under close supervision, and slavery as a labor system.

The fateful westward shift of sugar cultivation resulted from the Age of Discovery. How to sail south along the West African coast had long baffled mariners. Adverse northeast trade winds and strong southward ocean currents barred navigation below the Sahara. Discovery of a return route to Europe by sailing northwest far enough to catch westward winds made possible the Portuguese exploration of West Africa and the nearby Atlantic islands.[3]

The enterprising Portuguese quickly turned to sugar growing in the lush islands of Madeira and the Canaries. European navigational skill, capital, and experience in sugar production opened a new source. The plantation system and easily available African slave labor formed part of the transplanted economy.

All this had begun well before Columbus discovered America. But within thirty years after Columbus's first voyage the island of Hispaniola was exporting sugar back home to Spain. Sugar growing falteringly spread through the Spanish West Indies, hampered by the high death rate of the native Indian population, who were enslaved, coerced, and victimized by unfamiliar diseases.

The sugar empire next leaped to the mainland of South America, where the Portuguese learned they could grow sugar on the northeastern coast of Brazil. They resolved the labor problem not only by capturing Indians but also by carrying Africans across the South Atlantic to the extensive plantations on the fertile and broad Brazilian plains. The African laborer was not a mere captive but a commodity bought in a slave market. He was seen as property, an investment, a cipher in an accounting book, a unit of production.

The success of sugar plantations worked by imported African slaves impelled a vast expansion of the American sugar dominions.

3. F. W. Bovill, *The Golden Trade of the Moors,* 2d ed. (London: Oxford University Press, 1970), 112–19.

The Dutch, striving for empire and independence from Spain, conquered the sugar-growing region of Brazil and, holding it for nearly a quarter of a century, carried the lucrative plantation system, worked by African slaves, to the Caribbean. For their part the English appropriated St. Kitts and Antigua in the Lesser Antilles, and in a war with Spain seized the large island of Jamaica. The French took present-day Haiti on Hispaniola, as well as other islands. The "sugar revolution" had taken place, the center of cultivation having moved from the Mediterranean to the British and French West Indies, overtaking Portuguese, Brazilian, and Spanish contenders. By 1700 nearly three-quarters of the population of the British West Indies was African.[4]

An Atlantic commercial system comprising Europe, Africa, and the Americas had emerged, changing the face of the Western world. Exports of fish and fur predominated in the northern colonies of the western Atlantic, tobacco—the "hellish weed"—in the Chesapeake, and sugar—above all, sugar—in the Caribbean. Two of these three regions depended on African labor. For the British West Indian sugar growers a guaranteed market existed in Great Britain, consumer of one-third of all sugar entering Europe in the eighteenth century and protected by a heavy duty on foreign sugar. European capital, manufacture, shipping, credit, and insurance (and processing in the instance of sugar), African slavery, and American plantations formed the essentials of the system.[5]

It was a vastly extended system, its three corners separated by thousands of miles, unlike any the world had known. Why was it that laborers were transplanted across a wide ocean to work in America? The answer usually advanced is that black slave labor was cheaper than white labor, even that of indentured servants available for a term of years in return for ocean passage. African slave labor was indeed cheap. At the end of the seventeenth century British planters could buy a slave for the worth of 600 pounds of raw sugar on the London market. British slave merchants could buy a slave for the worth of sixteen guns.[6]

    4. Philip D. Curtin et al., *African History* (Boston: Little, Brown, 1978), 213–21; Farnie, "Commercial Empire," 211.
    5. Ralph Davis, *The Rise of the Atlantic Economies* (London: Weidenfeld and Nicolson, 1973), 255.
    6. Philip D. Curtin, "The Slave Trade and the Atlantic Basin," in *Key Issues in the*

But the cost of labor, important as it was, was only one factor behind the awkward arrangement of transporting millions of workers from the African continent to the distant Americas. Another factor was differences in disease environments. Native Americans who were exposed to diseases brought by whites died in dreadful numbers, reducing the local labor supply. So too did Europeans exposed to diseases in the tropics, particularly malaria and yellow fever. Africans, though they suffered a heavy mortality in America, enjoyed a much lower death rate than Europeans, having developed a degree of immunity to tropical diseases.[7]

Another factor helps explain the continuing flow of Africans into the New World. It is the unbalance of sexes, the larger proportion of men over women purchased in Africa. In general planters preferred young males, with their greater strength, to women and children. The low proportion of women, perhaps only one-third, diminished the possible birth rate in America. The low rate of birth, high rate of mortality in both infants and adults, harsh form of labor, scant knowledge of tropical medicine, and ready access to low-cost replacements fostered a prolonged reliance on African slave labor.[8]

We must consider one further factor—white racism. By the seventeenth century Englishmen had come to believe that Africans were inferior. An ethnocentrism emphasizing skin color—black standing for evil and the powers of darkness—set Africans apart not only from Englishmen but from red-skinned Native Americans. An English observer said that Africans "in colour so in condition are little other than Devils incarnate." An early impression of blacks was of "a people of beastly living, without a God, lawe, religion, or common wealth." With such factors at work, until the opening of the nineteenth century the Great Migration westward across the broad Atlantic was from Africa, not Europe.[9]

Afro-American Experience, 2 vols., ed. Nathan I. Huggins et al. (New York: Harcourt, Brace, 1971), 1:88.

7. Philip D. Curtin, "Epidemiology and the Slave Trade," *Political Science Quarterly* 83: (1968), 190–216.

8. David W. Galenson, *Traders, Planters and Slaves: Market Behavior in Early English America* (Cambridge and New York: Cambridge University Press, 1986); David Eltis and Stanley L. Engerman, "Was the Slave Trade Dominated by Men?" *Journal of Interdisciplinary History* 23 (autumn 1992): 237–57.

9. Winthrop D. Jordan, *White over Black* (Baltimore: Penguin Books, 1969), 24–25.

So far as Africa south of the Sahara was concerned, it was long unknown, a dark continent that barred access to the wealth of the East Indies. The first "scramble for Africa," starting in the seventeenth century and followed by a second scramble in the nineteenth and twentieth centuries, had a distinctive pattern. It did not aim for territorial annexation, settlement by Europeans, cultivation of lands, or dominion over conquered peoples. It was restricted to West Africa, omitting South Africa and East Africa except for Mozambique and Madagascar. It produced fierce rivalries, as Portugal, the Dutch Republic, France, and Great Britain competed in the quest for black workers.

How may this peculiar pattern be accounted for? One element was the existence of trade commodities—gold, slaves, pepper, ivory, etc.—that did not require exploitation of labor as did sugar, produced under white supervision. A second element was the presence of a native population that did not need to be conquered and enslaved as Native Americans were, but was of greatest utility by being left in its traditional role, providing commodities for export. The danger of disease barred access to interior markets. White traders found it far better to deal with Africans, paying their tolls and prices, than to vanquish the rulers and merchants who readily supplied what they desired. At the end of the seventeenth century only a few thousand whites resided in tropical Africa. On the Gold Coast, a center of English activity, only about 140 men occupied the forts and settlements in 1695. European influence in general flowed from a scattered configuration along the West African seaboard. An exception was Portugal, which sent out substantial numbers of men to settle in Portuguese-occupied areas to trade with the Africans.[10]

Portugal held a monopoly on trade with Africa until the middle of the sixteenth century, about a full century after the first explorations. When its Iberian rival, Spain, discovered the New World, the two Catholic countries allowed the papacy—wielder of international authority—to divide their discoveries. In 1493 Alexander VI issued a bull, followed by a treaty, that gave Portugal claim to Africa and Brazil, and Spain the remainder of the Americas, in-

10. K. G. Davies, *The Royal African Company* (London: Longmans, Green, 1957), 1–16, 247.

cluding the West Indies—excluding her from Africa, whose value as a source of labor was not yet recognized.[11]

The other European nations did not allow Portugal and Spain to hold their monopolies on Africa and America unchallenged. France was probably the first to poach in African waters, dispatching ships to Cape Verde and the Senegal and Gambia Rivers. Successful in procuring slaves in Portuguese Africa, France wrested valuable islands in Spanish America: Guadeloupe, Martinique, and St. Domingue on the western third of Hispaniola. The interconnections of West Africa, the French West Indies, sugar, and slavery formed the heart of the French colonial empire.[12]

The Dutch, aspiring to seapower, commerce, and empire, defied the Portuguese monopoly by acquiring the later notorious slave depot of Goree Island with its access to the Gambia trade, and making settlements on the Gold Coast. In 1638 they seized the fortress of Elmina ("the mine") and made it the headquarters of Dutch activity in West Africa. They also briefly occupied a portion of the Angola coast and of the Brazilian coast. In the West Indies they acquired Curaçao, St. Eustatius, and Tobago—all more important for the slave trade and other commerce than for sugar. By the middle of the seventeenth century the aggressive Dutch were perhaps the most formidable European power in Africa.[13]

England, aspiring to the riches of commercial empire, early in the seventeenth century explored the Gambia River region, questing in vain for gold. Englishmen soon acquired a fort on James Island, at the mouth of the river; in ensuing decades they established a string of settlements on the Gold Coast, particularly Cape Coast, a strong fort that became a center of English slaving in the Gulf of Guinea. The Gambia and the Gold Coast became nuclei of English enterprise in Africa.

---

11. James A. Rawley, *The Transatlantic Slave Trade: A History* (New York: W. W. Norton, 1981), 1–50.

12. Robert Louis Stein, *The French Slave Trade in the Eighteenth Century: An Old Regime Business* (Madison: University of Wisconsin Press, 1979), 3–12; Rawley, *Transatlantic Slave Trade*, 125–47.

13. Rawley, *Transatlantic Slave Trade*, 125–47; Ernst van den Boogaart and Pieter C. Emmer, "The Dutch Participation in the Atlantic Slave Trade, 1596–1650," in *The Uncommon Market: Essays in the Economic History of the Atlantic Slave Trade,* ed. Henry A. Gemery and Jan S. Hogendorn (New York: Academic Press, 1979), 353–75.

Nor did England lag behind in finding footholds in the West Indies. It took possession of islands small and large, including fertile Barbados in the southeast Caribbean—the first landfall of ships from Africa—and Jamaica, huge in size, rich in potential as a sugar producer, and near the Spanish market for reexport of slaves.[14]

Other small European nations—Denmark, Sweden, and German states—gained toeholds in Africa, and the first of these, Denmark, in the West Indies. By the last quarter of the seventeenth century four European nations—Portugal, the Netherlands, France, and England—maintained a presence in West Africa. In the West Indies, Spain, the Netherlands, France, and England occupied islands dependent on African slave labor.

The European nations had thrust themselves into Africa and America by occupation, purchase, and conquest. The Dutch had fought the Portuguese in both worlds, gaining strategic places for the slave trade. They had also fought the English in a series of wars, the second of these witnessing the first important fighting at Goree and the Gold Coast. By the end of the seventeenth century France and England were mortal rivals in a titanic struggle involving the European balance of power, commerce, empire, and maritime supremacy. The struggle endured for a century and a quarter, ending only at Waterloo.

In the first of these conflicts, the War of the League of Augsburg (1689–1697), West Africa was the theater of warfare. The English governor at Gambia seized the strategic islands of Goree and St. Louis. France retaliated by capturing James Fort, gaining control of the Gambia River. In the war's course France and England made prizes of one another's ships. The *Henrietta Marie* was apparently one prize taken in this war. By the Treaty of Ryswick in 1697 the seized territories were restored to their former possessors. But Anglo-French rivalry persisted during the peacetime years before war was renewed in late 1701. France continued to seize English slave ships, and it seems likely that the *Henrietta Marie* made its long, out-of-the way voyage off the Florida coast in order to escape French depredation.[15]

Well before the end of the seventeenth century all the sugar

14. Bovill, *Golden Trade*, 125; Davies, *Royal African Company*, 240, 45.
15. Rawley, *Transatlantic Slave Trade*, 149–69; Donnan, *Documents*, 1:445–51.

grown in English dominions was imported into England and the highly competitive Dutch had been excluded from the British empire. Parliament had so decreed and the Crown had conferred a monopoly of the African trade upon the Royal African Company. Wealth flowed into England, the outcome of exporting commodities to Africa, selling slaves in America, and importing sugar into England. No longer a luxury, sugar became a staple of confectioners, household bakers, and drinkers of tea and coffee.

When skeptics, including physicians, raised questions about the effects of sugar on the human body, including tooth decay and diabetes, Dr. Frederick Slare sprang to defend the sweet import. In his 1715 work entitled *A Vindication of Sugars . . . Dedicated to the Ladies,* Dr. Slare argued that sugar was a cure-all, valuable even as a dentifrice and appreciated by females, whose palates were more refined than those of males. He sang the praises of the West India merchant "who loads his Ship with this sweet treasure. By this commodity have Numbers of Persons, of inconsiderable Estates, rais'd Plantations, and from thence have gain'd such Wealth, as to return to their native Country very Rich, and have purchas'd, and do daily purchase, greate Estates."[16]

For a century and a half, until overtaken by cotton in 1820, sugar was Great Britain's largest import. The cost of sugar declined, the British population increased, consumption spread to embrace the poor, and the navy in 1731 authorized a half-pint of rum (a by-product of sugar) to each man per day. Historian Richard B. Sheridan estimates that sugar consumption increased fourfold between 1660 and 1700. In 1690 Sir Dalby Thomas, an English economist, said the greatest consumers of sugar were "the Rich and Opulent People of the Nation." A third of a century later, as the drinking of tea and coffee grew, a writer in the *Barbados Gazette* linked the rise in sugar consumption to the widening popularity of those beverages.[17]

West Indian fortunes, created by sugar and slaves, produced a British West India planter class, usually resident in England, that

16. Sidney W. Mintz, *Sweetness and Power: The Place of Sugar in Modern History* (New York: Penguin, 1985), 106–8.
17. Mintz, *Sweetness and Power,* 170, 160; Richard B. Sheridan, *Sugar and Slavery: An Economic History of the British West Indies, 1623–1775* (Baltimore: Johns Hopkins University Press, 1973), 21, 28.

became a power in Parliament, protective of its island interests and defensive about the merits of the slave trade. The merchants and planters who benefited from the sugar revolution lived lavishly in London. In stark contrast to the sweating Africans in the Caribbean, they flaunted their wealth through their great houses, finery, banquets and other entertainment, bribery of voters, and splendid carriages. King George III, on seeing a West Indian planter's expensive carriage and liveried servants, which were equal to his own, is said to have snorted to his prime minister, "Sugar, sugar, eh?—all that sugar! How are the duties, eh, Pitt, how are the duties?"[18]

At the turn of the century, when the *Henrietta Marie* was plying the slave trade, London was the center of British slaving. The capital of the nation, boasting a population of about 674,000, it was the country's largest port, its financial center, the hub of its international commerce. The Bank of England was organized in 1695, with insurers and shipping interests, both shipbuilding and owning, concentrated here. The bulk of the country's imports and exports flowed through the port of London. Not to be overlooked was the presence of substantial manufacturing and processing industries. Though sugar was grown in distant islands, from the late sixteenth century London was the refining center not only for Great Britain but also for Europe. The political, economic, as well as cultural capital, London was the great metropolis, dominating the English slave trade. It was about this time that an agreement was made in London to furnish the Spanish West Indies with slaves from Jamaica. London had the further advantages of enjoying a monopoly of the East India Trade with its textiles prized by Africans, large warehousing facilities, and a national policy that sometimes prevented use of the outports for both imports and exports.[19]

The economic thought of the time has been named the theory of mercantilism. Its doctrines looked to national self-sufficiency in a competitive, warring world. This goal was to be attained by restricting manufacturing to the mother country, acquiring colonies that supplied commodities not produced at home, maintaining a fleet useful in both peace and war, and having an excess of exports

18. Quoted in Mintz, *Sweetness and Power*, 156.
19. M. Dorothy George, *London Life in the Eighteenth Century* (New York: Capricorn Books, 1965), 24; Mintz, *Sweetness and Power*, 147; David MacPherson, *Annals of Commerce*, 4 vols. (London: Nichols & Son, 1805), 2:638.

over imports. A favorable balance of trade would result in the flow of bullion into the mother country. A strong company endowed with special powers and privileges seemed the best solution for promoting foreign trade. All slaving nations employed the privileged company as the means of conducting the slave trade. Portugal as early as 1481, the Netherlands in 1621, and France in 1633 made the trade a privileged one.[20]

England followed suit; after failed attempts at chartered companies earlier in the century, the Crown—not the Parliament—in 1672 gave the Royal African Company the monopoly of the African trade. Charles II, recognizing that the trade was "of great advantage to our subjects of this Kingdom," conferred sole rights upon the company for one thousand years, requiring delivery of two elephants to him and his heirs whenever the company set foot in the territories mentioned in the charter.[21]

From early days private traders—called interlopers or separate traders—illegally entered the trade. The Royal African Company proved to be a troubled and unpopular monopoly. Put to the expense of maintaining forts in Africa, criticized for failing to deliver adequate numbers of slaves to some colonies (especially in North America), suffering from losses during the 1689–1697 war, unable to compete with the separate traders who did not have to maintain forts, the company was assailed by the separate traders, merchants and manufacturers whose only legal market for African exports was the company, and dissatisfied West Indian colonists. The company lost its monopoly in 1698; the Glorious Revolution of 1688 had in fact discredited and suspended the royal charter.[22]

Antimonopoly sentiment was developing at this time—a century before Adam Smith gave classic formulation to free-trade doctrines in *The Wealth of Nations*. A number of economists voiced opinions opposing monopoly and, peering somewhat dimly toward free trade, favored increased production of sugar and other commodities with slave labor. Dalby Thomas, the economist, governor of Jamaica, and author of *An Historical Account of the Rise and Growth of the West India Colonies,* in 1690 argued for ending the

20. Davies, *Royal African Company,* 122–35.
21. Donnan, *Documents,* 1:178; the charter is on pp. 177–92.
22. Davies, *Royal African Company,* 122–35.

Royal African Company's monopoly. He declared, "[B]efore Sugars were produc'd in our Colonies, it bore four times the Price it does now" and went on to assert that the New England colonies, "could they readily get Negroes from Guinea," would become large-scale consumers of English wares, especially iron tools such as hoes and axes, and materials for ships. John Cary, writing five years later in his influential *Essay on Trade,* added his criticism of the monopoly: it required ready payment by the planters, while the separate traders offered long-term credit. The monopoly was unable to supply sufficient slaves and was generally inadequate, he concluded. Not long after, Daniel Defoe championed the extension of credit, which makes "the whole kingdom trade for many millions more than the national species can amount to." J. Pollexfen, in *A Discourse of Trade* (1697), pointed to the riches acquired in a short time from the colonies and asserted that *"the Original of moveable Riches is from Labour,* and that it may arise from the Labour of Blacks and Vagrants, if well managed."[23]

These thinkers based their arguments for a freer trade on the continued existence of the African slave trade and employment of cheap, black labor. The present-day reader is struck by the absence of humanity and morality in all this discourse. A few years later, when a bill for settling the trade to Africa came before a House of Commons committee, it included a provision for "the instruction of the negroes in the plantations, in the knowledge of the Christian religion." The Commons ignored the matter and, intent upon the lucrative slave trade, urged Queen Anne, "That she would be pleased to give directions, That such ships of war be appointed for protecting the trade to Africa as might be necessary for the preservation and security thereof."[24]

Parliament sought to resolve the dispute between the company and the separate traders in the Act of 1698. The act asserted that the

23. Mintz, *Sweetness and Power,* 40–41; Thomas quoted in William Darity Jr., "A Model of 'Original Sin': Rise of the West and Lag of the Rest," *American Economic Review* 82 (May 1992): 164 (though Darity transposes his name); Cary cited in Frank Wesley Pitman, *The Development of the British West Indies, 1700–1763* (New Haven: Yale University Press, 1917), 64; Daniel Defoe, *The Complete English Tradesman,* 2 vols., 2d ed. (1727; reprint, New York: A. M. Kelley, 1969), 1:33; Pollexfen quoted in Mintz, *Sweetness and Power,* 236.

24. *Cobbett's Parliamentary History of England from the Earliest Period to the Year 1803,* 36 vols. (London: T. Curson Hansard, 1806–1820), 6:896–97.

forts and castles were "undoubtedly necessary," siding with the company, and requiring the separate traders to contribute to their upkeep by paying a duty of 10 percent *ad valorem* on all exports to Africa. The separate traders, for their part, now could legally trade along the coast of West Africa, using the forts for protection and other privileges and erecting their own. The law disappointed both sides: the company, which had to recognize the legality of private trading, and the separate traders, who had to pay a duty on a trade they had been plying without a tax. Because most of the separate traders did not use the forts, relying instead on naval protection, they saw no gain in making the forts available. Discord, with rival claims in Parliament, continued until the middle of the eighteenth century.[25]

The new law almost exactly coincided with a jump in sugar prices. The rise began in 1700 and continued for several years. At the same time, the price of slaves to planters sharply increased. The separate traders vastly extended their trade, outpacing the company. A survey taken of the colonial governors a decade after the act revealed that the separate traders had imported about 75,000 slaves into the colonies, while the company had brought in only 18,000. The lush sugar islands of Jamaica and Barbados received the bulk of the black cargoes, taking 61,000 from the first group and 16,000 from the second.[26]

Separate traders, nearly all Londoners, participated in the trade in considerable numbers. During the decade 1702–1712, Robert Heysham, concerned in the Barbados trade, led in exporting goods to Africa, in nine of those years consigning £33,920 worth; Richard Harris, who became the principal spokesman of the separate traders as the acrimonious controversy with the company persisted, stood second, in nine years consigning £25,121 worth of goods. Isaac Milner, also active as a lobbyist for the separate traders, came third, in ten years consigning £21,475 worth of goods to the African coast. Many merchants took part in only one or two voyages and, it is to be stressed, engaged in the African trade only as a small part of their business.[27]

25. Donnan, *Documents*, 1:421–29; Rawley, *Transatlantic Slave Trade*, 161–64.
26. Public Record Office, *Calendar of State Papers, Colonial Series, America and West Indies, 1708–1709* (London, 1922); Davies, *Royal African Company*, 142–43, 336.
27. Davies, *Royal African Company*, 372–73; see also chap. 4 of this book.

The separate traders customarily pooled their capital in ships and goods, shared in insuring voyages, and had risk and profits in fractions, often one-sixth. Jean Barbot, a French Huguenot who fled to England after religious toleration was revoked in France, described a voyage to the Rio Real river in 1699 "aboard the *Albion* frigate, a ship belonging to the British government, then call'd the *Dover Prize,* which some merchants of London and I bought of the commissioners of the navy in 1698, and fitted out for New Calabar [in present-day Nigeria], with twenty-four guns, sixty men, and a cargo of two thousand six hundred pounds sterling." The *Albion* over a period of three and a half months purchased 583 slaves, whom it transported to Jamaica.[28]

Less fortunate for Barbot and his London coinvestors was the 1697 voyage of the frigate *Griffin,* which within three months after departing London bought 350 New Calabar slaves. As the *Griffin* sailed down the Rio Real channel, through the neglect of its officers it struck a bar and the entire crew abandoned ship, leaving it with full sail and the slaves still aboard. The ship tossed in the channel for three days until the African king of Bardy rescued from their misery the few survivors, who, helped by a Portuguese ship, made their way to England. The investors, expecting good news from Jamaica, where slaves were then selling for forty pounds a man, were greatly surprised to hear of the Africans' arrival in London.[29]

The instructions given to the ship *Blessing,* which cleared from Liverpool in late 1700—about the time of the *Henrietta Marie*'s fatal voyage—are revealing. The owners possessed a good deal of knowledge about markets, both African and American, behavior of crews, and what commodities they wanted returned to England. They repeatedly urged speed, aware of the heavy investment involved and eager to shorten the length of time before profits were in their pockets.

The *Blessing,* under Captain Thomas Brownbell, had a supercargo, John Murray, who managed the business of buying and selling slaves and a ship's doctor who was experienced in the trade.

---

28. P. E. H. Hair, ed., *Barbot on Guinea: The Writings of Jean Barbot on West Africa, 1678–1712,* 2 vols. (London: Hakluyt Society, 1992), 2:676, 704 n. 16.
29. Ibid., 679.

The captain and the supercargo were instructed to proceed first to the Gold Coast and, if finding "no Encouragement" there, to go directly to Whydah. "Slave yr ship to her full Reach, if you can," they were told, and, if any European cargo remained, "lay it out in Teeth [ivory] and [gold] Dust." If unsuccessful at Whydah, they were to go down to Angola "and slave the ship to her full Reach," and if any cargo remained to "lay it out in Teeth which are there reasonable."

The instructions continued: if the *Blessing* slaved at the Gold Coast and Whydah, it should sail for Barbados, and if the slave market proved "Dull," proceed leeward until a market could be found "to our advantage." In exchange for the slaves the *Blessing* should load sugar, cotton, and ginger. If the proceeds more than filled the ship, the captain and supercargo were to invest in the same commodities and freight them for England. In the event the *Blessing* slaved at Angola, it was ordered to sail for Jamaica, where Gold Coast slaves sold well and Angola slaves could be sent to Cartagena, "where there never fails of a good price." Cartagena also offered the opportunity to bring home pieces of eight, the Spanish dollars that featured the figure *8*.

"Wee leave the whole management of the concern to you," the owners said, after making these detailed instructions. They urged the captain to exercise caution when seeing other ships, to keep the crew sober, avoid embezzlement, proceed with "despatch," and invoke "the care and protection of the Almighty." Captain Brownbell subsequently unloaded 193 slaves in Barbados in December 1701 and 151 slaves in Antigua on May 4, 1702.[30]

London dominated British trade with Africa when the *Henrietta Marie* made its voyages. The port's place in the trade approached monopoly, with London enjoying 90 percent and above of almost every trade category. Handling exports and reexports of colonial and foreign goods, London in 1700 accounted for 95 percent of the total. London was the metropolis of Great Britain and the main entrepôt of external trade. In addition, a surprisingly substantial

---

30. Ralph Davis, *The Rise of the English Shipping Industry in the Seventeenth and Eighteenth Century* (London: Macmillan, 1962), 295–97 (from Norris MSS, Liverpool Public Libraries); Donnan, *Documents*, 2:25, 33.

share of goods sent to Africa came from India. In 1700 a total of £80,000 of British goods was sent out to Africa, and £34,000 of Indian goods (largely textiles).

As recorded by the customs office, textiles figured heavily in the trade, comprising a large amount of woolens, besides cottons, linens, and India piece goods. Metals, largely iron and copper but also brass, tin, lead, and pewter, figured importantly. Beads from Europe, coral from North Africa, and bead materials from India made up a significant portion of outbound cargoes. Alcohol and gunpowder were among other exports, though substantially lower in value than the above categories. Redwood (used in dyes), almonds, ivory, copper, and beeswax—measured in value—led the list of imports from Africa.[31]

The African trade was both bilateral and triangular, the latter predominating. Some traders, intent on a quick turnaround, preferred to exchange goods for valuable products to be returned home. The slave merchant Humphry Morice instructed one of his captains: "It is my earnest desire that you dispose of[,] at all Places upon the Coast of Africa, so many Goods as you can possibly of my Cargoe for gold. . . . If possible sell Negroes to Portuguese for gold. . . . You may take Brazil tobacco in part payment."[32] In the West Indies, separate traders exchanged slaves for sugar and other commodities; in contrast to the Royal African Company, they offered credit, thereby widening their markets.

The ships employed in the London trade were very small by present-day standards. Using the term of that day, "tons burden"— that is, "the number of tons weight which would laden a ship previously empty to her minimum safe freeboard, or loadline"—slave ships averaged 163 tons in the final decade of the seventeenth century and 138 in the next decade. War years and peace years made for variations in the ships used by London merchants. In general, larger ships prevailed in war years, crewed by more men and carrying more guns. By and large, slave ships were British-built— though wars produced prizes of war, of which the *Henrietta Marie* may well have been one—and peace years saw a greater number of

31. Statistics from Public Record Office, Customs 3, kindly provided by Marion Johnson.
32. Humphry Morice Papers, Bank of England, B46, quoted by permission.

American-built ships in the trade. At this stage slave ships tended not to be very old, or in "a leaky, worm-eaten condition," as has been charged of later Liverpool slavers.[33]

Was the slave trade profitable? Tales of great riches derived from the infamous traffic in human beings have long been popular. Recent research has tended to qualify these popular impressions. The trade was like a lottery, a gigantic gamble that could return sizable profits or cause complete losses. Many factors entered into the profit picture. Adverse weather and long passages, extended stays in Africa and America, heavy mortality, slave insurrections, and problems of payment by American buyers could skew results. The slave merchants were like fishers of men, with all the uncertainty of results involved in a fishing expedition. Undoubtedly some slave merchants became wealthy; others, as in the case of the Bristol merchants in the 1790s, went bankrupt. Yet the trade attracted persons willing to venture their capital and persisted over four centuries, ending only in the late nineteenth century.

The Atlantic slave trade went far to develop the resources of the New World, transplanted ten or more millions from Africa to the Americas, and changed the life patterns of Europeans and Americans, who ate sugar and rice, smoked tobacco, wore cotton, and used gold. At the same time, slave traders introduced new crops to Africa—maize and manioc, known as Indian corn and cassava—in some measure sustaining and possibly increasing the African population. The trade, moreover, gave an impetus to antimonopoly and free trade doctrines and supplied the formula for reform devised by abolitionists in the late eighteenth century and employed by reformers in the nineteenth century.

33. Christopher J. French, "The Role of London in the Atlantic Slave Trade, 1680–1776" (M.A. thesis, University of Exeter, 1970).

2

The Port of London and the Eighteenth-Century Slave Trade

HISTORIANS, SOURCES, AND A REAPPRAISAL

This chapter shows that for generations historians underrated the role of London in the trade. Even the surge of scholarly interest from the 1950s to 1980, when this essay first appeared, failed adequately to measure London's active participation. Drawing on the work of a series of scholars and my own research, I conclude that in the eighteenth century London held high rank among England's three major slaving ports: London, Bristol, and Liverpool.

In the late seventeenth century and during the first three decades of the eighteenth London dominated the British slave trade. Eclipsed by the West Coast ports of Bristol and Liverpool in midcentury, London recovered over Bristol in the last half-century of the trade. A recent estimate in a letter to me from David Richardson holds that between 1698 and 1809, 3,103 ships cleared from London, 740,145 slaves delivered by them.

$$\approx$$

The port of London's share in the eighteenth-century Atlantic slave trade was far greater than historians have realized. The aims of this paper are to review the historical literature, to point to neglected sources of information, and to make a general reappraisal of London's role in what is believed to be the first study to emphasize the

Originally published in *African Economic History* 9 (1980), 85–100. Research for this paper enjoyed the support of the National Endowment for the Humanities, the Henry E. Huntington Library, and the University of Nebraska-Lincoln. I am indebted to Philip D. Curtin, Richard B. Sheridan, and David Richardson for critical readings of the manuscript.

theme that London was a significant slaving port in the eighteenth century. In doing so we shall not attempt here to offer a precise estimate of the numbers of slaves loaded and landed by London ships, since some gaps in information remain. It may be stated, however, that from 1698, when the Royal African Company monopoly ended, to 1807, when the legal trade ended, more than 2,500 ships cleared the port of London for Africa—an astonishing figure, as we shall see, in the light of what some historians have argued.

Scholarly attention to the Atlantic slave trade has grown rapidly and rewardingly since the publication in 1969 of Philip D. Curtin's pathbreaking and stimulating book, *The Atlantic Slave Trade: A Census*. In that work Curtin made a series of estimates of the volume of the trade, sketched the patterns of incidence in time and participation by European nations, and outlined the African sources and the American destinations of slaves. Using the work of other scholars and making no pretense of having done original archival research, he produced a comprehensive scholarly analysis and synthesis, modestly described as an estimate, which offered new conclusions, notably about the volume of the trade.

At a series of conferences held since 1969 scholars have made important contributions to our knowledge of the Atlantic slave trade. International conferences have taken place at Rochester, New York, Copenhagen, Denmark, Colby, New York, and Aarhus. Meanwhile in the United States sessions on the Atlantic slave trade have figured in the programs of several professional associations. Many of these papers, as well as other significant scholarly research on the slave trade, have been published.[1] Yet, despite this burst of

---

1. Philip D. Curtin, *The Atlantic Slave Trade: A Census* (Madison: University of Wisconsin Press, 1969); Stanley L. Engerman and Eugene D. Genovese, eds., *Race and Slavery in the Western Hemisphere: Quantitative Studies* (Princeton: Princeton University Press, 1975); Walter E. Minchinton and Pieter C. Emmer, eds., *The Atlantic Slave Trade: New Approaches* (Paris, 1976); Henry A. Gemery and Jan S. Hogendorn, eds., *The Uncommon Market: Essays in the Economic History of the Atlantic Slave Trade* (New York: Academic Press, 1979); Vera Rubin and Arthur Tuden, eds., *Comparative Perspectives on Slavery in New World Plantation Societies* (New York: New York Academy of Sciences, 1977); Roger Anstey, *The Atlantic Slave Trade and British Abolition, 1760–1810* (Atlantic Highlands, N.J.: Humanities Press, 1975); Roger Anstey, "The Slave Trade of the Continental Powers, 1760–1810," *Economic History Review*, 2d ser., 30 (1977): 259–68; Roger Anstey and P. E. H. Hair, eds., *Liver-*

activity, including considerable work on the British trade, only incidental attention has been devoted to the port of London.

Historians' misunderstanding of London's role apparently dates from 1897, when Gomer Williams, an influential historian of the Liverpool slave trade, described how Liverpool became "the chief slaving town of the Old World" in the eighteenth century: "The merchants of London having almost relinquished the slave trade in 1720, the memorable year of the South Sea disaster, the only rival Liverpool had to fear in its fresh sphere of enterprise was Bristol."[2] There are four points of special interest in Williams's argument. First and foremost is his assertion that London merchants nearly abandoned the slave trade early in the eighteenth century; second is the dating of this fact in the year 1720; third is the association of this with the South Sea Bubble; finally there is the suggestion that after 1720 London was never a rival to Bristol and Liverpool in the competition for the Atlantic slave trade. Though Williams failed to document his assertion, he had obviously done a great deal of research in preparing his book, and historians to the present time have depended heavily on him. In his assessment of the role of London in the eighteenth-century slave trade, he fixed a stereotype which survived his work for at least seven decades.

Twenty years after Williams, the careful American scholar Frank W. Pitman, drawing mainly from the Public Record Office, cited statistics of ship clearances for Africa showing that in 1725 London sent out more ships than Bristol but was soon outdistanced by Bristol and Liverpool. In the third quarter of the eighteenth century, Pitman wrote, "London had greatly declined," an interpretation he supported with clearance statistics for the years 1747–1753. He then offered statistics for the isolated year 1771, which indicated that London far surpassed Bristol in employing ships in the African

pool, the African Slave Trade, and Abolition (Bristol: Historic Society of Lancashire and Cheshire, 1976). In a landmark article, Richard B. Sheridan described London's deep financial involvement in the slave trade but accepted the tradition of a negligible involvement in the carrying of slaves: "The Commercial and Financial Organization of the British Slave Trade, 1750–1807," Economic History Review, 2d ser., 11 (December 1958): 249–63.

2. Gomer Williams, History of the Liverpool Privateers and Letters of Marque, with an Account of the Liverpool Slave Trade (1897; reprint, New York, 1966), 467.

slave trade, but unaccountably continued to export fewer slaves.[3] The figures for 1771 derived from an anonymous pamphleteer of 1772 and were later cited frequently by historians.

Writing in 1928, Lowell J. Ragatz described London's dominance of the English slave trade at the opening of the century and furnished figures that indicated Bristol had outpaced London as early as 1704. London slaving rapidly fell off, he said, and "this intercourse virtually ceased in 1720 with the bursting of the South Sea Bubble." Though Ragatz possessed an extraordinary knowledge of British materials in the Public Record Office and the British Museum, for his view of the London slave trade he relied on Gomer Williams rather than drawing his own conclusions.[4]

Profoundly influenced by Ragatz, who, along with Pitman, read the manuscript of his 1944 book *Capitalism and Slavery,* Eric E. Williams did not deal interpretatively with the place of London in the eighteenth-century slave trade except to cite the remark made in 1788 by the English abolitionist Thomas Clarkson that from 1763 to 1778 "the London merchants avoided all connection with the Liverpool slave traders, on the conviction that the slave trade was being conducted at a loss." Williams disregarded ships' clearance figures for occasional years (burying them in a footnote) that he might have used to question the influential interpretation of Gomer Williams via Ragatz.[5]

In the next several years two scholarly studies offered materials that might have been used to challenge the now well-established interpretation. In 1950 the British economic historian T. S. Ashton edited a number of the letters and papers of the London West African trader Edward Grace, who sought to dispatch slaves to the New World from a base in Senegambia, though with little success. Eleven years later Conrad Gill, in his *Merchants and Mariners,* surveyed the commercial activities of the London merchant Thomas Hall and his associates, who in the 1730s and 1740s dealt

3. Frank Wesley Pitman, *The Development of the British West Indies, 1700–1763* (New Haven: Yale University Press, 1917), 67.

4. Lowell J. Ragatz, *The Fall of the Planter Class in the British Caribbean, 1763–1833* (New York: Century Co., 1928), 82.

5. Eric E. Williams, *Capitalism and Slavery* (1944; reprint, New York: Capricorn Books, 1966), 38, 219–22.

substantially in African slaves, establishing a floating factory off Anomabo. Despite these suggestive contributions, the old interpretation continued to flourish. C. Northcote Parkinson, writing in 1952 and ignoring Ashton's work, gave a slightly new twist to the stereotype by arguing that the participation of London merchants in the slave trade ended in 1716. A decade later Ralph Davis remarked on "the rapid disappearance of London interests from the slave trade after the eclipse of the Royal Africa [sic] Company." Davis did not date this disappearance, but it may be presumed to have occurred in the second decade of the century, when Parliament dropped indirect support of the company's African forts and the company was reorganized. K. G. Davies had already written that the company's history after 1712–1713 "is, on the whole, a record of decay and inactivity."[6]

The collaboration of Daniel P. Mannix and Malcolm Cowley on a popular history of the Atlantic slave trade did not disabuse its readership of the stereotype about London. The authors put an early end to London's place as the principal English slaving port, asserting that "after the trade was thrown open to independent vessels, or 'ten percenters,' in 1698 Bristol outdistanced London." They saw Liverpool leaping ahead of other ports by 1750 when Great Britain relinquished the *asiento* to Spain and the Royal African Company started formal dissolution proceedings. Following this, "the London and Bristol slaving fleets dwindled . . . During the last years of the legal slave trade, from 1794 to 1807, Liverpool enjoyed something close to a monopoly." To illustrate the point about monopoly the authors selected 1800—"a nearly average year"—when port clearances were: Liverpool 120 ships, London 10, and Bristol 3. The authors took most of their material from

---

6. T. S. Ashton, ed., *Letters of a West African Trader: Edward Grace, 1767–1770* (London: Council for the Preservation of Business Archives, 1950; the last letter edited by Ashton is dated April 23, 1770; Grace's out-letter book in the Guildhall Library, London, contains eleven more letters extending to November 21, 1774); Conrad Gill, *Merchants and Mariners of the Eighteenth Century* (London: Edward Arnold, 1961); C. Northcote Parkinson, *The Rise of the Port of Liverpool* (Liverpool, 1952), 91; Ralph Davis, *The Rise of the English Shipping Industry in the Seventeenth and Eighteenth Century* (London: Macmillan, 1962), 276; K. G. Davies, *The Royal African Company* (London: Longmans, Green, 1957), 344.

an anonymous work published in 1798, entitled *A General and Descriptive History of the Ancient and Present State of the Town of Liverpool,* and they also referred readers to Gomer Williams's account, which they described as "a colorful and dependable book."[7]

Taking up the question of the eighteenth-century London slave trade, Curtin was thus faced with a dearth of scholarship. He made a number of observations, which, as we shall see, are of striking historiographical interest. The first scholarly effort to assess the English slave trade for the entire eighteenth century, Curtin's work requires analysis of the author's sources and treatment of the London slave trade. He lamented that lack of data for the first half of the century made estimates based on shipping impossible. Following Pitman's findings, he examined the period 1750–1776, noting that Pitman had turned up data for only the years 1750–1753. Using the data for these four years, he projected an annual average of ten ships per year for London, or 270 ships for the entire period out of the aggregate figure for the three major ports of 2,726 ships.[8]

For the years between 1776 and 1787 Curtin used returns published in the British Parliamentary Papers, giving for each year not only the numbers of ships that cleared the three ports but also the annual tonnage of each. In contrast he found no full set of returns for the years 1788–1793, and resorted to two sets of figures for Liverpool published by Gomer Williams in order to project the national volume, with no reference to the respective shares of London and Bristol. He next stated that no ships sailed from Liverpool to Africa in 1794, and he assumed that this was true of the other English ports, on the grounds of a "critical juncture in the Napoleonic wars." His use of the tables in Gomer Williams led to his error for this year.[9] For the years 1795–1804 Curtin used aggregate tonnage figures, without reference to shares cleared by individual ports, and for the years 1805–1807 he declared that only Liverpool data were available.[10]

7. Daniel P. Mannix and Malcolm Cowley, *Black Cargoes: A History of the Atlantic Slave Trade, 1518–1865* (New York: Viking Press, 1962), 69–72, 290.

8. Curtin, *Atlantic Slave Trade,* 133.

9. Ibid., 134–35; Gomer Williams, *History of the Liverpool Privateers,* 678, 680, 685; Philip D. Curtin to author, October 30, 1979.

10. Curtin, *Atlantic Slave Trade,* 135–36.

It was on the basis of the data at that time familiar to scholars—incomplete, especially for the first half of the century, and shifting in base and varying in authority—that he was compelled to make his estimate for England in the eighteenth century. It should be reemphasized that Curtin's main concern was the whole of the English trade and not the place of London in it, but at the same time we should point out that the foregoing bases, the most carefully compiled to 1969, leave the London trade virtually undocumented for the eighteenth century. Though Curtin had taken the most comprehensive view of any scholar of the English trade, there was little, if anything, in his account to challenge the older orthodoxy of Gomer Williams, on whom he heavily depended, Pitman, and Ragatz. His conclusions were that London's share of the African slave trade was: impossible to estimate for the first half of the century; projectable for 1750–1776 on the basis of 1750–1753; well documented for 1776–1787; so poorly documented for 1788–1793 that he used Liverpool figures for both before and after these years to make his estimate for the nation; nonexistent in 1794; available only in aggregate figures in the years 1795–1804; and unknown in the years 1805–1807.

In a study published in 1975 Roger Anstey made a major breakthrough in the assessment of the London slave trade during the latter part of the eighteenth century. He used Board of Trade records which Pitman had failed to exploit and Ragatz had ignored; he used published Parliamentary Papers which previous scholars had neglected; and he unearthed manuscript materials in the House of Lords Record Office. Even so, Anstey's contribution to the study of the London slave trade was incidental to his larger theme of the volume and profitability of the British slave trade generally between 1761 and 1807.[11]

Anstey arranged his analysis of the British slave trade by decades, and in dealing with the first decade, 1761–1770, he offered perhaps his most startling revision of Curtin. The basis for this was a manuscript in the Public Record Office which listed ships clear-

11. Roger Anstey, "The Volume and Profitability of the British Slave Trade, 1761–1807," in *Race and Slavery,* ed. Engerman and Genovese, 3–12, 18 n. 44. Curtin substantially accepted Anstey's findings; see Philip D. Curtin, "Measuring the Atlantic Slave Trade," in *Race and Slavery,* 107–28.

ing Great Britain for Africa from 1757 to 1777 and which provided the names and tonnage of ships for each year. Confronted with
the fact that the London list showed much more activity than
Curtin had reckoned but did not distinguish between slave and
nonslave vessels, Anstey resorted to the estimate for the year 1771
made by the anonymous pamphleteer cited earlier. The estimate for
this year was that London had employed 58 ships and carried
8,136 slaves; Anstey decided that the best way to handle the problem was to apply the ratio of the unidentified data to the preceding decade, thereby doubling Curtin's estimate.

Taking up his estimate for the decade 1771–1780, Anstey stated that for 1771–1776 he had the same evidence and made the
same assumptions as for 1761–1770, and then surprisingly stated
that for the remainder of the decade there were no individual port
clearances, ignoring information on such clearances in printed Parliamentary Papers he had cited two pages earlier.[12] For this decade
Anstey did not segregate the London data, which could only have
increased Curtin's estimate, nor did he note that in every year of
the decade there were more clearances of London ships to Africa
than of Bristol ships and, in 1779, of Liverpool ships.

Observing that 1779 was the low point of the British slave trade
during the American Revolution, Anstey turned to the 1780s.
Lacking the kind of evidence that he used for the two preceding
decades, he estimated the national trade on the basis of projected
tonnage figures for Liverpool taken from Gomer Williams and a
Liverpool historian of the slave trade era who identified himself
only as "A Genuine 'Dickey Sam.'"[13] Again, surprisingly, Anstey
did not use the individual port clearances mentioned above, which
provide the numbers of ships and tonnage clearing for Africa
through 1787, though he did use another set for 1789–1790 that
had the merit of designating some ships as slavers. It is only for the
latter two years that he used documented data for London.

When he approached the decade of 1791–1800 Anstey remarked that the evidence "is better than ever." Here he had unexploited manuscript materials for 1791–1797 from the House of

12. Anstey, "Volume and Profitability," 6.
13. Ibid., 6–7; A Genuine "Dickey Sam," *Liverpool and Slavery* (Liverpool, 1884),
107, 137.

Lords Record Office, together with printed materials in the Parliamentary Papers. With an amplitude of data, he was not required by his purpose to distinguish individual port clearances. Nor for the years 1801–1807, in a decade cut short by abolition, did he distinguish individual port clearances, though he did note that for the interval after April 30, 1806, there were lists only for Liverpool. He assumed for that span of seven years that London and Bristol together possessed 15 percent of the whole national trade, and he made no attempt to apportion shares to either of the two ports.

Anstey's sources enabled him to make a more precise estimate than Curtin of the volume of the British slave trade for a period of less than half a century. He introduced documentation not previously used and, in the case of the House of Lords material, not previously known to historians. His study explicitly increased the volume of the London trade for the early years, raising Curtin's estimate by 10.3 percent and giving London an enhanced, though not individually described, role.[14]

Writing in 1976, D. P. Lamb introduced new materials into consideration for study of the London slave trade in the eighteenth century. Lamb pointed to neglected sources in the Public Record Office, notably in the Admiralty, Colonial Office, and Treasury classes, for the period before 1772. He also exploited the published Parliamentary Papers and the House of Lords Record Office papers for the period after 1772. Though his theme was the activity of Liverpool in the slave trade between 1772 and 1807, he presented a series of tables for parts of the century that served to give London a more precise and important place in the trade than before. In a table of clearances of vessels to West Africa for selected dates between 1710 and 1771, Lamb showed that London had the largest number of clearances as late as 1725; that in the years 1730–1739 London yielded supremacy to Bristol but remained ahead of Liverpool; and that in the years 1750–1759 London dropped to third place with average clearances of thirteen vessels annually (compared with Curtin's estimate of ten). For 1771 he cited the familiar undocumented figures.

A second table, of clearances of all vessels in both the slave and

14. Anstey, "Volume and Profitability," 7–12.

nonslave trades for the years 1772–1804, was arresting, for it showed London to be consistently ahead of Bristol and therefore the second port in importance during the period. "Clearances from London to West Africa exceeded those from Bristol by an average of 6–18 vessels" annually during these years, Lamb wrote. The table, with its challenge to the traditional interpretation that relegated London to unimportance after 1720, became less arresting when, in the following table, Lamb offered clearances for 1789–1795 for vessels designated as *slaving* vessels. This table listed 118 clearances from London, 157 from Bristol, and 610 for Liverpool. So, while London continued to be actively involved in sending out slave ships, often rivaling Bristol, it nevertheless was third in importance.

Another of Lamb's tables suggested a new perspective on London's place in the African slave trade. Here slaving vessels as a percentage of all vessels clearing to West Africa between 1789 and 1795 were examined. Although slaving vessels formed a large majority of the whole, the table showed varying percentages for the three ports: from 94 percent to 98 percent for Liverpool, from 72 to 100 percent for Bristol, and only from 42 to 67 percent for London. Like Anstey before him, Lamb was concerned with the problem of distinguishing between ships in the slave trade and others. When faced with tonnage figures for all clearances, Anstey had reduced the figures to 95 percent, which was acceptable, Lamb demonstrated, for Liverpool, but tended to inflate the total volume for Bristol, and markedly so for London.[15]

In summary, using a better set of sources than any previous scholar, Lamb suggested that throughout the eighteenth century London continued to play a significant part in the British slave trade. He outlined a pattern: London stood foremost in the slave trade in the first quarter of the century, then experienced a decline in the 1730s, a sharp drop by the 1750s, a marked rise by the 1770s, and activity at a substantial level thereafter until abolition. Intent on his own theme, however, Lamb attempted no general revision of previous writing on London's role.

15. D. P. Lamb, "Volume and Tonnage of the Liverpool Slave Trade, 1772–1807" in *Liverpool, the African Slave Trade, and Abolition,* ed. Anstey and Hair, 91–112; see esp. 91–98.

However, Lamb distorted the place of London vis-à-vis Bristol when he referred to "the failure of London's and especially Bristol's West African trades to recover fully following the outbreak of war in 1793." He explained, "[I]t appears that London merely withdrew from the shipping of slaves and retained an important financial interest in the trade." Actually, London made a surprising recovery in shipping slaves; and it should be noted that the authority on whom Lamb based his explanation, Richard B. Sheridan, was describing the longer period 1750–1807.[16]

J. E. Inikori, writing in 1976, sought primarily to examine Curtin's methods and data, particularly for the period between 1750 and 1807, but also discussed Anstey's modifications of Curtin. Inikori made a broad-ranging study of slave-carrying nations, and his work displayed the most thorough archival research on the British slave trade to date. With respect to the London slave trade, Inikori made a specific contribution. He also dealt with two general problems, without applying his conclusions directly to London. His specific contribution was to point out unexploited sources for London sets of shipping figures covering the whole period from 1750 to 1776 and for Great Britain generally, Customs 17, giving numbers and tonnages of British ships clearing for Africa between 1777 and 1807.[17] Curtin, it will be recalled, projected his estimate for the period from figures for 1750–1753 only. Anstey began his estimate with the year 1761, using a basic source and making a dramatic increase in London's share of the trade.

Inikori noted that Curtin had not used all the official figures that were available for London from 1750 to 1776, or the British national shipping totals for the years 1777–1807. In addition to the primary source for the figures for the years 1750–1753, Inikori pointed out that figures for 1754–1756 could be found in a history of Liverpool published in 1795, and that figures for 1757–1776 were available in the Board of Trade Records in the Public Record Office which Anstey had cited. On the basis of these figures, Iniko-

16. Lamb, "Volume and Tonnage," chap. 2; Sheridan, "Commercial and Financial Organization."

17. J. E. Inikori, "Measuring the Atlantic Slave Trade: An Assessment of Curtin and Anstey," *Journal of African History* 17:2 (1976): 197–223, esp. 210–21; for comments by Curtin and Anstey and a rejoinder by Inikori, see *Journal of African History* 17:4 (1976): 595–627.

ri argued that Curtin's use of the 1750–1753 figures to estimate London shipping for 1750–1776 had "produced an underestimate of almost 200 per cent."[18] This compared with Anstey's implication that Curtin had underestimated by almost 100 percent.

Inikori has since qualified his assertion that the gap in London figures can be filled by the 1795 account. The author of that account, James Wallace, had calculated figures for Great Britain and Liverpool but did not list London separately. Moreover, he did not give any figures for 1754–1756, but only a seven-year average for 1752–1758. Inikori used the seven-year average to deduce figures for 1754–1756, subtracted figures for Liverpool and Bristol from the total for Great Britain, and achieved, in his words, "a rough indication of the London volume, making due allowance for the lesser ports."[19]

The two general problems to which he addressed himself pertained to the numbers of slaves carried by British ships. One was how to distinguish slave ships from nonslave ships on the basis of products brought back from Africa. The Office of the Register General of Shipping, which recorded clearances and entrances of vessels, assumed that all African products had been brought directly from Africa by nonslave ships. The office then calculated the number of ships importing African products from the total number clearing *for* Africa. This bookkeeping practice, which excluded the possibility that some slave ships returned with African products, inevitably diminished the number of slave ships.

On the basis of other evidence about the number of ships employed in the direct trade, Anstey had concluded that one-half of the value of these products had been brought in slave ships, thereby raising the number of ships in the slave trade accordingly. Inikori agreed that much of the African importation had been in slave ships, but from an analysis based on Customs 17 he raised the number of slave ships further. Neither author sought to distinguish individual ports in the importation of African products. It will be remembered that Lamb's paper, published in the same year but

18. Inikori, "Assessment of Curtin and Anstey," 210–12; James Wallace, *A General and Descriptive History of the Ancient and Present State of the Town of Liverpool* (Liverpool, 1795), 255.

19. J. E. Inikori, letter to author, December 19, 1978.

unknown to Inikori, showed that London had a much higher percentage of nonslave ships than the other two major ports, at least for 1789–1795.

The other general problem that Inikori took up was the thorny one of calculating the number of slaves carried by applying an estimated ratio of slaves to tons of shipping as known from the records. Inikori claimed that Anstey, especially for the period after 1781, had not only placed the number of slave ships too low, but also had employed too low a ratio of slaves per ton. In response Anstey hailed the Customs 17 Series as an "important discovery" and raised his own estimate of the volume of the British slave trade by 7.3 percent. He declined, however, to accept the bases of Inikori's slaves-per-ton ratio. Neither author distinguished individual port clearances in their exchange. In 1977, employing the Customs 17 Series but making no direct application to London, Seymour Drescher offered a series of estimates of the volume of the British slave trade from 1777 to 1807, each of which raised Anstey's estimate.[20]

From the foregoing examination we may note that very little has been published on the London slave trade in the eighteenth century per se; that writers early fixed a stereotype which has long been repeated by historians; that the estimate by Curtin underestimated the volume of the trade; and that several scholars have recently pointed to neglected sources showing that this volume was considerably more than the stereotype indicated, but that they have not exploited these sources specifically for London.

Having surveyed the historiography of the eighteenth-century London slave trade, we may now suggest a fresh appraisal of London's place in the trade. Our approach will be substantially chronological, pointing to the scholarly sources for each period, and comparing the evidence of these sources with previous interpretations.

Historians are agreed that until the end of the seventeenth century London dominated the English slave trade. London was the headquarters of the Royal African Company, which from 1672 to 1689 enjoyed a royal monopoly on the trade; and, though separate

20. Inikori, "Assessment of Curtin and Anstey," 214–21; Roger Anstey, "The British Slave Trade 1751–1807: A Comment," *Journal of African History* 17:4 (1976): 606–7; Seymour Drescher, *Econocide: British Slavery in the Era of Abolition* (Pittsburgh: University of Pittsburgh Press, 1977), 25–28.

traders appeared in the 1690s, they were nearly all Londoners. Looking to the maintenance of the company's forts in Africa, Parliament in 1698 enacted a law that opened the trade to all merchants, with the stipulation that separate traders were to pay an *ad valorem* duty of 10 percent on all their exports to Africa. The act continued in effect until 1712 and it is during this period that some historians have suggested Bristol surpassed London.

Ragatz and the collaborators Mannix and Cowley, who have put forward this view of a very early rise to dominance of Bristol, rely on the undocumented authority of Gomer Williams. Elizabeth Donnan, whose knowledge of the Atlantic slave trade was unrivaled in her time, noted in 1931 that Williams's figures for Bristol for 1701–1709 "are probably much too large." Official clearance lists of ships going to Africa for 1708–1709 and 1709–1710 (in each instance from one Michaelmas to the next) yield these results: in the first of these years, Royal African Company (London) 3 ships, London separate traders 28, and Bristol 12;[21] in the second year, Royal African Company 3 ships from London and 2 from the plantations, London separate traders 24, Bristol 20, Liverpool 2, Whitehaven 1, Jamaica 2, and Barbados 3.[22] At the end of the decade, then, London remained the leading English port, though competition was increasing.

As to the claim that by 1720 London had virtually abandoned participation in the slave trade, there is abundant proof to the contrary. A little-known list of ships that cleared for Africa from London in the years 1714 to 1724 demonstrates continuing activity: 29 clearances in 1721, 38 in 1722, 27 in 1723, and 43 in 1724, compared with 25, 21, 21, and 30, respectively, for Bristol.[23] For 1725 there is evidence that London employed 87 ships in the African trade and was still the most active English port, with Bristol employing 63 and Liverpool 21.[24]

The linking of the disappearance of London from the slave trade

21. Elizabeth Donnan, ed., *Documents Illustrative of the History of the Slave Trade to America,* 4 vols. (Washington: Carnegie Institution, 1930–1935), 2:92–95.

22. Public Record Office (hereinafter PRO), *Calendar of State Papers, Colonial Series, America and West Indies,* 42 vols. (London, 1860–1954), 1710–1711, no. 544, 310–11.

23. PRO, Colonial Office (hereinafter CO) 390/7, no. 1.

24. PRO, CO 388/25, 574.

with the South Sea Company debacle in 1720 is a curious error. After Great Britain had secured the contract to sell slaves in Spanish America, the Crown bestowed the *asiento* on the South Sea Company. The events of 1720 did not put the company, whose headquarters was in London, out of the business of selling slaves. With interruptions in trade, the *asiento* remained in English hands until 1750, was administered by the company, and accounted for a measure of London's continuing activity. For instance, from February 12, 1723, to October 31, 1724, the company delivered 3,052 slaves to its agents in Jamaica, and from 1727 to 1730 it transported about 5,000 slaves to Spanish America.[25] In the 1730s the London mercantile firm of Thomas Hall and Associates displayed a lively interest in the African slave trade conducted by the South Sea Company, delivering large numbers of slaves to America, especially to Buenos Aires, for the company. Securing the company's slave business was very competitive among London merchants. Captain James Pearce, one of Hall's associates, exhorted him: "[A]s there are so many people pushing 'tis time to begin in earnest for Buttler [that is, secure a contract for Captain Butler to carry slaves]. You should not loose [*sic*] a day in doing it."[26]

Pitman had remarked that the London slave trade had greatly declined since 1725, basing his statement upon figures for 1747 and 1753, when only three and thirteen ships, respectively, were reported as clearing for Africa. The broad generalization is quite true, but better figures are available, showing a pattern to the decline in the second quarter of the century and providing a comparison with the Bristol and Liverpool trades. The figures include data from the Naval Office Shipping Lists kept by naval officers at the main ports in the colonies and the Mediterranean passes, which were issued by the Admiralty after 1730 to vessels clearing for Africa as well as for the Mediterranean. Drawing on these two sources, Michael Atkinson made a study of the English slave trade from 1698 to 1739; using the shipping lists, Christopher J. French made a study of the London slave trade from 1680 to 1776.[27] Although neither of these

25. Donnan, *Documents*, 2:xxxv, xxxvii n. 120, xxxvi.

26. Pearce to Hall, November 5, 1734, PRO, CO 103/130–33. These materials are tied together in bundles and are not properly sorted and classified.

27. Michael Atkinson, "The English Slave Trade, 1698–1739" (M.A. thesis, Uni-

studies has been published, the findings are particularly valuable for the neglected first half of the century. To begin with, the figures show that by 1730 Bristol had surpassed London in the slave trade, at least in terms of numbers of slaves transported to America. In that year Bristol shipping accounted for 9,982 slaves, London 8,553, and Liverpool 2,538.

The London trade dropped sharply after 1730, with a partial resurgence in 1735–1737, followed by a precipitous drop at the end of the decade. Throughout the 1730s Bristol was the preeminent English slave port, while Liverpool was on the rise, moving ahead of London by 1737. It was in the 1740s and early 1750s that London stood at ebb tide; in only one year between 1740 and 1751 did London send more than ten ships to Africa. Meanwhile, Liverpool had overtaken Bristol in the trade.

As noted, in making his estimate of the English trade in the years 1750–1776 Curtin used figures for London only for 1750–1753. These figures were not typical, but represented a low period of activity in the span of twenty-seven years. In any case Curtin need not have based his estimate on these years alone since other figures were available, which varied sharply with those he used. The figures for 1771 had frequently been printed; they disclosed that London in that year sent out 58 ships to Africa, nearly six times the average Curtin employed. A list in the Parliamentary Papers which he used for the period 1776–1787 actually begins with the year 1772.[28] The available six-year run of figures (1771–1776) gives London an average of 42 ships per year, over four times the figure of 10 that Curtin projected. In addition to these sources, *Lloyd's Register of Shipping*, though incomplete, listed London ships insuring for African voyages at a significantly higher average than 10 per year for the years from 1764.[29]

Beyond these published materials there exists a manuscript return in the Board of Trade papers for the years 1757–1776, giving

versity of Exeter, 1974); Christopher J. French, "The Role of London in the Atlantic Slave Trade, 1680–1776" (M.A. thesis, University of Exeter, 1970).

28. *Parliamentary Papers, Accounts and Papers*, 1789, 24 (633), 60–63.

29. *Lloyd's Register of Shipping*, 1760–1900, 132 vols. (London, 1965–68). See volumes for 1764, 1765, 1766, 1768, 1769, 1770, 1771.

the names and tonnage of ships for the three major ports.[30] This shows that the number of ships clearing from London rose from 11 in 1757 to 22 in 1758 and continued at a high rate; in fact, the average for this run of years was 35, not 10. Moreover, in each of these years except for 1759 and 1760, the number of London ships was greater than that for Bristol, and except for 1759 the tonnage of London ships was greater than that for Bristol. Anstey incorporated this evidence into his decennial estimates. It is clear from this evidence that the years 1750–1753 by no means represented the average for the period 1750–1776, and that after a quarter of a century of low activity by the 1760s London had become England's second leading port in the African trade.

However, it is one thing to learn that London was second in the African trade and another to argue from this that London was also second in the African *slave* trade. The return does not distinguish between slave and nonslave ships, which would have made possible a direct comparison between Bristol and London in slaving. Lamb's research on a later period showed that London enjoyed a heavy proportion of the nonslave trade with Africa. During the earlier years the nonslave trade with Senegal, particularly the gum trade, increased. In 1763, when Great Britain acquired Senegambia from France, the number of London ships clearing for Africa rose to 42, compared with a previous high for the period of 22. At the same time, in many of these years the numbers of London ships and tons so greatly exceeded the numbers for Bristol that it is doubtful that this excess was accounted for entirely by the nonslave trade.

The year 1776 marked the formal declaration of war between the United States and Great Britain, which by 1780 had become a world war. A writer in the *New Cambridge Modern History* observed that "the British slave trade was itself brought to a standstill during the American War."[31] In light of this observation, the role of London during the years 1776–1783 is interesting. To begin with, the British slave trade as a whole did not come to a standstill, though the number of ships clearing for Africa fell from 151

30. PRO, Board of Trade (hereinafter BT) 6/3, ff. 150–89.
31. *New Cambridge Modern History,* 14 vols. (Cambridge: Cambridge University Press, 1957–1979), 7:570.

in 1775 to a low figure of 28 in 1779. London sent out 27 percent of all ships and 28 percent of all tonnage during the war years. In 1779 London was the leading port in the African trade, sending out 17 ships, as against 11 for Liverpool and none for Bristol. In each of the war years but two London sent out more ships than Bristol, and in each year but one more tons of shipping.[32]

Though these figures are for ships in the African trade, the number of clearings is too great to be accounted for wholly by the direct trade between Great Britain and Africa. Anstey has questioned the credibility of official figures for the number of ships in the direct trade; on the basis of the value of imports of African produce, combined with tonnage figures, he assumed, as we have seen, that one-half the value was imported from Africa indirectly by slave ships. The number of vessels described as in the direct trade varied widely from year to year, from 71 aggregating 8,037 tons in 1775 to 8 aggregating 1,180 tons in 1782. In this last year 69 vessels totaling 9,311 tons cleared British ports for Africa, 10 of them from London.[33] If all direct imports had been carried by London ships, which is unlikely, there would still have been space for slaves. Moreover, the remaining 59 vessels clearing for Africa were probably in the slave trade. Whichever set of figures one accepts—the official one or Anstey's—it demonstrates that the British slave trade was not entirely dormant during the American Revolution.

That the London slave trade continued during the war is also evidenced by a petition to the Board of Trade in 1777 from the London merchants trading to Africa. Laying blame on the committee elected to administer the Company of Merchants Trading to Africa and the governors of the forts on the Gold Coast, they complained not of the disappearance of the trade but only of its decrease, forcing them to purchase inferior Negroes.[34]

As we turn to the last quarter-century of the legal slave trade, we are struck by how misleading it is not only to say that London disappeared from the slave trade, but also to say merely that London declined after 1725, leaving the matter there, or to select the

32. *Accounts and Papers,* 1789, 24 (633), 60–63.
33. David MacPherson, *Annals of Commerce,* 4 vols. (London: Nichols & Son, 1805), 4:154.
34. PRO, BT 6/3 ff. 33–34.

year 1800 as exemplifying London's place in the trade between 1794 and 1807.[35] Clearance figures for vessels from English ports to Africa from 1783 through 1788 show that in every year but 1787 London sent out more ships and tonnage than Bristol.[36] For the years 1789 through 1795 we have a more precise set of figures, manuscript lists of slaving vessels clearing for Africa, which demonstrate continuing activity by London merchants in the slave trade.[37] Interestingly, they also reveal a somewhat higher level of slaving for London than do the figures in the published Parliamentary Papers. For example, the latter lists only 9 ships clearing from London to purchase slaves in 1789, whereas manuscript Treasury returns list 14. According to these records, London sent out 118 vessels in the slave trade during these years. The returns also show, in contrast to the figures for African clearances only, that Bristol was more active than London, sending out 157 slave ships. London clearances accounted for 13 percent of all slaving vessel clearances, and Bristol 18 percent. In 1793, however, London sent out as many slave ships as Bristol, and in 1795, more ships than Bristol.

These two sets of figures suggest strongly that London sent out a larger proportion of nonslave ships than did the other two ports. It is possible to analyze the second set of figures and show that this is indeed the case: slaving vessels as a percentage of all vessels clearing from Liverpool amounted to 95 percent, from Bristol about 88 percent, and from London only about 54 percent.

This pattern began to change in 1794 when London sent out as much tonnage as Bristol, while in the following year London surpassed Bristol both in numbers and tonnage of slave vessels. It was Bristol which now nearly relinquished the slave trade. The House of Lords list, which extends only through 1797, indicates not only that London far exceeded Bristol in 1796–1797 in the slave trade, but also did so by a greater margin than suggested by the published Parliamentary Papers. For 1796 the latter lists 8 ships for London and 1 for Bristol, and the former lists 12 and 2, respectively; for 1797 the latter lists 12 and 2 and the former lists 16 and 0. For the

35. For the selection of 1800, see Mannix and Cowley, *Black Cargoes*, 71–72.
36. *Accounts and Papers*, 1789, 24 (633); 1790, 31 (705); 1792, 35 (768).
37. PRO, Treasury 64/286, House of Lords Record Office, 5/J/11/2.

years 1798–1804, the Parliamentary Papers show a heavy dispro-
portion in favor of London over Bristol in ships and slaves allowed.[38]

Moreover, the year 1800 is unrepresentative of London's place
in the British slave trade in the last years of legal activity. The figures used by Mannix and Cowley were from the Parliamentary
Papers for the period 1795–1804. In seven of those ten years,
London sent out more than 10 slave ships, the number taken as
representative of London, and in 1802 three times as many. In the
last six years of the period, 10 was the *lowest* number of slave ships
clearing from London, and during these years London sent out 113
slave ships as against 17 for Bristol. In 1800 London clearances accounted for only 7 percent of the English total; but for the period
1795–1804 they accounted for 12 percent, and Bristol clearances
came to only 2.2 percent.[39] Thus by the end of the century London
was the second slaving port of Great Britain and it continued in this
place until the end of the legal slaving era.

In conclusion it is clear that historians have long neglected the
London slave trade in the eighteenth century, confining themselves
to echoing a misleading interpretation set forth without documentation in 1897. That interpretation nearly dismissed London from
the slave trade in the eighteenth century, linking its disappearance
to the collapse of the South Sea Bubble in 1720 and eliminating
London as a rival to Bristol. Data for a fuller treatment have been
thought to be lacking, and historians have not always consulted the
data known to be available. The classic census of the English slave
trade in the eighteenth century was based on the belief that printed materials were not available for the first half of the century, existed for only four years for the third quarter of the century, and,
though much fuller, were incomplete for the years 1776 to the end
of the legal trade. The census did not advance knowledge of the
London slave trade much beyond the place to which it was consigned by Gomer Williams.

Since 1969 historians have pointed to rich resources for understanding the place of London in the eighteenth century trade. No
historian, however, has attempted to exploit these resources. On

38. *Accounts and Papers,* 1806, 13.
39. Ibid.

the basis of this material it is evident that London remained the leading English slaving port until the late 1720s; that it continued as a slaving port until the close of the legal trade; that it yielded supremacy to Bristol by 1730 and sank to a low level of activity until the late 1750s; that it experienced a resurgence in the 1760s and 1770s when it apparently closely rivaled or surpassed Bristol, at least in some years; that it was an active port during the American Revolution; that for a period of years until 1793 it again yielded to Bristol for second place after Liverpool; and that in the final years of the legal trade it was again England's second most important slaving port.

The above findings fit in with those of other investigators who have revised Curtin's 1969 estimates.[40] The findings demonstrate that published sources have been inadequate in documenting the trade, that extrapolation from one or a few years can be the cause of serious error, that arrangement of figures by decades or quarter-centuries can conceal fluctuations in the trade, and that as a result the estimates for London must be substantially raised.

40. In addition to the works by Anstey, Inikori, and Drescher previously cited, important revisionist studies include David Eltis, "The Direction and Fluctuation of the Transatlantic Slave Trade, 1821–1843: A Revision of the 1845 Parliamentary Paper" in *Uncommon Market,* ed. Gemery and Hogendorn, 273–301; David Eltis, "The Transatlantic Slave Trade, 1821–1843" (Ph.D. diss., University of Rochester, 1978); Jay Coughtry, "The Notorious Triangle: Rhode Island and the African Slave Trade, 1700–1807" (Ph.D. diss., University of Wisconsin, 1978); and Robert Louis Stein, *The French Slave Trade in the Eighteenth Century: An Old Regime Business* (Madison: University of Wisconsin Press, 1979).

David Richardson, professor of history at the University of Hull and a leading authority on the British transatlantic slave trade, supplied me with a sophisticated table of estimated numbers of slave ship clearances and slaves delivered. His work, more than twenty years after my article originally appeared, represents the sort of evidence on which my paper was based.

Arranged by decades and divided among ports, it illustrates the rise and fall of the three major ports: London, Bristol, and Liverpool. The totals support my claim made in 1980 that London played a larger role in the trade than was previously assigned to it.

Table 1
The British Slave Trade in the Eighteenth Century

Years	London Number of Clearances	London Slaves Delivered	Bristol Number of Clearances	Bristol Slaves Delivered	Liverpool Number of Clearances	Liverpool Slaves Delivered
1698–1709	539	116,592	60	10,070	2	262
1709–1719	313	75,499	194	34,490	79	10,349
1720–1729	435	95,467	332	69,438	120	19,080
1730–1739	282	71,910	405	96,312	231	48,510
1740–1749	81	24,543	239	60,378	322	78,890
1750–1759	164	27,716	215	49,950	521	118,267
1760–1769	335	72,025	256	62,422	725	170,375
1770–1779	370	92,500	154	34,519	703	170,126
1780–1789	190	58,520	112	29,311	660	214,500
1790–1799	156	46,153	130	29,603	1,042	318,839
1800–1807	132	36,427	17	3,988	896	224,880
Totals	2,997	717,352	2,114	480,481	5,301	1,374,078

3

Humphry Morice

FOREMOST LONDON SLAVE MERCHANT OF HIS TIME

In 1985 slave trade scholars gathered at the University of Nantes to share their research on the Atlantic slave trade. This paper was my contribution. Humphry Morice's mercantile papers had been deposited at the Bank of England, of which he was governor. The bank's authorities generously granted me permission to examine the papers, and subsequently to publish this essay.

The recently released *Trans-Atlantic Slave Trade* database discloses that over the years 1718–1732 Morice dispatched 53 voyages to Africa for slaves. In nearly all instances he was the sole owner, rare in his time when a number of investors shared the financing of a voyage and the risk. One of his vessels disappeared without leaving a record. The remaining 52 ships embarked 14,019 Africans and suffered a loss of 2,576 lives. Crew losses—usually heavy, in part because of the long, three-part voyage from England to Africa, to the Americas, and back to England—are not given.

The length of the middle passage, Africa to America, notorious in slave-trade history, is available for only four voyages, with a mean of 83 days. The share of adult males, available for only two voyages, has a mean of 72.90 percent, of children 59.40 percent. The pattern of slave embarkation is highly irregular: 2,249 in 1772 and 2,326 in 1724, peak numbers in each case preceded and succeeded by low numbers.

The database is a rich lode of information, though there are still many gaps in the record. The totality, however, strongly sustains my assertion made in 1985 that Morice was the foremost London slave merchant of his time.

≈

This chapter first appeared in *De la Traite a l'Esclavage*, Serge Daget, ed. (Nantes: Centre de Recherche sur l'Histoire du Monde Atlantique and Société Française d'Histoire d'Outre-Mer, 1988).

The role of London in the eighteenth-century slave trade was long thought by historians to be negligible. The influential historian of the Liverpool trade, Gomer Williams, in 1897 wrote: "The merchants of London having almost relinquished the slave trade in 1720, the memorable year of the South Sea disaster, the only rival Liverpool had to fear in its fresh sphere of enterprise was Bristol." Three decades later this undocumented assertion was affirmed by the meticulous scholar Lowell J. Ragatz, who possessed intimate knowledge of British archival material on the Caribbean: "London's participation [in the trade to Africa] was at first even more promising [than that of Bristol], but soon fell off. In 1701 a total of 104 bottoms cleared out from that port for Guinea; in 1704, fifty; in 1707, only thirty. This intercourse," he continued, echoing Williams, "virtually ceased in 1720 with the bursting of the South Sea Bubble."[1]

In recent years historians have adduced evidence demonstrating the falsity of these assertions. They have shown that London did not relinquish the slave trade in 1720, that the port had an irregular pattern of slaving, sometimes surpassing Bristol in volume, and in sum was a significant carrier of slaves in the eighteenth century. The full dimensions are not yet established; however, over 2,500 vessels cleared from London for Africa in the years 1698–1807. There is good ground for the conjecture that London, not Bristol, was England's second most important slaving port in the eighteenth century.[2]

Much of this recent investigation has centered on the years after 1750. We will concentrate here on a London merchant's slaving activities in the 1720s, the decade when Williams believed London merchants had almost relinquished the trade and Ragatz believed the trade from London had virtually ceased.

Humphry Morice (1671?–1731) may well have been England's foremost slave merchant in the 1720s. The author of the sketch of Morice in the *Dictionary of National Biography*, whether out of ig-

---

1. Gomer Williams, *History of the Liverpool Privateers and Letters of Marque, with an Account of the Liverpool Slave Trade* (1897; reprint, New York, 1966), 467; Lowell J. Ragatz, *The Fall of the Planter Class in the British Caribbean, 1763–1833* (New York: Century Co., 1928), 82.

2. See chap. 2. The figure of over 2,500 clearances from London for Africa is based on my research files.

norance or a fastidious distaste for the slave trade, described him as "a Turkey merchant," but threw out a hint of possible involvement in the trade by referring to his debts due "for Gold and Elephants' Teeth." Morice was, like a number of London slave merchants, a member of Parliament, serving from 1713 to 1731. A suggestion of his implication in the slave trade may be found in his parliamentary profile, which states that he carried on "an extensive trade with Africa, America, Holland and Russia."[3]

The eldest son of a Broad Street merchant, Morice took over his father's business at the age of eighteen. He married twice, each time taking to wife a daughter of London merchants. His first wife was Judith, daughter of Thomas Sandes, by whom he had five children. His second wife was Katherine, daughter of a fellow African merchant, Peter Paggen; by her he had two sons, one of whom, Humphry, became a baronet and sat in Parliament. In 1716, rising in influence, he became a director of the Bank of England, and in 1727–1728 served as its governor. A portrait at Hartwell, Buckinghamshire, limns "an intelligent-looking middle aged gentleman." After his sudden death in 1731—"'Tis supposed he took poyson"—Morice's reputation was damaged by revelations that he had defrauded the Bank of England and embezzled trust funds held for his daughters. Protracted litigation over his estate, involving, among others, claims made by a number of his slave-ship captains and their heirs, ultimately went to the House of Lords for adjudication.[4]

Historians' knowledge of Morice has been sparse. William Snelgrave, who sailed in Morice's service for a number of years, in 1734 wrote *A New Account of Some Parts of Guinea and the Slave Trade,* in which he occasionally referred to his employer. A witness before the Board of Trade in 1750 gave a clue to Morice's preeminence in the slave trade—which historians have not pursued—when he testified: "Mr. Morris [sic] imported more Gold Coast ne-

3. "Humphry Morice," in *Dictionary of National Biography,* 22 vols., ed. Sidney Lee (London: Oxford University Press, 1921–1922), 13:941 (my essay on Morice is forthcoming in the *New Dictionary of National Biography*); Romney Sedgwick, ed., *The History of Parliament: The House of Commons, 1715–1754,* 2 vols. (New York: Oxford University Press, 1970), II, 277.
4. "Humphry Morice," in *Dictionary of National Biography; Notes and Queries,* CWCII, May 3, 1947, 178–80, British Library, Addit. MSS 21, 500:f. 62.

groes into our Colonies in two or three years about twenty-eight
years ago, than all the merchants of Bristol and Liverpool." The
governor of Cape Castle, John Roberts, in 1779 drew on a Board
of Trade listing of slave ships in 1726 to declare: "[M]any of those
Ships belonged to Humphry Morris Esqr of London that went to
Whydah for from 4 to 500 Slaves." A legal document written in
1737 in part stated that Morice "at his Death had many Ships on
the Sea bound for *Africa* and the *West Indies,* with rich ladings."
For nearly a quarter of a century Morice was as well as a slave merchant a principal spokesman of the London separate traders, and
his views may be followed in the journals of the Board of Trade.[5]
The main source for this chapter is the heretofore unexploited
Humphry Morice Papers in the Bank of England. These papers include instructions and orders to ship captains, invoices of cargoes
dispatched to Africa, and journals of trade along the African
coast.[6]

In the early years of the eighteenth century Morice appears to
have been involved in the slave trade as owner mainly of fraction-
al shares in ships, as insurer of cargoes, and as consignor of cargoes on ships clearing for Africa. He actively opposed efforts of the
Royal African Company to regain its monopoly, witnessed the expiration of the 10 percent duty act that had benefited the company, unsuccessfully sought creation of a regulated company, and after England gained the *asiento* endeavored to get a share of the
Spanish slave trade.[7]

By 1720 Morice had no fewer than eight vessels actively employed in the African slave trade. Of the eighty-seven London ships

5. William Snelgrave, *A New Account of Some Parts of Guinea and the Slave Trade*
(1734; reprint, London: Frank Cass, 1971), 193, 288; *Journal of the Commissioners
for Trade and Plantations, 1704–1782*, 14 vols. (London: Stationery Office, 1920–
1938), 5:8; British Library, Egerton MSS 1116B:f. 115 (incorrectly cited in Elizabeth
Donnan, ed., *Documents Illustrative of the History of the Slave Trade to America*, 4
vols. [Washington: Carnegie Institution, 1930–1935], 2:348 n. 8); British Library, Addit. MSS 36, 153.

6. Other manuscript materials are in the Public Record Office, the British Library,
and Columbia University Library. I am grateful to the staffs of these repositories, especially to J. M. Keyworth and the staff at the Bank of England. Humphry Morice was
a director of the bank from 1716 to 1725 and from 1729 to 1731, deputy governor
from 1725 to 1727, and governor from 1727 to 1729. His personal papers appear to
have come to the bank after his death in 1731.

7. Public Record Office (hereinafter PRO), Treasury 70/1199.

in the trade in 1726, he owned seven, designed to carry 2,500 Negroes, or 9.4 percent of the port's intended total of 26,440. Four of these ships were very large: one was designed to carry 400 Negroes, two to carry 450, and one to carry 550. His preeminence in 1726 was rivaled by Richard Harris, whose seven vessels were designed to carry 2,180 Negroes, or 8.2 percent of London's capacity, and Francis Chamberlayne, whose five vessels were designed to carry 2,100 Negroes, or 7.9 percent. Together, these three merchants, of a group of forty-nine, owned 25.5 percent of London's slave-carrying capacity. Thirty-three merchants owned only one ship each; eleven owned two. Concentration of ownership, which has been shown to be characteristic of the London trade toward the end of the century, is also apparent early in the century. In the later period partnership dominated the trade, but in 1726 individual entrepreneurship was the pattern, and single owners of ships were able to mobilize the capital to engross a sizeable fraction of the trade.[8]

Some of Morice's vessels were constant traders throughout the decade. The *Judith Snow,* 130 tons, made her first voyage in 1721 and her seventh in 1730; the *Katherine,* 170 tons, made her first voyage in 1724 and her sixth in 1730, setting a pattern of an annual voyage; the *Portugall* embarked on her sixth voyage in 1729. Other names recur; new ones appear and old ones disappear. Fond of naming vessels for his wives (Judith and Katherine) and his daughters (Anne and Elizabeth), Morice owned a brigantine *Anne* in 1720, recorded the fourth voyage of the *Anne* Gally in 1724 and the first voyage of another *Anne* Gally in 1730.

Similarly, the captains often were continuingly in his service. The most famous of these, William Snelgrave, in 1718 commanded the *Bird,* whose capture by pirates he recounted in his book, and he subsequently commanded the *Henry,* the *Portugall,* and the *Katherine.* He was among those slave-ship captains—including John Dagge, Jeremiah Pearce, Thomas Grosse, and Robert More, all of whom had commanded several voyages for Morice—who filed claims against the estate for adjudication by the House of Lords.[9]

8. Humphrey Morice Papers, Bank of England, COU B43, B44; PRO, CO 388/25; Roger Anstey, *The Atlantic Slave Trade and British Abolition, 1760–1810* (Atlantic Highlands, N.J.: Humanities Press, 1975), 6.

9. Snelgrave, *New Account,* 193–288; *The Journals of the House of Lords,* 57 vols. (London, n.d.; hereinafter *LJ*), 25:27.

The cargoes exported from London in Morice's vessels importantly included metal and wares made from metal, including voyage iron (for working by Africans), pewter (often in the form of "Guinea basins"), brass (often in the form of pans and referred to as "battery"), swords, guns, beads, textiles (including woolens and cottons), and India goods. The average investment in ten cargoes was £3,008, including insurance and various charges. The exports from London were of domestic origin, except for the India goods, and reflected advantages England had in conducting the African trade.

A prominent feature of Morice's trade was loading a second cargo in Holland, where he maintained a close connection with the Rotterdam merchant Bastiaen Molewater. The *Sarah,* clearing from London in 1722, loaded a cargo in Rotterdam made up of beads, cloths, guns, powder, and spirits, valued at 14,776.6 guilders. The *Katherine,* clearing from London in 1729, loaded a cargo in Rotterdam made up of gunpowder, malt brandy, cloths, brass pans, iron bars, tobacco pipes, and knives, valued at 32,407.14 guilders. The average value of five cargoes exported from Holland was 27,158.4 guilders. A Captain Hill, who had been in the slave trade for many years and who may have been Captain Thomas Hill, commander of Morice's *Anne* in 1730–1731, told the Board of Trade in 1750, "Mr Morris's ships amounted from 6 to £12,000."[10]

Concerned that English ships were carrying foreign goods in the African trade, the Board of Trade in 1730 asked Morice about the practice. Morice responded that gunpowder and spirits were cheaper in Holland, in both instances the price having been raised by English government policies. So far as other wares were concerned, Morice testified that iron and beads and old sheets were cheaper in Holland, but that German exports from Hamburg were cheaper in England because they came by water, the Dutch importing them by land.

Was it true, the board asked, that Dutch factories on the coast of Africa sometimes seized English vessels because they were carrying Dutch goods? "Far from it," replied Morice, explaining that English vessels loading in Holland received passes from the Dutch West India Company.[11]

10. *Journal of the Commissioners, 1749–1753,* 9–10.
11. *Journal of the Commissioners, 1728–1729–1734,* 100–101.

Morice, however, may have enjoyed the special favor of the Dutch. William Smith, author of *A New Voyage to Guinea*, published in 1744, wrote: "I had heard that all the *Dutch* Chiefs, at the Outports, were ordered to supply no *English* Ship whatsoever with either Wood or Water, except the Ships belonging to a certain worthy and eminent Merchant of *London*."[12] Whatever the situation, Morice paid special heed to his Dutch loadings and Dutch connection in Africa.

Morice was equally zealous to sell Dutch wares in Africa, cultivate good business relations with Dutch traders in Africa, and acquire gold from Dutch traders on the Gold Coast. Material prepared for a hearing at the bar of the House of Lords after his death in part read that Morice "carried on a very extensive Trade to the Coast of Africa . . . and also to Holland."[13]

After instructing Captain Snelgrave of the *Katherine* in 1729 to take on a cargo in Holland, Morice continued: "I am in hopes you will be able to dispose of a considerable part of your Dutch Cargoe to the Windward for Gold, Especially at Cape Lahoe, where by all accounts I am informed there is a good trade Stirring and plenty of Gold . . . I would have you touch at the Mine [Elmina, a Dutch fort] and deliver my Letters to the Dutch gentlemen there, and you must take aboard under your care and charge whatever Gold those Gentlemen or any others will load aboard you. Possibly you may be able to sell part of your Cargo at the Mine for Gold, which I would have no endeavors on your part be wanting to accomplish."[14]

The voyage patterns of Morice's ships often involved, as we have seen, a stop at Rotterdam; his vessels customarily put in for supplies at the start of trading in Africa. The master of the ship *Henry* was instructed to take on rice, wood, and water at Sestos or thereabouts, corn at Axim, and then sail to specified locations. At least one vessel was dispatched directly to Antigua in the West Indies to load rum and other wares and then proceed to Africa. The *Judith*, after transporting 100 Negroes from Africa to Jamaica in

12. William Smith, *A New Voyage to Guinea: describing the customs, manners . . .* (London, 1744), 118.
13. British Library, Addit. MSS 36, 153:f. 76.
14. Morice to Captain Snelgrave, September 22, 1729, Morice Papers, COU B49.

1722, cleared for Africa laden with the remainder of its original cargo and 4,945 gallons of rum taken on at Jamaica. On this bilateral voyage the *Judith* purchased 165 slaves in Africa. Some of Morice's vessels lingered in African waters, as we shall see, resupplied there by other Morice vessels, buying and selling among themselves and foreigners.[15]

At his office in Mincing Lane, Morice gave detailed and well-informed advice to his captains about trade conditions in Africa. Take care, he told one captain, that you are not imposed on in your customs at Whydah, where "the Natives seem to advance and increase their Dutys." To another he gave instructions to try to sell his entire cargo to the governor of the Royal African Company's Gambia fort, Robert Plunkett, "for I am of opinion Mr. Plunkett having no Stock of Goods or provisions by him; or has any prospect of having any Supplies from the African Company, he may under these Circumstances be willing & desireous to trade with you."[16]

To Captain Snelgrave he explained a technique of trading and an attitude of Africans in a particular part of the coast: "You must endeavour to hire or buy at Commenda or any other place a good large Canoe and Secure Canoe men to go down the Coast along with you for at Quittah and Popoe they will be of singular use to you to land and gett ashore your Goods, and carry off your Negroes, which will tend greatly towards your dispatch at those places, but if you proceed down to Jacqueen you must discharge your Canoe men, for they will not admitt them to work your ship there . . ."[17]

He enjoined a captain, who was sailing for the Gambia River to trade for Negroes, gold, ivory, beeswax, and other commodities, to go up the river where goods were to be purchased more cheaply, avoiding the African Company. He further advised, do not "unsort" your cargo by selling only the best Negroes at the first stop; reserve part of your prime goods for the last; dispose of your worst goods first. Expressing the hope the captain would be able to buy 150 Negroes besides gold, ivory, and other wares, Morice instructed him

15. Morice to Captain Snelgrave, October 20, 1722, Morice Papers, COU B43; Morice to Capt. Jeremiah Pearce, March 30, 1730, Morice Papers, COU B43, B51; PRO, CO 142/14, f. 109.
16. Morice to Capt. William Boyle, May 11, 1724, Morice Papers, COU B47; Morice to Capt. Edmund Weedon, March 25, 1725, Morice Papers, COU B47, B48.
17. Morice to Captain Snelgrave, September 22, 1729, Morice Papers, COU B49.

that if he was unable to slave at Gambia, he should go to Sierra Leone and as far as Whydah and Jaquin.[18]

Morice's instructions to his captains were not only explicit and well-informed but also suggested a distinctive pattern in the African trade. His main interest was not in the slave trade, though he was perhaps the foremost English slave trader of his time. He operated a complex network of vessels in the trade, often having several ships simultaneously in African waters. When his captains did buy slaves, he preferred to have them sold in Africa. The slave purchasers of his first choice were the Portuguese in Africa and not the English or Spanish in America. Contrary to the conventional wisdom about the profits and pattern of the triangular trade, he was neither eager to sell his slaves in America nor to engage in the importation of American products.

If you must buy Negroes, he told the commander of the *Sarah Gally*, try to sell them to the Portuguese in Africa. Sell your cargo for gold and your Negroes for gold to the Portuguese, as Captains Boyle and Dagge (commanders of his vessels the *Portugall* Gally and the *Whidah,* respectively) did lately, he urged a captain departing London in 1722. "It is my earnest desire that you dispose of[,] at all Places upon the Coast of Africa, so many Goods as you can possibly of my Cargoe for Gold, and to sell to the Portuguese and others what Negroes you can for gold. If possible sell Negroes to Portuguese for gold, because they give 6 & 7 and 7 1/2 ounces of gold for males. You may take Brazil tobacco in part payment," he instructed one his captains.[19]

The operation of a number of vessels simultaneously in the African trade gave Morice several advantages. Though perhaps not as efficient as the floating factory maintained by Thomas Hall in the 1730s and 1740s, his method made possible the exchange of goods and information among his captains and often expedited the movement of his ships.[20]

18. Morice to Capt. William Clinch, September 13, 1721, Morice Papers, COU B44.

19. Morice to Capt. Stephen Bull, October 30, 1722, Morice Papers, COU B45; Morice to Captain Snelgrave, October 20, 1722, Morice Papers, COU B46; Morice to Captain Snelgrave, September 22, 1729, Morice Papers, COU B49; Morice to Captain Clinch, September 13, 1721, Morice Papers, COU B44.

20. For Hall, see PRO, CO 103/130–33, and Conrad Gill, *Merchants and Mariners*

A contemporary noted how Morice's method met special demands of the African trade. Writing in 1735, John Atkins observed: "The Success of A Voyage depends first, on the well sorting, and on the well timing of a Cargo . . . First, on the Timing of a Cargo: This depends at several places much on Chance, from the fanciful and various Humours of the Negroes, who make great demands one Voyage for a Commodity, that perhaps they reject next, and is in part to be remedied either by making the things they itch after, to pass off those they have not so much mind to, or by such a continual Traffick and Correspondence on the Coast as may furnish the Owner from time to time with quick Intelligence, to be done only by great Merchants, who can keep imployed a number of Ships, that like a Thread unites them in a knowledge of their Demands, and a readier Supply for them, as well as dispatch for their Master's Interest, by putting the Purchases of two or three Ships into one. The late Mr. Humphry Morice was the greatest private Trader this way, and unless Providence had fixed a Curse upon it, he must have gained exceedingly."[21]

In his instructions to his captains, Morice often listed the names and commanders of his vessels whom they might meet. He urged full cooperation among them, wrote out signals to be observed among ships in his service, gave them a large measure of discretion, and at the same time required that a signed record be submitted to him. Thomas Hill, commander of the *Anne* Gally, read in his instruction: "It being my Orders that when you meet with any Ship in my Service upon the Coast of Africa that you consult and advise with the Commander thereof what may be best to be done for my interest in both Ships, and to make disposition of each Vessell accordingly . . . and you are to observe that your Selfe and any Commander in my Service, are at Liberty to deliver any Goods, Stores, Provisions, Negroes, or any thing on board, out of one Vessel into the other giving Receipts to each other . . . [and] it is my directions that the Results of your Consultations be put down in writing and Signed by each of you; to be produced to mee when required."[22]

---

of the Eighteenth Century (London: Edward Arnold, 1961), 74–97. For comment on the two methods of doing business, see *Journal of the Commissioners, 1749–1753,* 10.

21. John Atkins, *A Voyage to Guinea, Brazil, and the West Indies . . .* (London, 1735), 158–59.

22. Morice to Captain Hill, September 30, 1730, Morice Papers, COU B50.

To take one illustration of Morice's policy of collaboration, the ship *Henry,* Captain Snelgrave, in 1721–1722 supplied the *Sarah,* Captain Bull, and the *Elizabeth,* Captain Sharpe, with goods; received 120 slaves from the *Elizabeth;* delivered 100 slaves to the *Sarah;* and sold 76 slaves to the Portuguese before making its way to the slave market at Kingston, Jamaica. On her next voyage the *Henry* received two invoices of goods, one for the *Sarah,* which was clearing for Africa by way of Rotterdam, and one for the *Portugall,* Captain William Boyle, which departed London two and a half weeks later. The captains were to consult one another and exchange goods in Africa.[23]

Not only did Morice sometimes send cargoes for two trading vessels in one vessel, but he also sought by exchange of cargoes to expedite the voyage of a vessel he had earlier sent out. Captain Boyle, departing for Africa again in the *Portugall* in 1724, was told he might meet Captains Snelgrave and Dagge and exchange with them, completing their cargoes, and that if he should meet Captain Blincko of the *Squirrel,* he was to load Negroes and whatever commodities were appropriate "in order to dispatch her away so soon as you and Capt. Blincko see each other." Trading at Whydah, the *Portugall* turned over to Snelgrave the gold it had received for slaves, and at the same time took on board 170 slaves from Snelgrave.[24]

The efficiency of Morice's handling of his ships made it possible for some of them to conduct a voyage a year. He was at pains to shorten the length of voyages. Trade wherever you touch, he often advised his captains. Sell to the Portuguese or other purchaser in Africa, was another steady injunction. Try to get 200 Negroes in 14 days or three weeks. If you can't buy from Mr. Plunkett, the Royal African Company governor, try the natives, but not longer than three weeks, and then try up the river where the Negroes are cheap. "I am in hopes you will meet with a good Sale and quick dispatch for your Cargo," he told one captain, and to another he wrote characteristically, "I should be glad to have you turn your whole Cargoe of Goods and Negroes into Gold and so proceed home directly to London."[25]

23. Morice Papers, COU B43, B45.
24. Morice to Captain Boyle, May 11, 1724, Morice Papers, COU B47.
25. Morice to Captain Weedon, March 25, 1725, Morice Papers, COU B48;

When a captain was to buy Negroes and could not sell them in Africa but had to carry them to America, Morice sought to reduce the turnaround time in the New World. "It is my positive Orders," he instructed, "that after the delivery of your Cargoe of Negroes at Virginia or Maryland, that you do not stay longer at either place to get a freight home of Tobacco, than fourteen days, or three weeks at farthest." In lieu of tobacco the ship was to load pipe staves or walnut tree planks.[26]

The short distance between London and Rotterdam—an advantage that London held over Bristol and Liverpool—extended the voyage only three weeks. Voyage time between London or Rotterdam and the first stop in Africa varied from five to ten weeks. The length of stay in Africa sometimes lasted five months, but perhaps owing to Morice's distinctive methods could last only three weeks. Similarly, the crossing time for the Atlantic leg varied because of differences in length and voyage conditions, taking from less than one month to over two and a half months.

In selecting slaves captains were given precise instructions about age, sex, and health. They were to choose Negroes between 12 and 25 years of age; the sexual ratio was two males for each female; and as to physical condition, "let your doctor mind they are sound, good, healthy and not blind, lame or blemished." Analysis of several slave cargoes totaling 1,658 slaves discloses that slave purchases were substantially in keeping with Morice's orders, except for the ratio between boys and girls. The breakdown is 911 men, 425 women, 237 boys, and 85 girls.[27]

Morice's captains, with their names recurring voyage after voyage, were not only experienced mariners, but also experienced in buying and selling slaves. They were paid in part through a captain's commission, involving a portion of the slaves and sometimes other

Morice to Capt. Anthony Overstall, July 8, 1728, in "Book containing Orders and Instructions to Anthony Overstall commander of the *Judith Snow* . . ." Columbia University microfilm, University of Nebraska–Lincoln; Morice to Captain Snelgrave, September 22, 1729, Morice Papers, COU B49.

26. Morice to Captain Weedon, March 25, 1725, Morice Papers, COU B48.

27. Morice to Captain Clinch, September 13, 1721, Morice Papers, COU B44. The cargoes analyzed are those of the *Judith*, 1721–1722; the *Henry*, 1721–1722; the *Sarah*, 1722–1723; the *Henry*, 1722–1723; the *Anne*, 1725–1726; and the *Judith*, 1728–1729.

produce, and the opportunity to make a limited investment on their own account and to transport slaves free of freight. Similar arrangements often were made with other officers. Captain William Clinch of the *Judith* on her voyage of 1721–1722 was allowed a commission of four Negroes in every 104 sold; 5 percent of all gold, ivory, and other commodities; and permission to carry free of freight "an adventure" of £300 and four Negroes. Clinch was authorized to allow his chief mate and doctor whatever he agreed on with them. For the voyage of the *Anne* in 1730, Morice allowed "adventures" to Captain Hill of £600 and four Negroes, to the chief mate and the surgeon £50, and to the second mate £40—all freight-free.[28]

Morice necessarily placed great reliance upon his captains, who often were out of his sight for a year or more. He required them to keep a daily account of trade and to secure the signatures of other officers. He also threatened forfeiture of commission, wages, and all privileges should a captain exceed the investment that had been authorized. At the same time, recognizing the contingencies of the voyage, he acknowledged: "I must therefore referr to your prudence and care and good management the Conduct of this Ships Cargoe and Investment which I leave entirely to you to dispose of as you find most for my benefit and advantage depending on your Integrity and experience to do your best for mee."[29]

His loyalty was seldom misplaced and he was solicitous about captain and crew. After Captain Snelgrave's *Bird* was seized by pirates, on his return in a Bristol vessel Snelgrave found waiting for him a letter from Morice offering words of comfort, command of another ship, and an order to Morice's Bristol correspondent to distribute money among the *Bird*'s crew. Morice was careful to obey the law about paying sailors when their wages were due: "Lett your Officers and Seamen be well used by you and have everything that is necessary and Convenient for them especially if sick and out of Order and let them have such refreshments as are proper for them when they work hard and are fatigued with hard labour in the Warm Climate of Africa."[30]

28. Morice to Captain Clinch, September 13, 1721, Morice Papers, COU B44; Morice to Captain Hill, September 30, 1730, Morice Papers, COU B50.

29. Morice to Captain Overstall, July 8, 1728, in "Book containing Orders."

30. Snelgrave, *New Account,* 288; Morice to Captain Overstall, July 8, 1728, in "Book containing Orders."

A major aim in Morice's continuing injunctions to sell cargoes and Negroes for gold in Africa was to reduce losses by death and accident on the Middle Passage, "whereby the hazard of mortality and innumerable accidents will be avoided that happens in a voyage to the West Indies." His ship *Henry* in its 1721–1722 voyage had a disastrous loss; it sold to the Portuguese in Africa 76 slaves, delivered to another Morice vessel 100 slaves, and embarked for Jamaica with 591 slaves, of whom 232 died. This was perhaps the heaviest mortality loss Morice suffered. The *Henry* on its next voyage lost only 19 of its cargo of 426, reducing the loss from 39 percent to 4.5 percent.[31]

Long before Parliament in 1788 required slave ships to carry surgeons and ordered them to keep a journal of numbers of slaves, deaths of slaves and crew, and causes of death, Morice customarily placed a surgeon on each ship and had him certify the number of deaths. Well before Dr. James Lind in 1754 published *A Treatise on the Scurvy*, describing the effectiveness of oranges, lemons, and limes as antiscorbutics, Morice had his captains purchase limes before starting the Middle Passage. One measure of concern about the health of the Negroes is the notation made by the master of the *Anne Gally* in 1725 that he had paid forty bars of iron to "Mr. Rodon Surgeon of the Samuel for his attendance and Medicines in the time of my Surgeon's sickness." Morice adjured a departing captain, "Be carefull of and kind to your Negroes and let them be well used by your Officers."[32]

It was perhaps because of these practices—the employment of surgeons, the supply of antiscorbutics as well as ample provisions, and exhortation of care and kindness—that Morice's losses on the Middle Passage were usually small. The *Judith* in her voyage of 1728–1729 appears to have lost 13 of 227 Negroes; on her voyage of 1730–1731 she lost 13 of 280, and of these, three died on the African coast and three in Barbados. The *Judith*'s losses and those of the *Henry* on its second voyage, averaging about 4.5 percent, compare very favorably with those of the later period

---

31. Morice to Captain Snelgrave, September 22, 1729, Morice Papers, COU B49, B43, B46.

32. Morice Papers, COU B48; Morice to Captain Snelgrave, September 22, 1739, Morice Papers, COU B49.

1761–1791, when mortality rates varied from 8.5 to 9.6 percent.[33]

If his captains failed to sell their slaves in Africa, Morice customarily ordered them to proceed to the British West Indies. They were instructed to leave behind any unsold goods with other Morice captains or responsible factors, and in particular to dispose of Dutch goods, because carrying them to the plantations and London risked seizure and forfeiture to the British government. A frequent voyage pattern involved a stop at Barbados either to sell slaves or to inquire about markets elsewhere in the British West Indies.[34]

Most of Morice's American sales were made in Jamaica, with Barbados the second most important market. A number of ships disposed of their slaves at both islands. The *Anne* in 1725 had orders to sail to Virginia and then Maryland, unless detained in Africa or on the Middle Passage, but she in actuality sold her cargo in Jamaica. Morice's Barbados factors on at least one occasion consigned his Negroes to Maryland merchants.[35]

In each of the American markets Morice had merchants with whom he customarily did business. In Barbados it was the firm of Withers and Harrison and in Jamaica a firm headed by a Mr. Bassnett, who over the decade had a series of partners. These merchants would not only handle the sale of Negroes, but also supply money to pay the seamen their half wages which the law directed to be paid, pay charges for refitting the vessel, and provide a load for the return voyage to London.[36]

Eager to get as high a price as possible, Morice instructed his captains to present his human cargoes in the most favorable manner. "I would have you be mindfull so soon as you come in sight of Barbadoes or Jamaica," he told one captain, "to get your Negroes shaved and made clean to look well and strike a good impression on the planters and buyers . . . whereby there may be hopes of selling them at a better price and may prove a considerable advantage

33. "Book containing Orders"; Morice Papers, COU B51; Anstey, *Atlantic Slave Trade and British Abolition,* 31, 415.
34. "Book containing Orders"; Morice Papers, COU B49.
35. Morice Papers, COU B48; Morice to Withers and Harrison, June 29, 1731, Morice Papers, COU D542.
36. Morice to Captain Snelgrave, October 20, 1722, Morice Papers, COU B46.

to me in their sales, for as they appear at first sight the planters represent their quality and goodness to one another as they are affected with their looks and appearances."[37]

He prescribed certain principles of selling slaves in America. One was to preserve the assortment of the cargo; do not unsort your cargo, he instructed. A second was to continue the voyage in case the cargo remain unsold, making inquiries of designated merchants. A third principle was to avoid a long wait for a return cargo. "You must be expeditious as Possible to take in a Loading of Sugars, for to Lye long at any of the Islands to take in a Loading, will be very detrimental to mee, And the great charge your Ship Sails at will eat up the freight," he told the master of the *Katherine,* which was designed for 550 Negroes.[38]

On occasion he specified prices to be gotten for the cargoes. Sell at £30 per head, he ordered the master of the *Portugall* on May 11, 1724; less than a year later, on March 25, he ordered the master of the *Anne* to sell at £25; on July 8, 1728, the master of the *Judith* received instructions to get £28–£30. Details of sales and return cargoes are sparse in the Morice papers. Load sugar, a captain was told, and we may suppose that sugar was the normal cargo from Barbados and Jamaica. The instructions notably do not speak of bills of exchange. The *Anne,* with orders to proceed to Virginia or Maryland, had instructions, as we have seen, to bring home tobacco or pipe staves and walnut wood.

The materials seen by this writer do not make it possible to document profits and losses. The fact that Morice long continued in the trade suggests he thought the trade to be profitable. However, the fact that he died deeply in debt (he owed nearly £150,000) suggests either mismanagement of his affairs or losses in the trade.

Humphry Morice has been little known, though he perhaps was the foremost English slave trader in his time. But his time was the first half of the eighteenth century, which has been little studied in this connection; perhaps only one other English slave merchant in that half-century has been studied in detail: Thomas Hall. The volume of his trade alone does not make Morice important. Beyond this there are distinctive attributes of his trade. He frequently ac-

37. Morice to Captain Boyle, May 11, 1724, Morice Papers, COU B47.
38. Morice to Captain Snelgrave, September 22, 1729, Morice Papers, COU B49.

quired a portion of his African cargo in Holland. He conducted a system of multiple-ship operations in Africa that enabled him to exchange information and wares among his captains. His main interest in African commerce was in gold and silver and only secondarily in Negroes. Yet the demands of African commerce often required his captains to trade their European wares for Negroes. In this event Morice preferred to sell the Negroes in Africa. He urged sale to the Portuguese, who paid in gold, rather than to the South Sea Company or the Royal African Company. He preferred a bilateral rather than a triangular trade, hoping to avoid the Middle Passage, with its perils, and the problems of a returning cargo. He evinced concern for the care and treatment both of his crews and human cargoes.

His contemporaries recognized Humphry Morice as a very substantial slave merchant who carried on his business in distinctive ways. The separate traders frequently sent him before the Board of Trade to represent their views. On one occasion Morice explained why his ships sometimes took on part of their loading in Holland, although the wares were available in England. John Atkins described him as "the greatest private Trader" among those who were able to maintain "a continual Traffick and Correspondence on the Coast." William Smith believed him to be the beneficiary of orders to the Dutch West India Company chiefs to supply only his ships. The magnitude of Morice's slaving is suggested by testimony before the Board of Trade that he imported more Gold Coast Negroes into the British colonies than all the merchants of Bristol and Liverpool and that the capital in each of his ships amounted from £6,000 to £12,000. Well known in his day, Humphry Morice deserves to be better known by students of the transatlantic slave trade.

4

Richard Harris,
Slave Trader Spokesman

A contemporary of Humphry Morice, Richard Harris was an active slave merchant, especially in shipping slaves from Africa to Jamaica. He frequently was called before the Board of Trade to supply information and act as liaison with his fellow merchants. Harris was probably the chief spokesman of the London slave merchants for the first three decades of the eighteenth century. No biography of him exists, but my sketch of his life will appear in the *New Dictionary of National Biography.*

Between 1702 and 1712 Harris made nine consignments to Africa valued at £25,121. During the same period, Morice made four consignments with a sworn value of £5,720.

The Trans-Atlantic Slave Trade: A Database lists Harris as first of the owners of slave ships that made eight voyages between 1718 and 1733, and second owner of one. In all, Harris's nine ships embarked 1,931 slaves in Africa with a mean of 215 slaves and disembarked 1,626 with a mean of 181 in the Americas.

The *Crocodile,* built in New York in 1718, registered in London in 1723, 164 British measured tons, disembarked 200 slaves in Kingston, Jamaica, in 1728. The *Antelope,* to provide another example, built in Shoreham, Sussex, registered in London in 1724, the year of its build, 254 British measured tons, after buying slaves in Angola, arrived in Virginia with 286 slaves. It had departed London on October 3, 1733, and dropped anchor in the York River on October 22, 1734.

≈

"So little is known of the separate traders," lamented the historian of the Royal African Company, K. G. Davies, that he was reduced

This chapter first appeared in *Albion* 23:3 (fall 1991): 439–58.

to perceptive speculation about their activity. Basil Williams, writing about the period 1714–1760, asserted, "The traffic in negro slaves was carried on mainly by the Royal African Company."[1] In actuality a great deal can be discovered about the separate traders and their activity. The papers of Humphry Morice provide a rich source for a merchant who was perhaps London's and Great Britain's foremost slave trader in the 1720s. The assertion that the traffic in Negro slaves was carried on mainly by the Royal African Company is easily refuted by materials in the Public Record Office. London separate traders dominated the trade for the first three decades of the eighteenth century, giving way to Bristol traders in the 1730s, who in turn gave way to Liverpool in the 1740s.[2]

The English slave trade between 1699 and 1729, energized by the end of government monopoly and the booming international market for slaves in America, grew prodigiously. In these years England accounted for nearly one-half of all slaves exported from the west coast of Africa. London alone accounted for two-thirds of all slaves delivered by English ships.[3]

Although the period falls more than half a century before Adam Smith's classic exposition of the advantages of free trade over monopoly, an English free trade doctrine had found expression in Sir Dudley North's pamphlet *Discourses upon Trade* (1691) and in parliamentary proceedings. Interlopers in the slave trade, smugglers in the lucrative Spanish-American trade who opposed parliamentary restriction on their activity, separate traders whose participation in the trade became legalized in 1698, and a variety of commercial, industrial, and planting interests all contributed in their fashion to an outlook favoring free trade in slaves. When England won the *asiento* from Spain in 1713 and conferred it upon the South Sea Company, separate traders sought to share in the monopoly's delivery of slaves to the Spanish market.

Free trade advocates argued their case for free trade not in terms

---

1. K. G. Davies, *The Royal African Company* (New York: 1970), 148; Basil Williams, *The Whig Supremacy, 1714–1760* (Oxford: Clarendon Press, 1939), 296.

2. James A. Rawley, *The Transatlantic Slave Trade: A History* (New York: W. W. Norton, 1981), chap. 10.

3. David Richardson, "The Eighteenth-Century British Slave Trade: Estimates of Its Volume and Coastal Distribution in Africa," *Research in Economic History* 12 (1989): 185–87.

of theory but in practical results for the British economy. Compared to monopoly, they said, free trade could foster greater employment and production in England, export more English goods to Africa, employ more shipping, carry more slaves, more successfully meet labor needs in all importing colonies (some of which had been neglected by the Royal African Company), sell slaves more cheaply, stimulate more production of plantation crops, and import more African and American products. Sundry merchants and other Londoners in 1696 told the House of Commons that "the trade to Africa is of great importance to England and might be much enlarged if all persons had free liberty to trade thither without molestation." Davies concludes, "Free trade was given its chance by one of the least ideological of all revolutions."[4]

The present-day student is struck by the absence of moral considerations in discussing the slave trade. Parliament, opening the trade to separate traders in 1698, described it as "highly beneficial and advantageous to this kingdom, and to the Plantations and Colonies." Without pricking of conscience, it united free trade and the slave trade. The Church of England sanctioned the union; in 1727 the bishop of London advised American masters that conversion to Christianity would place their slaves "under stronger Obligations to perform those Duties with the greatest Diligence and Fidelity, not only from the Fear of Men, but from a sense of Duty to God." Whatever compassion was felt for the slaves moved in the direction of conversion rather than emancipation. At the close of the period in 1729 both the attorney general and the solicitor general declared that neither baptism nor presence on English soil freed a slave. Not until the second half of the century did slavery significantly stir the English conscience.[5]

The case of Richard Harris, London slave merchant and spokesman for the private traders, often referred to as the separate traders,

4. *The Journals of the House of Commons* (London, 1547–; hereinafter *CJ*), 11:622; Davies, *Royal African Company*, 152. David W. Galenson demonstrates that "a large competitive market existed in the late seventeenth and early eighteenth century." Galenson, *Traders, Planters and Slaves: Market Behavior in Early English America* (Cambridge and New York: Cambridge University Press, 1986), 153.

5. Elizabeth Donnan, ed., *Documents Illustrative of the History of the Slave Trade to America*, 4 vols. (Washington: Carnegie Institution, 1930–1935), 1:42; David Brion Davis, *The Problem of Slavery in Western Culture* (Ithaca: Cornell University Press, 1966), 210, 209.

illuminates the vigorous political activity of the London separate traders both in their routing of the Royal African Company's efforts to regain its monopoly and in their wielding influence to secure economic advantages for conduct of the trade. Harris's career extended over four decades, beginning as early as 1694 when he was at Barbados and observed that French privateers, cutting off provisions from the British North American mainland, were causing the planters to "suffer much & the Negroes perish for want." Never a member of Parliament, unlike many of his colleagues, nor an alderman, he has not been the subject of biographical sketches; details of his life remain obscure. He was, however, a familiar figure before the Board of Trade and parliamentary committees. A pamphleteer in 1728 recognized the depth of his knowledge and the height of his trustworthiness, alluding to "Mr. Richard Harris, a Merchant . . . than whom no Body understands this [slave] trade better, or is more to be credited." The *Gentleman's Magazine* in 1734 noted "the death of Mr. Richd Harris, on Tower Hill, an eminent Trader to Africa and the West Indies."[6]

Probably no man exerted himself more in the interests of the London separate traders during the first third of the eighteenth century than Harris. Heavily engaged in the trade, he made consignments to Africa of sworn value of £25,121—second only to Robert Heysham—in the years 1702–1712. The owner of seven ships in the African trade in 1726, he stood second to Humphry Morice in number of ships owned and Negroes intended to be purchased.[7] The London separate traders used him to present their case, together with other principal slave merchants, but none so persistently over the years of Harris's career. He possessed intimate knowledge of the Jamaica trade and familiarity with nearly all aspects of slaving: British, African, Spanish American, Caribbean, and North American.

The Board of Trade turned to Harris as an avenue to ascertain

6. "A Defence of the Observations on the Assiento Trade. By the Author of the Observations on the Assiento Trade" (London, 1728); *Gentleman's Magazine* 4 (September 1734): 511. Searches for information on Harris at the National Register of Archives and the London Record Office proved unproductive; perhaps subsequent investigation will add biographical details.

7. Davies, *Royal African Company,* 372–73; Public Record Office (hereinafter PRO), CO 388/25.

the views of the London separate traders. It summoned him to speak for his associates and to convey queries back and forth between the Londoners and the board. He responded to a broad range of queries touching the trade, as we shall see. The board's far-reaching reliance on him may be illustrated by inquiries it made about minor matters. The board in 1719 asked him whether the English were the first discoverers of Newfoundland, particularly whether Sebastian Cabot was there before the Spaniards. Harris replied that he could not find proof about Cabot, but remarked that the navigator had always been so reputed, and he referred the board to Peter Heylin's *Cosmography* (Heylin was a historian who in 1618 began lecturing on cosmography at Oxford University). Asked on another occasion about removing a certain colonial governor, Harris dismissed "bagatel storys" concerning the man and went on to make a ringing endorsement of the governor's rare merit, observing, "I doubt there is no better reason for his remove then [*sic*] ye pressing instance of another for his post." At another time the board requested his opinion about a proposed lighthouse at Cape Henry, Virginia. The extent of his interests is suggested by a letter he wrote Sir Hans Sloane, renowned collector of curiosities, offering a live tortoise and a "ginny fowle" brought by "One of my Ginny masters."[8]

Harris's political activities focused mainly on combating the untiring efforts of the Royal African Company to recover its monopoly on the slave trade and the persistent tendency of colonial legislatures to impose duties on the importation of slaves. Besides these matters Harris concerned himself with the slave trade's need for naval protection, the French competition, debt collection in the slave colonies, and the Molasses and Credit Acts.

Following the overthrow of the royal monopoly under which the Royal African Company had conducted business, Parliament for a decade failed to put the African trade on a new footing. In 1698 Parliament passed a law that fell between the demands of the company for restoration of its monopoly and the demands of private traders for free trade. The act addressed the matter of maintaining

8. PRO, *Calendar of State Papers, Colonial Series, America and West Indies,* 42 vols. (London, 1860–1954; hereinafter CSPC), 1719–1729, 187, 211; ibid., 1728–1729, 186–87; British Library, Addit. MSS 4045:f. 37.

the company's forts and settlements in Africa with a recognition that they were "undoubtedly necessary." Private traders, many of whom made little use of the African installations, were obliged to share in paying for their upkeep. Together with the company they were required to pay a duty of 10 percent *ad valorem* on all exports to Africa and a lesser duty on certain imports from northern Africa. Parliament fixed responsibility for maintaining the installations on the company. Private traders were to enjoy the protection and privileges of the forts and settlements and were allowed to set up installations of their own. The act had a life of thirteen years, expiring at the close of the parliamentary session of 1711–1712.[9]

Neither party was satisfied with the legislation; the company failed to regain its monopoly and the private traders were compelled to pay a duty, though some of them had plied the trade for years without being forced to do so. A spirited struggle between the rivals broke out in 1707 and endured until expiration of the act. During these years the London separate traders prospered and formed a community of interest in opposition to the ambition of the company. Merchants in Bristol and Liverpool entered the trade, but in Harris's time they did not attain the prominence they later enjoyed. Lobbying against monopoly and for free trade came largely from the London separate traders, who won support for a variety of interests inside and outside the metropolis.

The Royal African Company, suffering under the legalized competition, developed its case in 1705–1706. In the fall of 1707 it appealed to the Board of Trade, launching a campaign that lasted five years without remission, and was revived in 1725–1726. The company addressed a petition to the queen, who referred it to the Board of Trade. Here and in following papers the company laid out its basic arguments: the 10 percent duty did not suffice to maintain the forts, and the company was paying a disproportionate share of the costs; ruinous competition in Africa for slaves had pushed up the price so that trade stood in danger of being lost by England; other nations, especially the Dutch, were taking advantage of the ensuing confusion; the remedy could be found in restoring the monopoly. Nothing if not thorough, the board formulated queries, held hearings, collected masses of material, and wrote reports. Topics it

9. 9 and 10 Wm. III. c. 26. The text is in Donnan, *Documents,* 1:421–29.

investigated included company finances, condition of the forts, prices of slaves, numbers of ships employed and slaves carried by each party, and the value of English manufactures, especially woolen, exported to Africa. The board made inquiries of the slave-buying colonies, and in turn received petitions and letters from the colonies.[10]

Throughout these investigations Richard Harris was active, a leader of the small body of London merchants who spoke for the slave merchant community. In the first inquiry he and others attended board meetings and answered queries addressed to them by the board. The London separate traders on January 2, 1708, offered evidence that from midsummer 1698 to December 3, 1707, the Royal African Company had employed 87 ships in the African trade, the separate traders 522, most of which had cleared from London. The separate traders, they claimed, had delivered 130,500 slaves, the company 30,450.[11]

In this initial inquiry Harris played a distinctive role. He presented observations he had made before the separate traders had received the board's queries. Among other points, he declared: "There are carried about 4 or 500 Negroes p[er] ann[um] to Carolina and as many to New York, by the Private Traders, whereas none were carried before." He made at least three appearances before the board at this inquiry.[12]

The board on February 3 presented to the Privy Council a report that was damaging to the company's cause. Rebuffed, the company turned to the House of Commons, petitioning for consideration of its case. Faced with the Board of Trade report as well as petitions on behalf of the separate traders, the Commons adjourned without devising a bill.[13]

Continuing to hold hearings in 1708, the board among other matters gathered materials from colonial governors. The separate traders were no less busy, and on December 6, Harris and Thomas Smith presented to the board a memorial signed by themselves and three other prominent slave merchants. They offered papers

---

10. *Journal of the Commissioners for Trade and Plantations, 1704–1782*, 14 vols. (London: Stationery Office, 1920–1938), 1704–1734.

11. *Journal of the Commissioners, 1704–1709*, 436, 437, 444.

12. PRO, CO 388/11; I. 13, 16, 17.

13. British Library, Addit. MSS 14034:ff. 99–108; *CJ*, 15:599.

demonstrating that the separate traders had delivered far more slaves to Jamaica than had the company, questioning the expenditures of the 10 percent duty at the African forts and providing information from ship's masters, including Samuel Bonham, a rising figure in the London slaving community. They submitted an extract of a letter to Harris, dated Gambia, January 20, 1707, from John Freeman, master of a sloop belonging to a separate trader, in which Freeman asserted he had seen an order to the captain of a company ship forbidding any attempt against any French vessel, pursuant to an agreement between the company and the French.[14]

The board sent a letter to Harris, enclosing several queries to be communicated to the separate traders to Africa, an implicit recognition of his leadership among the London separate traders. In their replies, the separate traders provided impressive statistics in their favor. On the question of how much 10 percent duty had been paid by each party between Michaelmas 1707 and Michaelmas 1708, the traders declared they had paid £3,757, the company £944. The traders had dispatched thirty-four ships, the company four. The traders' exports had been valued at £39,580 and the company's at £9,440. But for "Calamity's of the War," the separate traders having lost twenty-one ships worth nearly £70,000 and the company one ship, the figures would have been higher.[15]

In its report to the Commons the board incorporated these materials, including a reference to Captain Freeman's letter to Harris. Summarizing evidence reaching back to 1698, the board feared that restoration of monopoly would restrict the trading area in Africa, decrease the number of ships in the trade, insufficiently supply Negroes to the plantations, and prejudice trade in general with a single exporter of British manufactures and a single buyer of plantation commodities abroad.[16]

Both parties petitioned the House of Commons, and twenty-seven London separate traders, including Harris, signed the group's plea—a "chorus against the company," snorted the company apologist Charles D'Avenant, who doubted whether some of the sign-

14. PRO, CO 324/9, 165–70; PRO, CO 388/11; *Journal of the Commissioners, 1704–1709*, 560–61.
15. *Journal of the Commissioners, 1704–1709*, 562; PRO, T70/175, 68–69.
16. PRO, CO 390/12, 172–82.

ers had ever sent goods to Africa. The Commons, after hearing from both parties, moved a bill for a regulated company with provisions for maintaining the African forts through a second reading, but the bill died through prorogation.[17]

Not long after Parliament met for the session of 1709–1710 the London merchants took the initiative, petitioning the Commons for a free trade measure. The merchants asserted that "the well-being and support of the plantations in America wholly depends upon their being well-supplied with negroes from Africa," and that the Royal African Company obstructed the trade. Petitions again poured in, over three to one in favor of free trade. The Commons asked the Board of Trade to report. The board, having held hearings, was prepared. In October it had addressed queries to the company and to the separate traders through Harris. He saw to it that the separate traders responded; the company failed to answer. Not surprisingly, the board's report to the Commons was unfavorable to the company. "Our Trade to Africa might have been in danger of being lost ... had not the Seperate [sic] Traders supply'd the American markets," it declared.[18]

By order by the Commons, the Royal African Company and the separate traders each presented their proposals on January 24, 1710. The company, which earlier petitioned for restoration of its joint stock basis, now proposed that it be required to export to Africa £100,000 in manufactures and merchandise each year, the price and number of Negroes delivered to the plantations being left to Her Majesty in Council. To its proposal the company introduced a new element: should England acquire the *asiento* to supply Spanish America with slaves, the nation required a strong joint stock company. Through Harris and his colleague, Humphry Morice, the separate traders offered their proposal: so far as the controversial matter of the African forts and settlements was concerned, the queen should take them over, making recompense to the company by a duty laid on the African trade. On the principal point at issue, the traders asked that the trade be laid open to all Britons subject to the duty. The usual flurry of petitions, thirteen for free trade,

17. CJ, 16:71, 160; PRO, T70/175, 100.
18. CJ, 16:235, 242, 246; Journal of the Commissioners, 1709–1715, 77 ff.; PRO, CO 389/21, 7–16 (in Donnan, Documents, 2:102–7).

four for the company, accompanied the parliamentary proceedings.[19]

The committee of the whole on February 9 reported two resolutions: the forts were necessary for the African trade, and the trade should be free to all. Worried creditors of the company petitioned the Commons, requesting that their security be safeguarded. In response the House ordered the company to produce a valuation of its property and the separate traders to submit their scheme for carrying on the trade. The company gave an account totaling £279,555, assigning more than one-third to Cape Coast Castle. The separate traders, through Harris, Morice, and their London colleague Isaac Milner, offered four propositions, amplifying their proposals of January 24. First, the traders would be incorporated in a regulated company, open to any subject who paid dues determined by Parliament. Second, the company would be compensated for its African forts, which would become national property maintained and defended by the Crown. Third, masters of Africa-bound vessels would be required to carry provisions and supplies for support of the forts and settlements. Fourth, duties would be paid to the queen, no governor or officer would be allowed to trade, and no development of agriculture would be permitted. These "fresh suggestions," as Davies called them, failed to win enactment.[20]

The Board of Trade in late October resumed consideration of the African trade. It wrote to the secretary of the Royal African Company for several accounts and sent to Harris queries to be communicated to the separate traders. The board directed Harris to report how much had been paid to the company for the 10 percent duty from Michaelmas 1709 to Michaelmas 1710, how many ships the separate traders had dispatched in that period, and how many Negroes had been delivered at what prices in that period.[21]

Over the signatures of Harris, Morice, Milner, and others, the separate traders made their replies. The duty paid by the separate traders exceeded £6,000, by the company about £400. The separate traders had sent out fifty-one ships, twenty-four of them from

19. *CJ*, 16:319–20 passim.
20. *CJ*, 16:300, 310, 312, 317–19; Davies, *Royal African Company*, 150.
21. *Journal of the Commissioners, 1708–1715*, 191; CSPC, 1710–1711, 247.

London, and the company five, two of them from the plantations. The separate traders had delivered 8,040 Negroes to the plantations, receiving depreciated colonial money. The company announced its willingness to unite with its creditors and carry on the trade on any reasonable terms, provided it had its charter privileges restored. The board sent the company scheme to Harris for his and other separate traders' observations.[22]

Harris and Morice replied at length for the separate traders, again urging royal annexation of the African settlements and placing the trade in a regulated company. Harris, always in close communication with Jamaica, presented a letter from merchants, planters, and legislators in Jamaica, saying they had been better furnished by the separate traders than by the company and urging a policy of open and free trade.[23]

The Board of Trade recommended a policy of free trade, calling for prompt action because the Act of 1698 would soon expire. Both parties now turned to the Commons, presenting their petitions, with that of the separate traders bearing the signatures of Harris, Morice, Milner, and others. Once more a bill failed to win enactment.[24]

With the prospect of the 10 percent act expiring the next year, the House of Commons requested the queen to have the Board of Trade examine the manner of carrying on the African trade. The board concerned itself mainly with the security of the African settlements, receiving testimony from the Royal African Company and the separate traders represented by Harris, Morice, and Milner. In late July 1711 the board made a response to the queen, but in January 1712 it received a mass of additional materials. It resumed its succession of hearings, attended by Harris, Morice, and others. On February 28 Harris and Morice, on behalf of the separate traders, described their proposal for a regulated company obliged to export each year goods to the value of £100,000 and subject to the queen's instructions about the number of Negroes to be supplied to the plantations. The company would supply the *asiento* trade, giving security for performance of responsibilities;

22. PRO, CO 388/13, no. 102; *CSPC*, 1710–1711, 306–8, 326.
23. *CSPC*, 1710–1711, 336–37.
24. PRO, CO 389/21; Donnan, *Documents*, 2:134–40.

appoint consuls on the African coast to pay rent and other expenses; and make gifts to African leaders. The African forts would be supported by the 10 percent duty, and if it should prove insufficient the traders would raise further sums among themselves.[25]

The board made its report to the queen, and on March 31 a committee of the House of Commons resolved in favor of a regulated company. A bill to create such a company failed to pass, the 10 percent act expired, and Parliament passed an act giving the company relief from its clamorous creditors. The separate traders, after a long, time-consuming struggle, had won a victory for free trade and themselves.[26]

Now obliged to maintain the African establishments without the 10 percent duty, the company threatened to sue the separate traders. The traders appealed to the Commons, asking for a declaration that the trade be continued free and open. The Commons responded with a resolution that the trade should be open, subject to duties for maintaining the forts. When the Lords took up the resolution, Harris pushed the separate traders' cause. He introduced a supporting address from "the Planters abroad," evidence about the number of ships in the trade, and "spake a long time in general." He offered a proposal on behalf of the separate traders, for which the papers no longer survive. The Lords rejected the resolution.[27]

The separate traders had won a nonideological victory for free trade and a material one for themselves. No longer need they pay duty on exports to Africa. The company bore financial responsibility for the African forts, which decayed until rescued by a legislative subvention in 1730. The slave trade continued without a statutory basis; nearly four decades would pass before Parliament provided one.

Why had the separate traders prevailed? Three factors aid in answering this question. One was the abysmal record of the Royal African Company. In comparison with the separate traders, it had dispatched few ships to Africa, exported modest amounts of British manufactures, poorly maintained the forts, and delivered a small

25. *Journal of the Commissioners, 1709–1715*, 288–89, 293, 333, 335, 344–46.
26. *CJ*, 17:164–65; 10 Ann. c 24.
27. *CJ*, 17:319; *The Manuscripts of the House of Lords*, n.s., 10 (1712–1713) (London, 1953), 73–74.

number of slaves to the plantations. Second, the evidence drawn together over the years of inquiry strongly showed that the commercial interests of England had been advanced by the separate traders. Free trade on its face was more successful than monopoly. Third, widespread counteraction to the appeals of the Royal African Company marked the contest. Opposition to monopoly came from the outports, Bristol and Liverpool, both growing in importance in conducting the slave trade. It came also from municipal corporations and local economic interests, particularly woolen, iron, shipwright, and ship-outfitter interests. It came further from plantations, especially Jamaica, which was "more concern'd in the Negro Trade, than all the other British Plantations," as the Board of Trade advised the queen.[28] Of great importance was the assiduous opposition of the London separate traders, at this time the major slave merchant community. They gathered evidence for their cause, peppered the Board of Trade and committees of the House of Commons and House of Lords with petitions, and perseveringly appeared before those bodies. Humphry Morice, Robert Heysham, Francis Chamberlayne, and other separate traders were members of Parliament. At the forefront of the leadership stood Richard Harris, flourishing as a trader, well-connected in Africa and America, astute and energetic—a man whose qualities were recognized by his colleagues and the government.

Aided by contracts to supply the *asiento* and an infusion of capital by the Duke of Chandos, the Royal African Company obstinately clung to the slave trade for about a decade. In 1724 the company initiated a series of petitions complaining of foreign and domestic competition that had pushed up the price of slaves, declaring it had resolved not to trade any longer and threatening to abandon the forts. The Board of Trade sent copies of these petitions to Humphry Morice, who now assumed a more prominent role as spokesman for the separate traders than heretofore. The board also addressed a series of queries to Morice, Harris, and others.

The London merchants, over the signatures of Morice, Harris, Chamberlayne, and Randolph Knipe, replied in forthright opinions and a documented memorial. "We are unanimously of opinion that

28. PRO, CO 389/21, 441–57; Donnan, *Documents*, 2:137.

it will be for the service of the public and the benefit of the plantations and colonys in America, that the trade to Africa should re-
maine free & open," they asserted. "Forts & settlements on the
coast of Africa, are not necessary or usefull to trade," they continued. Asking for a hearing before the board, they offered a list of
ships owned by Londoners, enumerating eighty-seven ships capa-
ble of carrying 26,440 Negroes.[29]

The Board of Trade began its hearings in mid-April 1726, with
Harris and Morice attending. Morice served as principal spokesman among the traders, but Harris "read his observations upon the
African Company's petition and memorial." The two slave merchants attended intermittent hearings for a month; the board apparently delayed its report to the Crown until March 17, 1727.[30]
The report concentrated on two points in dispute: the nature and
condition of the trade and the utility of the forts and settlements.
Noting a great increase in the numbers of Negroes transported, the
board concluded that the plantations had been "much better supplied, and very near as cheap as formerly." Although the forts and
settlements were not absolutely necessary for carrying on the trade,
if abandoned they might fall into the hands of unfriendly foreign
nations. The government accordingly should offer to buy the forts
and settlements; if the company refused, the government should lay
a duty on ships trading to Africa in order to maintain the locations.
On the crucial question, the board emphatically asserted that "the
trade ought always to continue free and open."[31]

Free trade in African slaves continued, but the government did
not buy the settlements or impose a duty. In 1730 the moribund
company, inciting fears that the forts might fall into the grasp of
the Dutch, French, or Portuguese, petitioned Parliament for relief.
Parliament complied with a subsidy that continued for several
years.[32]

If the prosperity of the London separate traders rested in part on
maintaining free trade, it rested also on selling slaves in the plan-

29. Chandos Papers, Henry E. Huntington Library; PRO, T70/172, 8–9, 11–14,
15–17, 21–23 (for quotation); PRO, CO 388/25.
    30. *Journal of the Commissioners, 1726–1727*, 232 ff., especially 250, 251, 257,
267 for Harris.
    31. PRO, CO 389/28, 305–12; Donnan, *Documents*, 2:337–39.
    32. *CJ*, 21:522–23 ff.

tations without paying onerous import duties. A number of slave-employing colonies passed Negro duty laws. Their motive was not moral, as Virginians and other colonists claimed when the trade fell into disrepute, but sprang from different considerations. A primary motive was the necessity to raise revenue for a colony's needs. Colonial indebtedness and dislike of monetary drain to the mother country also figured in imposing the duties. Less worthy motives included the desire of large slaveholders to raise the prices of slaves, and fears of insurrection and miscegenation. All North American colonies but four passed Negro duty laws; Virginia and South Carolina were the most persistent. In the British West Indies, Jamaica presented an abiding problem to the separate traders.[33]

As he had in the struggle to resist monopoly, Harris played a major role in opposing colonial Negro duty laws. A letter from a Virginia correspondent in 1723 informed Harris that the colonial assembly had laid a duty of 40 shillings per head on imported Negroes. The Virginian hoped Harris might organize opposition by the separate traders. Harris's first move was to make his own protest to the Board of Trade. Such duties, he pointed out, were borne by the importers, that is, the slave merchants. Because the profits from the sale of Negroes came from the freight, he continued, the tax was an oppression on British navigation. A previous Virginia law that levied a duty of £5 per head so discouraged traders that they discontinued trade with the colony. The tax revenue was for colonial expenses and therefore ought to be obtained from the colonists, not the merchants. The board, he said, should consider prohibiting colonial duties on British trade and navigation, in view of the advantages the colonies derived from the fleet and power of the mother country.[34]

Harris and Francis Chamberlayne on December 5, 1723, presented to the board a memorial from merchants trading to Virginia, which the board read together with the letter from Virginia. The merchants complained that the duty would reduce the growth of tobacco, production of naval stores, revenue from importation of

33. Lewis Cecil Gray, *History of Agriculture in the Southern United States to 1860*, 2 vols. (Washington, 1933), 1:356; Darold D. Wax, "Negro Import Duties in Colonial Virginia: A Study in British Commercial Policy and Local Public Policy," *Virginia Magazine of History and Biography* 79 (January 1971): 29–41.

34. PRO, CO 5/1319, no. 31, 128–29.

tobacco, and importation of Negroes into Virginia, while raising the price of British tobacco sold in the competitive foreign market. The duty law, they charged, had been passed by the great planters in order to discourage tobacco production by the small freeholders. Moreover, it contradicted an Order in Council dated July 31, 1717.[35]

Several weeks later Harris, Chamberlayne, Morice, and others representing merchants of London and Bristol came before the board to argue their cause. Harris added to his previous arguments the statement that the merchants would not object to the act were the duty paid by the planters. Virginia planters required about 1,500 new slaves each year, half of whom now were being supplied by London and half by Bristol. Harris reminded the board of the Privy Council's 1717 order. The board supported the merchants' position and the Privy Council disallowed the law.[36]

The Virginia legislature again in 1728 passed a law levying a duty of 40 shillings per head on imported Negroes. Aroused by this fresh threat to their trade, merchants in London, Bristol, and Liverpool protested to the Board of Trade. Harris appeared among the petitioners, who again won disallowance of the law. South Carolina, where slaves far outnumbered whites, enacted Negro duty laws between 1730 and 1734, late in Harris's career. He joined in protesting the laws, figuring at the hearings. Here, too, the merchants prevailed, the Privy Council concluding that the duty was excessive.[37]

By the third decade of the eighteenth century Jamaica had become the largest market for slaves in the British empire. The South Sea Company and the separate traders formed the main suppliers of this market, the former often using the island as a refreshment station for slaves en route to the Spanish colonies. The Jamaica assembly in the late seventeenth century had levied a duty on imported Negroes. An act imposing a duty of 20 shillings on all Negroes reexported provoked a protest from the South Sea Company.

35. CSPC, 1722–1723, 384.
36. Journal of the Commissioners, 1723–1728, 64–66; W. L. Grant and James Munro, eds., Acts of the Privy Council: Colonial Series, 1613–1783, 6 vols. (London: Public Record Office, 1908–1912), 3:64.
37. Journal of the Commissioners, 1723–1728, 64–65; Journal of the Commissioners, 369–70; Grant and Munro, Privy Council, 3:393, 395.

Ordered by the Board of Trade to attend, Harris in March 1716 observed that except for the past two years the duty was no higher than it had been for twenty years; the money went to defray expenses of the island government. The South Sea Company prevailed and the Privy Council in disallowing the law instructed the governor of Jamaica not to allow a duty on Negroes imported for refreshment only.[38]

The Jamaica assembly persisted in imposing duties on the Negro trade. A law of 1724 levying "great duties" on the import and export of Negroes sparked a petition from merchants trading to Jamaica over the signatures of Harris, Morice, and two other merchants. The Board of Trade commanded Harris and Morice to appear in connection with the protest. In late February 1725 they heard from the board that the law had expired; moreover, the board had exempted Negroes landed for refreshment only.[39]

Within a month Harris complained to the board that Jamaica authorities had charged an import duty of £10 on two of his ships' cargoes, and the assembly, he had been informed, intended to renew the duty and require payment after the fact. Such a law removed the profit from slave trading, he said, and he reminded the board it had recommended disallowance of a similar Virginia law. The duty on reexports to the British colonies should be excused, he argued; the remedy for Jamaica's financial problems lay not in levying duties on the Negro trade but in encouraging settlement on lands deliberately kept unoccupied by the great planters, which discouraged small planters and new settlers. Greater numbers of settlers would pay more taxes and provide manpower for the defense of the island.[40]

In recommending that reexports to British colonies be excused from duties, Harris was separating the separate traders' case from that of the South Sea Company, which mainly sold to the Spanish colonies. A memorial from the merchants trading to Jamaica at this

38. Philip D. Curtin, *The Atlantic Slave Trade: A Census* (Madison: University of Wisconsin Press, 1969), 140; *Journal of the Commissioners, 1715–1718*, 121–22; Grant and Munro, *Privy Council*, 2:728–29.

39. PRO, CO 137/16, 17–18; CSPC, 1724–1725, 282; *Journal of the Commissioners, 1723–1728*, 149–50.

40. *Journal of the Commissioners, 1723–1728*, 150–51; CSPC, 1724–1725, 347–48.

time declared that the South Sea Company bought up the best Negroes and sold them to the Spaniards, to the detriment of Jamaica planters and the island's future.[41]

The South Sea Company and the separate traders in 1727 joined in protesting Jamaica duties on Negroes. The company also requested exemption from duties for slaves landed for refreshment only. The Privy Council complied with the company's request by instructing the governor not to approve any duties on Negroes landed for refreshment only. This action displeased the separate traders who landed slaves for sale on the island and then reexported those slaves not sold. On behalf of the separate traders, Harris objected that they were not relieved from the burden of the duty on Negroes. The separate traders, he argued in vain, "for the last three years . . . have paid more for their import duty than most of them have got by their voyages."[42]

In 1731 the Jamaica assembly, now encumbered by a slave rebellion, laid a duty of 15 shillings on all Negroes exported, except those on whom the import duty had been paid and who had not been sold. Harris, attending a Board of Trade hearing about protests from London, British, and Liverpool merchants, participated in a widespread assault on the new law. As a result, the Privy Council ordered the governor not to assent to any law imposing duties on slaves imported into the island payable by the importer, or upon any slaves exported that had not been sold and had been there for twelve months.[43]

The Jamaica legislature continued its practice of annually passing a law taxing the slave trade. In January 1732 it imposed a tax of 10 shillings a head on slave imports and 20 shillings on exports. Slave merchants of the three major slave ports petitioned against the new law. Attending the Board of Trade hearing on behalf of the petitioners, Harris pursued his theme that high duties on slave commerce inhibited settlement on the island. Even if white people went to Jamaica, he declared, they would be unable to find employment. Acting with unusual promptness, the Privy Council

41. PRO, CO 137/16 R 5; Frank Wesley Pitman, *The Development of the British West Indies, 1700–1763* (New Haven: Yale University Press, 1917), 81–82.

42. *CSPC, 1726–1727,* 393.

43. *Journal of the Commissioners, 1728–1734,* 223; Grant and Munro, *Privy Council,* 3:164.

disallowed the law and repeated its earlier instructions to the governor.[44]

Undeterred by royal disapproval, the Jamaicans in August 1733 laid a duty of £10 on every Negro imported and sold in the island, payable by the purchaser. Harris headed a list of fifteen London merchants who protested to the Privy Council that the law was "destructive of the commerce of Great Britain[,] a discouragement to the increase of its colonys," and contrary to His Majesty's instructions that no duties be levied on importation or exportation. The colonial legislature, ever trying to keep one step ahead of the home government, continued the law in March 1734. Harris died before resolution of the matter. In July 1735 the Privy Council, recognizing the island's expenses in putting down the slave rebellion, ruled that "a reasonable duty may be imposed."[45]

Besides the struggles to maintain free trade in slaves and to combat colonial Negro duty laws, Harris engaged his abundant energies in numerous other matters related to the slave trade. If the Royal African Company was a recurring concern, the South Sea Company, holder of the *asiento,* found him in the position of both opponent and client. The company and the separate traders often opposed the Negro duty laws, but when an instruction prohibited duties on slaves imported for refreshment, he objected on behalf of the separate traders. On the other hand, when the company secured the *asiento,* he and others discussed with the company the contract's terms for furnishing 4,800 Negroes annually. At a later time the company invited him, Morice, and others to make proposals for supplying Negroes to Buenos Aires. He also received licenses to deliver slaves in Puerto Rico, agreeing to pay the company 80 pesos per slave. Harris sought these licenses and one for Caracas in order to recover debts owed him in the two markets.[46]

Slave-ship owners incurred a risk of losing their vessels and valuable cargoes to foreign foes and pirates. During the War of the Spanish Succession the British navy provided convoy service to slave ships. After the war, slave traders continued to turn to the

44. *Journal of the Commissioners, 1728–1734,* 307–9; Grant and Munro, *Privy Council,* 3:164.
45. CSPC, 1734–1735, 62–63; Grant and Munro, *Privy Council,* 3:165.
46. Donnan, *Documents,* 2:156; British Library, Addit. MSS 25556:ff. 34, 172–73.

government for naval protection, with a split apparent between the Royal African Company and the separate traders. The company evinced concern about security in African waters, while the separate traders were concerned about the West Indies.

In 1715 the company requested naval assistance, saying its trade was in as great danger as during the war. African, Dutch, and French rivals, company officials professed, threatened their trade. The Board of Trade summoned Harris, Morice, and Robert Heysham to give their opinions. These leading merchants stated there was no need for a man-of-war on the African coast. Injuries done by Africans could not be redressed by a ship; those done by the French should be redressed by the king of France. The merchants suspected that the company's request masked a desire to use a naval vessel as a means to carry stores and provisions to Africa. The board continued to consider the request and asked Harris to present in writing his views on the advantages of having a warship on the African coast with instructions to protect British trade in general. The next day Harris appeared in person to speak about his letter, reaffirming his view that a warship was not necessary and adding that if one were assigned it should be far from the Gambia River, with its sickly climate and worms that ate through the hulls of ships.[47]

The following year the company again appealed for naval protection, expressing apprehension about the "Sallee Rovers" (Moors based at the port of Sallee) and other pirates. Summoned to testify before the Board of Trade, Harris and Morice said the Sallee Rovers could be avoided by sailing westward of them. The separate traders had no news of pirates on the African coast since the peace, and they suspected the request was aimed "to promote the stock jobbing of some particular persons."[48]

The West Indies were a different case for the separate traders. There the French held strategic islands and the Spanish coast guard seized English ships, often alleging they were violating the *asiento*. Moreover, pirates preyed on English merchant ships. As early as March 1715, Harris and others presented the Crown with "an account of ships and vessels taken by the Spaniards in the West In-

47. *Journal of the Commissioners, 1715–1718*, 91–93, 99.
48. Ibid., 190–91.

dies since the peace and made prize of under the most frivolous pretences."[49]

In the spring of 1717, when Bristol merchants complained about pirates in the West Indies, particularly around Jamaica, Harris and others were ordered to speak with the Board of Trade. All present agreed that "the case was very desperate" and two or three men-of-war should immediately be dispatched. At the same time they believed it was almost impracticable to reduce the number of pirates by force, and therefore a pardon should be offered to all pirates who surrendered within a given time.[50]

Several years later the crews of two ships were captured by the notorious pirate Bartholomew Roberts and forced to become pirates. The English victims later escaped and petitioned the Crown for pardon. The Board of Trade, to whom the petition was referred, asked Harris to consult with West Indian traders about a suitable policy. After speaking with fellow merchants and insurance officials he advised the board that most persons "are clear of opinion that the soonest endeavours should be used to get the pirats [sic] called in or pardoned."[51]

The Spanish coast guard continued to take English ships. In June 1728 English merchants listed forty-five ships lost to the Spaniards since the Peace of Utrecht. The sloop *Griffin,* owned by Harris, fell into Spanish hands on its homeward voyage from Jamaica in 1722. Desirable as naval protection might be, trade must go on. When, fearful of a Spanish attack, Jamaica embargoed one hundred ships then in Jamaican harbors, Harris and others petitioned that the ships be permitted to return to their respective ports. In the year of his death Harris testified on the weak and defenseless condition of the Leeward Islands. He did not live to see the outbreak of the trade war with Spain in 1739.[52]

Foreign competition, especially by the French, deeply concerned Harris. In 1697 France acquired St. Domingue and rapidly turned its new possession into a large-scale producer of sugar and a market for slaves. A dozen years later, during the War of the Spanish

49. Ibid., 118.
50. Ibid., 236–37.
51. *CSPC,* 1722–1723, 182.
52. PRO, CO 389/28, 356–57; *The Journals of the House of Lords,* 57 vols. (London, n.d.; hereinafter *LJ*), 33:523.

Succession, Harris presented his thoughts relating to the French in the Caribbean: "By being fixed att martinico & Guadeloupe . . . they intercept all ships coming with provisions from New England & other our [sic] Northern colonies[,] without a supply whereof . . . the planters must suffer much & their Negroes perish." It was absolutely necessary, especially for Jamaica, to remove the French from among settlements in America, he exhorted.[53]

The peacemakers at Utrecht did not remove France from among British settlements in America, but France did lose the *asiento* to Great Britain. Even so, French merchants using Spanish names continued to ply an illegal trade in Spanish America, and British merchants exceeded the privileges of the *asiento* in a number of ways, including cutting logwood in Spanish America. A proposal to prevent the French clandestine trade in exchange for preventing the British clandestine trade prompted a retort from Harris. The proposal, he thought, was aimed against the logwood trade, which was "essentially necessary in dying [sic] our manufactures." He was especially troubled about Britain's consequent loss of capacity to dye woolens, an important export to Africa in the slave trade. "It seems rather absolutely necessary to support this pretended clandestine trade," he advised. Instructed to complain about the French trade to South America, the British ambassador in Madrid got no satisfaction.[54]

Merchants, planters, and others interested in Jamaica shared Harris's anxiety about the French success in exploiting the fruitful soil of St. Domingue. They protested the expansion of French influence over the island of Hispaniola, of which St. Domingue formed the western part. They asserted that the French had made "an unlawfull encroachment." To this representation Harris attached his own remarks condemning "the great schemes formed by France for founding a universall power in America as well as in Europe." The protesters were unable, of course, to dislodge France from her strong position in Hispaniola.[55]

French encroachments on British trade in Africa brought Harris and others before the Board of Trade in 1720. Louis XV had grant-

53. PRO, CO 137/8, 40.
54. *CSPC*, 1714–1715, 58–60.
55. Ibid., 115–18.

ed exclusive trade to Africa to the Company of the Indies, and the French had seized British ships on the African coast. In his testimony Harris declared that a private agreement in James II's time had relinquished the English privilege of ascending the Senegal River in exchange for the French privilege of going into the Gambia River.[56]

French competition in producing low-priced sugar troubled slave and sugar merchants, who often were one and the same and depended upon sugar imports into England to finance slave exports from Africa. Harris and a dozen other merchants trading to Jamaica in 1724 explained why British sugar production had decreased. Heavy indigo production in St. Domingue had caused Jamaica planters to shift slaves from sugar production. The drop in British exports to foreign markets resulted from French improvements in their colonies and freedom from government impositions on French trade.

The remedies, Harris and his colleagues suggested, lay in reducing such English encumbrances on trade as fees and duties and the large number of holidays. The slave and sugar trades should be protected against pirates on the African coast and the Spanish coast guard off Jamaica and Hispaniola, they said. "The greatest mischiefs which hath of late years attended our Colonys have been caused by the Spanish guard de coast vessels and pirates, not only by the havock and destruction of the ships employed in the negro trade on which the being of our Colonys chiefly depends, but also by the great interruption given to our navigation in bringing home the Plantation products, *etc.*"[57]

Distress in the British sugar colonies persisted, sharpened by the illegal trade carried on between British North America and the French West Indies. Barbados, suffering keenly, petitioned the Privy Council for relief, and, receiving none, appealed to Parliament. In 1731 Harris testified before a Commons committee that the fall in sugar prices resulted from the large increase in French production, made possible by the New England trade. Later in the year he told the Board of Trade that the French could sell their sugar 7½ percent cheaper than the English in Barbados and the Leeward Islands,

56. *Journal of the Commissioners, 1719–1720,* 199–200.
57. *CSPC,* 1724–1725, 104–5.

and that if the French islands were not supplied with provisions and lumber from the northern colonies, they could not "undersell us at market as they now do." He advocated prohibiting all trade between the northern colonies and the French islands for lumber, rum, sugar, and molasses. His testimony contributed to the Molasses Act of 1733, which imposed a prohibitive duty on foreign molasses imported into the northern colonies.[58]

Harris also played a significant role in securing passage of the Credit Act of 1732. In August 1731 several London merchants, with Harris as the first signer, petitioned the Privy Council for relief in recovery of debts owed them in the colonies. The Board of Trade, to whom the petition was referred, asked for particulars, which Harris, Morice, and six others provided. The merchants pointed out that lands and houses were not liable to pay debts in Jamaica and some other colonies. Though this immunity was contrary to the laws of England and instructions sent to the governor, the Jamaica assembly declined to remedy the grievance. The board reported to the Privy Council that although several of the colonial laws were unreasonable, they were of long standing and had not been the object of previous complaint. The board recommended no action.[59]

The merchants now resorted to Parliament, which responded with the Credit Act of 1732, later hailed as "the Palladium of Colony credit, and the English Merchant's grand security." The law made lands, tenements, and Negroes owned by colonial debtors payable for debts in the same manner that such properties were liable in England. The harsh feature of the law making Negroes subject to sale by creditors was repealed in the more humane climate of the century's end.[60]

At his death in 1734, Richard Harris probably had exerted more influence over British slave trade policy than any other person in the first three decades of the eighteenth century. Never a member of Parliament, he was sought out by the government for his knowledge, his connections with leading merchants, and his remedies for

58. *Journal of the Commissioners, 1728–1734,* 253–54.

59. Ibid., 223; Grant and Munro, *Privy Council,* 3:162.

60. *Journal of the Commissioners, 1728–1734,* 347; CSPC, 1731, 224–25, 293–95; Sheridan, *Sugar and Slavery,* 288–89.

a host of problems. The problems mainly concerned the African slave trade. He was a leader of the struggle to maintain free trade in slaves, oppose colonial Negro duty laws, and develop policy with respect to naval protection of the trade against pirates and foreign nations. He contributed significantly to two major pieces of legislation—the Credit Act of 1732 and the Molasses Act of 1733. Richard Harris, in retrospect, was an unacknowledged legislator for the transatlantic slave trade.

5

Henry Laurens and the Atlantic Slave Trade

Henry Laurens for nearly three decades was a leading figure in South Carolina, continental, and national commerce and politics. He joined a Charleston commission firm in 1749 and saw it expand to three members in 1759 and dissolve in 1762. More than a merchant, he was a planter, owning Mepkin Plantation, 3,143 acres, about thirty miles up the Cooper River. In the troubled 1760s, three of his schooners were seized by British customs and vice admiralty officials. In 1776, he had 797 slaves.

Active in politics, he was seventeen times elected to provincial and continental legislatures. South Carolina sent him to the Continental Congress where he succeeded John Hancock as president. Congress in turn appointed him to help enlist the Dutch in the Revolutionary cause and later to serve on the peace commission ending the war. Returning to the new United States, he declined to assume public service or to serve as a delegate to the Constitutional Convention. His later imprisonment and the death of his brave, patriotic son John in 1782 enfeebled the gout-ridden, grieving father and brought on his death.

Citing new materials and studies, I have endeavored to reappraise Henry Laurens and his part in the Atlantic slave trade in the light of recent research and perspectives. This paper has not been previously published. An early version, since substantially revised, was delivered at the 1970 Tricentennial Symposium on South Carolina in Columbia.

≈

Upon the port at the narrow neck of low-lying land between the Ashley and the Cooper Rivers converged the exports of the lower South, brought from the forests and field and swamps of the Carolinas and Georgia. Through Charleston in turn flowed the wares of England, which was just entering the Industrial Revolution, and the captive labor from Africa, long suffering the depredations of Europeans.

Henry Laurens, a slave merchant functioning in the Atlantic community of the mid-eighteenth century, is our concern. That he was active in the foreign slave trade has long been known. David Duncan Wallace, his skillful biographer, in 1915 devoted an excellent chapter to Laurens and the trade. When Elizabeth Donnan published copious quantities of Laurens materials in her invaluable volumes of documents on the slave trade, she observed that "from this point the history of the Carolina trade is largely to be written from the Laurens letters." The South Carolina Historical Society has added to the largesse by publishing his papers. David Eltis, Stephen D. Behrendt, and others have compiled all the documents on the Atlantic slave trade they could discover and have published their findings, further enriching the materials.[1]

Laurens's participation in the trade needs to be placed in historical context. Modern scholarship has qualified the charges that parliamentary acts of navigation and trade exploited the colonies during the period when Laurens was a slave merchant. When it came to needed raw materials, South Carolina benefited from the imperial preference for the principle of enumeration, bounties, English shipping, and naval protection. Laurens's letters are singularly free from complaint concerning these matters.

However, in August 1776, not long after Thomas Jefferson's famous attempt to fasten the blame for the external slave trade on King George III, Laurens fulminated:

> [T]hese Negroes [owned by him] were first enslaved by the
> English—Acts of Parliament have established the Slave Trade
> in favour of the home residing English & almost totally pro-
> hibited the Americans from reaping any share of it—Men of

---

1. David D. Wallace, "The Foreign Slave Trade in South Carolina in the Eighteenth Century, 1703–1807," chap. 6 in *The Life of Henry Laurens* (New York: G. P. Putnam's Sons, 1915); Philip M. Hamer, ed., *The Papers of Henry Laurens*, 15 vols. (Columbia: University of South Carolina Press, 1968–2000; hereinafter *Laurens Papers*), 1:2 n. 7; Elizabeth Donnan, ed., *Documents Illustrative of the History of the Slave Trade to America*, 4 vols. (Washington: Carnegie Institution, 1930–1935), 4:300; David Eltis, Stephen D. Behrendt, David Richardson, Herbert S. Klein, *The Trans-Atlantic Slave Trade: A Database on CD-ROM* (Cambridge and New York: Cambridge University Press, 1999).

> War Forts Castles Governors Companies & Committees are
> employed & authorized by the English Parliament to protect
> regulate & extend the Slave Trade—Negroes are brought by
> English Men & sold as Slaves to Americans—Bristol Liver-
> poole Manchester Birmingham &c$^{a.}$ & c$^{a.}$ live upon the Slave
> Trade . . . I was born in a Country where Slavery had been es-
> tablished by British Kings & Parliaments as well as by the
> Laws of the Country Ages before my existence . . .[2]

Laurens's pinning responsibility for the institution of slavery
upon the English instead of the colonials must be seen in light of
recent investigations of the origins of the southern labor system. It
seems clear that Virginia and Maryland—the first of the southern
colonies—saw Negroes as perpetual servants. They had no body
of English law to invoke: slavery may be considered a colonial in-
vention, abetted by the English traders in slaves.

In the case of South Carolina, slavery was coeval with the founding of the colony in 1670, being provided for in the Fundamental
Constitutions; slaves imported by the Barbadians figured prominently in creating the colony. M. Eugene Sirmans has shown that
South Carolina over the course of seventy years uniquely evolved
its peculiar institution from a freehold concept borrowed from Barbados to the more conventional legal status of chattel slavery.[3]
Bondage in Laurens's colony underwent distinctive development by
local law. The institution of slavery was not established by the
British Parliament, nor by the laws of the country ages before Laurens was born. It was accordingly misleading for him to declare
that "these Negroes were first enslaved by the English."

Nor was Laurens on firm ground in asserting that "Acts of Parliament have established the Slave Trade in favour of the home re-
siding English & almost totally prohibited the Americans from
reaping any share of it." Parliamentary efforts to establish the slave
trade with other groups appear to have resulted in a record of failure. As far as the English Navigation Laws are concerned, their historian has judged that "the Acts appear to have had no great effect
upon the trade with Africa." Beyond this, the monopoly on the

2. *Laurens Papers,* 10:224.

3. M. Eugene Sirmans, "The Legal Status of the Slave in South Carolina, 1670–
1740," *Journal of Southern History* 28 (November 1962): 462–73.

slave trade conferred by Parliament in 1672 on the Royal African Company ended in 1698, when, according to the historian K. G. Davies, "[f]ree trade won a notable triumph."[4] When in 1713 there was a move to restore the monopoly, South Carolina merchants and planters joined other interested groups in petitioning Parliament not to do so, a wish that was respected.

After England secured the *asiento* from Spain in 1713, Parliament assigned it to the South Sea Company. The story of that ill-fated company is one of difficulties and failure, and England surrendered the *asiento* in 1750, when Laurens was entering the trade. Well before this date, concerned over the decay of castles guarding English stations on the African coast, Parliament had begun to subsidize them. In 1750, resolving that the African trade "ought to be free and open to all His Majesty's Subjects," Parliament formed the Company of Merchants Trading to Africa, a loose association whose members were forbidden from carrying on any private trade.[5] This company failed in supervising the trade and suffered severe criticism, not from Americans but from merchants in Bristol and Liverpool—flourishing centers of slaving—who thought they did not have a sufficient voice in the company.

Indeed, throughout the pre-Revolutionary period, objections to Parliamentary measures regarding the merchants' respective positions in the slave trade came mainly from English, not American, traders. Laurens himself did not complain on this score while he was busy selling slaves. English laws did not prevent him from reaping a share, both as a commission merchant and as owner of ships plying the trade. Laurens, in fact, found the trade not unprofitable.[6] Virtual free trade in slaves for Englishmen had triumphed nearly half a century before Laurens became a slave merchant. The merchants of English ports and cities, enjoying an advantage conferred less by Parliament than by an advanced economy, predominated in the slave trade, but not by acts prohibiting enterprising colonials, who were numerous in New England and

---

4. Lawrence Harper, *The English Navigation Laws* (New York: Octagon Books, 1964), 240; K. G. Davies, *The Royal African Company* (London: Longmans, Green, 1957), 152.

5. Donnan, *Documents,* 2:474, xxxii–xxxvii.

6. For Laurens as investor in ships and cargoes, see Donnan, *Documents,* 4:317, 369, 415, 617.

South Carolina, from enjoying a share. Economic forces, not acts of government, made most American slave merchants, who had slender capital, do business as commission merchants.

The Royal African Company, in point of fact, never imported many slaves into South Carolina. Importation on a sizable scale commenced only after the act of 1698, when separate traders could lawfully operate. Moreover, a direct trade between South Carolina and Africa existed from about that time forward. A Carolina slaver stood into the Gambia River in 1700 and Colonel William Rhett of Charleston appears to have ventured a Guinea voyage in 1711. Henry Laurens was a Johnny-come-lately in getting his share.

The Atlantic trading community in which Laurens conducted his slave business was, then, not one in which Parliament discriminated in favor of the home-residing English. English wars of trade against European slave-trading competitors—Dutch, French, and Spanish—had widened opportunities for slave merchants. The preamble to the parliamentary measure of 1750 for extending and improving the trade to Africa in order that it "be free and open to all his Majesty's Subjects" is more nearly an accurate description of the political environment in which British American traders operated. Throughout his slaving career, Laurens looked to the British navy for protection against "that haughty tyrannical People the French who are the pest of all human Society in every part of the Globe."[7]

To the extent that Laurens in August 1776 was indulging in revolutionary rhetoric, he may perhaps be indulged. To the extent that he intended to voice reality, he may be censured. His statement tends to nourish a myth—actually, a double myth: one, of the Revolutionary era, that England foisted the slave trade on the hapless colonials, and the other, of the first half of the nineteenth century, that New England foisted the institution of slavery upon the South. The meticulous research of K. G. Davies makes abundantly plain that the English monopoly failed and that only the policy of open trade provided the planters with a large supply of slave labor. The mercantile system in which Laurens functioned was, on balance, beneficial to his slaving business.[8]

7. Laurens to John Knight, July 24, 1755, *Laurens Papers*, 1:300–301.
8. Davies, *Royal African Company*.

Turning to what Philip D. Curtin has called "the numbers game," we may, with the help of his study *The Atlantic Slave Trade: A Census,* better appraise Laurens's place in executing the vast involuntary migration that endured for more than four centuries. Curtin's monograph is a quantitative study of the dimensions and sources of the international slave trade. Emphasizing that he had reached "only approximations where a result falling within 20 per cent of actuality is a 'right' answer," he essayed a new synthesis of the data on the number of slaves brought across the Atlantic.[9]

Perhaps the most important, and most startling, finding is his reduction of the numbers transported from 15 million to about 10 million, subtracting one-third from the figure widely accepted by historians. Curtin shows that Laurens participated in the trade at nearly its peak, both for the trade as a whole and for British activity in it. He also shows that Laurens dropped out of the trade during a decade of high demand.[10]

Examining slave imports into British America during the decade of the 1750s, when Laurens was most active, Curtin demonstrates that an estimated 21.4 percent of the total was imported into southern mainland North America.[11] We may be confident that Charleston merchants had a large share of this one-fifth of the flow from Africa, and we shall take recourse to another scholar's finding that Henry Laurens garnered a substantial share.

In respect to ethnic origins, South Carolina buyers had a strong bias for slaves from the Gambia. "Gold Coast or Gambia's are best, next to them the Windward Coast are preferred to Angola's," Laurens advised a St. Christopher's correspondent. Slaves from Biafra's port of Calabar were "quite out of repute from numbers in every Cargo that have been sold with us from destroying themselves," he observed in businesslike fashion.[12]

Curtin's estimates disclose how far South Carolina, over the period 1733–1807, was able to secure supplies in terms of these preferences. Senegambia contributed 19.5 percent to the colony's slave

9. Philip D. Curtin, *The Atlantic Slave Trade: A Census* (Madison: University of Wisconsin Press, 1969), xviii.

10. Ibid., 266, 142.

11. Ibid., 158.

12. Laurens to Smith & Clifton, July 17, 1755, *Laurens Papers,* 1:295; Laurens to Peter Furnell, September 6, 1755, ibid., 1:331.

population, the Windward Coast 16.3 percent, and the Gold Coast 13.3 percent—these three preferred sources producing one-half the total. Only 2.1 percent came from the Bight of Biafra, and the largest single source was Angola, which furnished 39.5 percent. These estimates affirm that the principal provenance of South Carolina slaves was the West African coast area from the Senegal River to the southern boundary of Angola. A mere 0.7 percent derived from Mozambique and Madagascar.

Drawing on the research of one of his students, Curtin projected an estimate of South Carolina's share of the southern mainland slave trade for the years 1701–1775. It is to be remembered that South Carolina supplied many of the slaves for North Carolina and Georgia. The ports of the Chesapeake Bay area supplied the upper South. Dividing the trade between these two centers, Curtin estimated that the share of South Carolina merchants was about 46 percent.[13]

With this census having brought into sharper perspective the size and sources of the slave trade, we may next turn to a closer examination of Henry Laurens and the portion he held. Elizabeth Donnan found that more than one hundred Charleston firms offered cargoes of Negroes for sale before the American Revolution. For the limited span of 1752–1756 she determined that the firm of Austin and Laurens "was advertising more cargoes than any other firm in Charleston."[14]

W. Robert Higgins subsequently studied Charleston merchants and factors dealing with the external Negro trade during the period 1735–1775. Reminding us that Charleston enjoyed the importation for not only nearly all the colony, but for its environs as well, he asserted that South Carolina supplied Negroes for some thirty places. Importers were subject to duty on cargoes of Negroes. Higgins's list exceeds Donnan's, running to 405 names, many of whom, to be sure, paid duty on but one cargo. Of chief interest to us is the placing of Laurens's firm at the head of the list. Austin and Laurens, the first partnership of which Laurens was a member, during

13. Curtin, *Atlantic Slave Trade*, 157, 158.
14. Elizabeth Donnan, "The Slave Trade into South Carolina before the Revolution," *American Historical Review* 33: 810.

its eight years from 1751 to 1758, paid a duty on forty-five cargoes in the amount of £45,120 current money. To this must be added the expanded partnership of Austin, Laurens, and Appleby, which during the period of their activity is now established beyond dispute.[15]

In recent years economic historians have questioned the slave trade's traditional reputation for huge profits. They have documented the financial failure of the politically advantaged Royal African Company and disclosed the complexities of ascertaining profitability.[16] The Laurens papers underscore the hazards of a business whose gambles included the loss of a ship at sea, the uncertainties of supply, the ravages of an epidemic among the slaves, the outbreak of war, the activities of privateers, a fall in crop prices leading to a fall in slave prices, and the ineptitude of a ship's captain. On the eve of the Seven Years' War, referring to a report that a slaver at Angola might not be able to purchase enough slaves to pay for the cost of her cargo and "outset," Laurens remarked: "The African trade is more liable to such Accidents than any other we know of, so it highly concerns such as become adventurers in that branch to fortify themselves against every disappointment that the trade is incident to."[17]

Despite the absence of his business accounts, one can draw certain conclusions from the Laurens papers. For one thing, he shared the risks of slaving by always acting in partnership. Moreover, in its early years the firm of Austin and Laurens enjoyed the participation of the wealthy merchant Gabriel Manigault in some of its ventures. It is perhaps significant that Laurens abandoned the slaving trade in 1762, when he no longer had partners. The next year we find him, in declining the "African trade," saying: "[L]ess Capital than I have in my possession have [sic] often been employ'd to

15. W. Robert Higgins, "Charles Town Merchants and Factors Dealing in the External Negro Trade, 1735–1775," *South Carolina Historical Magazine* 65 (October 1964): 205–7, esp. 206.

16. Davies, *Royal African Company;* Stanley Dumbell, "The Profits of the Guinea Trade," *Economic Journal* (supplement 1931): 254–57; Francis E. Hyde, Bradbury B. Parkinson, and Sheila Mariner, "The Nature and Profitability of the Liverpool Slave Trade," *Economic History Review,* 2d ser., 5:3 (1953): 368–77.

17. *Laurens Papers,* 1:259.

wield more business than three or four Cargoes of Negroes per annum can create, but I would in this uncertain Climate and for other considerations endeavor to avoid embarrassment."[18]

Although, as we shall see, he assigned many reasons for giving up the traffic, Laurens never suggested it had been unprofitable. On the contrary, while he was in England in 1772, he wrote his brother James, to whom he had earlier offered his slave business: "I have already refused the offers (unask'd by me) and without security, of Negro Cargoes from three Houses . . . but these Branches, the most profitable, I have quitted to people who are more eager for them. You know I have given away many Thousands of pounds, which I might have added to my Stock in that way."[19] It seems impossible to discover how much of Laurens's great wealth sprang from the Negro trade, how much from his other mercantile operations, and how much from his land speculations. But of the various branches of business in which he engaged, slaving, we have on his testimony, was "the most profitable."

Still another concern of research in economic history has been the pattern of international trade. The well-known 1953 study of the Liverpool trade by Francis E. Hyde and others concluded: "As far as the Davenport Papers are concerned, the most important fact revealed is the great variety of the trade. No two voyages were identical. The trade did not conform to any rigid pattern." Subsequently Gary Walton argued that the triangular trade routes described in school textbooks did not exist for New England and the middle colonies. He found, moreover, that the stereotyped view of the trade between Great Britain and the southern colonies was essentially correct.[20]

On this issue of trade routes, however, the Laurens papers make abundantly clear that Laurens's slave trade essentially followed the familiar triangular pattern: home port, African slaving station,

<hr>

18. Laurens to Richard Oswald and Co., February 15, 1763, *Laurens Papers,* 3:260.

19. Laurens to James Laurens, February 6, 1772, *Laurens Papers,* 8:177–78.

20. Hyde et al., "Nature and Profitability of the Liverpool Slave Trade," 372; Gary Walton, "New Evidence on Colonial Commerce," *Journal of Economic History* 28 (September 1968): 363–89; Gary Walton, "Trade Routes, Ownership Proportions, and American Colonial Shipping Characteristics," *Anuario de Estudios Americanos* 25:71–505.

Charleston, back to home port. In both African and American waters, a slave ship might touch at several ports.

The home ports of vessels that brought slaves to Laurens included Bristol, Liverpool, London, Lancaster, and Newport, Rhode Island. Laurens's papers further corroborate the view that the African trade was usually triangular. Yet there were exceptions, as we have noted, earlier in the century. At least twice, slave ships from Bance Island returned to their African port of departure.

Historical tradition has long made Bristol and Liverpool the English centers of the mid-nineteenth-century slave trade. With the failure of the Royal African Company, London was supposed to have lost its predominance. The two outposts, with their advantages of shipping lanes and proximity to the wares of industrial England, were thought to have captured the trade. So far as the West Indies are concerned, Richard Pares and Richard B. Sheridan have found that London in this period maintained a major interest. Sheridan wrote: "A careful reading of the literature leads one to the conclusion that London was as deeply involved in the trade as the much maligned Liverpool."[21] Laurens's papers reveal that London held major importance for the portion of the Charleston trade that passed through his hands. He numbered among his correspondents at least eight London merchants, including the house of Lascelles, which Pares studied, and Richard Oswald and Co.

His relationship with Oswald was especially significant, not alone in the slave trade, but also in personal and diplomatic affairs. Oswald was born in Scotland and migrated to London, establishing a business in Philpot Lane. He amassed a fortune through marriage to the only daughter of Alexander Ramsey of Jamaica, by whom he acquired estates in the West Indies and on the mainland. For a number of years he lived on the mainland. He became a proprietor of Bance Island off the west African coast, from where he exported slaves. From 1754 to 1773 he sent six slave ships to Charleston for sales by Laurens.[22]

21. Richard Pares, "A London West-India Merchant House, 1740–1769," in *Essays Presented to Sir Lewis Namier,* ed. Richard Pares and A. J. P. Taylor (New York: St. Martin's Press, 1956), 75–107; Richard B. Sheridan, "The Commercial and Financial Organization of the British Slave Trade, 1750–1807," *Economic History Review,* 2d ser., 11 (December 1958): 249–63 (quotation on 263).
22. Sidney Lee, ed., *Dictionary of National Biography,* 22 vols. (London: Oxford University Press, 1921–1922), 14:1223–24.

The *St. Paul* in 1754 departed from Gambia with 150 slaves. The *Carlisle* sailed in 1755 with another 150. The *Betsey*, departing in 1757, arrived the next year with 230 slaves. Three hundred slaves after an interruption by the Seven Years' War arrived in 1764 on the *Queen of Barra*. The *Charlotte* arrived in Charleston in 1771 with 118 slaves, and the last of these cargoes, 230 slaves, disembarked in 1773 in Charleston from the *Amelia*.

The *Carlisle*, 70 tons, Captain Thomas Osborne, had an illustrative voyage. Departing from London on December 18, 1755, it purchased 35 slaves in Gambia, and completed its purchases in Sierra Leone. Sailing for South Carolina it arrived on the night of June 28 with a cargo of 151 slaves.[23]

Expecting the arrival, Laurens wrote Oswald and his partner, starting an extended correspondence: "[I]t would give us much pleasure to transact the Affair for you had we a prospect of doing it successfully but really the Scene is so much alter'd for the worse the last 3 or 4 months & which we hope cannot escape your knowledge that we sincerely wish you order the Sloop to a much better market than at present seems to promise."[24]

Just before the sale the rumor circulated that England had declared war. "This prov'd an unfortunate piece of Intelligence," Laurens wrote. He explained, "Our people to a man were determin'd not to buy without a Considerable abatement." With the market seeming every day to grow worse, "we again flatter'd ourselves with a pretty good Sale for them."[25]

From the beginning of this transaction Laurens had worried about what freight to return to Oswald. In the end he determined to send rice, an important South Carolina crop, along with logwood from Central America for his own firm's account. Later, he found, "we are in advance" on the *Carlisle* account. His commission for his work was 5 percent. In late March he wrote Oswald, "We have the pleasure by a ship arrived from Portsmouth that the *Carlisle* was got safe home." The voyage from origin to disembarkation had lasted 195 days.[26]

23. Eltis et al., *Database*.
24. *Laurens Papers*, 2:169.
25. Ibid., 2:272.
26. Ibid., 2:507.

Henry Laurens left off selling slaves about 1762. Four years later he wrote a letter that has become an exhibit of antislavery sentiment:

> I abhor Slavery, I was born in a Country where Slavery had been
> established by British Kings & Parliaments as well as by the
> Laws of that Country Ages before my existence, I found the
> Christian Religion & Slavery growing under the same authori-
> ty & cultivation—I nevertheless disliked it—in former days
> there was no combatting the prejudices of Men supported by In-
> terest, the day I hope is approaching when from principles of
> gratitude as well as justice every Man will strive to be foremost
> in shewing his readiness to comply with the Golden Rule . . . [27]

Writing to a Quaker Friend, William Fisher of Philadelphia, about
abandoning the slave trade, he said, "I quitted the Profits from that
gainful branch principally because of many Acts from the Masters
and others concern'd toward the wretched Negroes." A year later,
however, engaged in a bitter argument with slaveholder Egerton
Leigh, he denied the impeachment of humanitarian hypocrisy and
retorted he gave up slave dealing because he had no partner and
business was too heavy.[28]

Yet if his motives were mixed and his avowals inconsistent, his
conduct contradicted his professed philanthropy. Though himself
not acting as a slave merchant, he assiduously attended to placing
consignments for English firms, collecting commissions for his services. He vacillated on the question of reentering the trade, writing
a correspondent in 1770, "If you send any Slaves to this place con-
sign'd to me, you may depend upon it, that I shall either sell them
myself, or put them into such hands as will do you the most Service
in the sale." He opposed the acts of Parliament that prompted South
Carolina to pass nonimportation resolutions, and lamented that
"these resolutions remain a Bar to the importations of Negroes," observing that "Negroes would make not only a saving but a gainful
Remittance if our Resolutions did not prohibit the importation."[29]

27. Ibid., 10:224.
28. Laurens to William Fisher, November 9, 1768, *Laurens Papers,* 6:149.
29. Laurens to John Holman, September 8, 1770, and Laurens to Richard Oswald,
September 10, 1770, *Laurens Papers,* 7:344.

During the American Revolution, Laurens served in the Continental Congress. That body chose him to negotiate a loan from Holland and also a treaty of amity and commerce. His ship was captured by the British and he was taken captive along with incriminating papers. Made a prisoner in the Tower of London, he was detained despite pleas from Benjamin Franklin and Edmund Burke that he be released. Richard Oswald eventually effected his release on bond. Not long after, Laurens learned that he, together with John Adams, John Jay, Thomas Jefferson, and Franklin, had been named to negotiate a peace.

He arrived late, "the last day of the conferences," Adams recorded. The American commissioners first met at Jay's house on that day and then repaired to Oswald's. The preliminary articles were well advanced when Laurens said "there ought to be a stipulation that the British troops should carry off no negroes or other property." The other Americans agreed, and Laurens's British colleague in slave trading, Oswald, consented. "I was very happy that Mr Laurens came in," Adams continued. "The article he caused to be inserted . . . would most probably, in the hurry and multiplicity of affairs, have escaped us." Laurens dealt a double blow for the rights of private property and for slave owners.[30]

Not only did he make this contribution to the Peace of Independence, but also, for all his putative antislavery zeal, he stands in contrast to John Jay, who a few months later asked Great Britain to agree not "to carry or import into the United States any slaves from any part of the world; it being the intention of the said States entirely to prohibit the importation thereof."[31] Lastly, in reassessing Laurens's attitude toward slavery, we must point out that at the time of his death in 1792, although he had announced his intention to manumit his slaves, he had freed only a few—despite the ease of emancipation in contemporary South Carolina.

Laurens told William Drayton, a jurist, that "true policy lies on the side of the abolition of slavery." Then, referring to a famous incident in South Carolina history involving Col. George Gabriel Powell and a free man of color, apparently a mulatto, Laurens re-

---

30. Francis Wharton, *The Revolutionary Diplomatic Correspondence of the United States*, 6 vols. (Washington: Government Printing Office, 1889), 6:90–91.
31. Ibid., 6:460; Wallace, *Life of Henry Laurens*, 456.

vealed an ambivalence on race and human rights. "Reasoning from the colour carries no conviction," he affirmed.

> By perseverance the black may be blanched and the "stamp of Providence" effectually effaced. Gideon Gibson [the man of color] escaped the penalties of the negro law by producing upon comparison more red and white in his face than could be discovered in the faces of half the descendants of the French refugees in our House of Assembly. . . . The children of this same Gideon, having passed through another state of white-wash[,] were of fairer complexion than their prosecutor George Gabriel. But to confine them to their original clothing will be best. They may and ought to continue a separate people, may be subjected to special laws, kept harmless, made useful and freed from the tyranny and arbitrary power of individuals.[32]

In Laurens's outlook, sufficient blanching of his skin secured to a man, on the basis of his fading color, the right to escape the penalties of the Negro law, but still consigned him and his descendants to separate and unequal status. Winthrop D. Jordan, the historian of colonial racial attitudes, has commented: "Laurens showed both sides of the coin. He defended an individual's white status on the basis of appearance and at the same time expressed the conviction that colored persons 'may and ought to continue a separate people.' Once an Ethiopian always an Ethiopian, unless he could indeed change his skin."[33]

It seems plain that however much Laurens may have criticized the cruelties of the slave trade, abhorred slavery, and favored the abolition of slavery, he nonetheless confused his motives in abandoning the slave business, denied his philanthropy in his roles of slave owner and diplomat, and shared the ethnic prejudices of his time, which were, as Jordan shows, probably rooted in Elizabethan England rather than in the France of his forebears.[34]

The law of England offered no positive support for slavery, as Chief Justice Mansfield acknowledged in Somersett's case in 1772.

32. Laurens to William Drayton, n.d., *Laurens Papers*.

33. Winthrop D. Jordan, *White over Black* (Baltimore: Penguin Books, 1969), 173–74.

34. Ibid., 173.

In South Carolina the law of human bondage evolved through colonial legislatures over a period of seventy years. Despite Laurens's protests, it seems clear that the institution of slavery fundamental to his mercantile activities was not "established by British Kings & Parliaments as well as by the Laws of that Country Ages before my existence." Nor does it seem historically accurate to say that "acts of parliament have established the slave trade in favour of the home-residing English." Open trade to all merchants within the realm seems a more just description of English commercial policy in the eighteenth century.

The new estimates for the Atlantic trade afford a more dependable basis for determining the dimensions and directions of the flow of blacks from Africa, reducing the volume and pointing out the peaks and the sources.

With full assurance we now may say that Henry Laurens stood foremost in the slave trade of mid-eighteenth-century South Carolina, if not of the lower South. To the question of whether he found the slave trade profitable, he himself answered with a resounding "yea." Hazardous in the extreme, this branch of his business was "the most profitable." The contours of shipping routes formed a triangle that normally began in England, the African and American angles often being flattened, as it were, by calls at more than one port. An occasional ship returned directly to Africa.

London, far from losing out as a major slaving center, upheld an important role, both directly as a vendor of slaves and indirectly as a center of commerce and capital. Laurens, far from becoming a conspicuous foe of the slave trade and slavery, actively supervised the consignments of slaves in Charleston for years after he gave up accepting cargoes, kept most of his blacks in servitude, used his office as a peace commissioner to secure the slave property of Americans, and favored separation of the black and white races.

At the beginning of his life he was a British subject, at its close an American citizen. In early manhood he almost became an English resident. He had much to do with the political events that sundered trans-Atlantic ties and transformed his nationality. In a crowded career, this colonial merchant benefited from the English commercial system, though he was once victimized by administrative officials, and greatly contributed to the economic growth of his home country. He found vents for its products and furnished large supplies of black labor. As a patriot—or rebel—he promoted the schism in the Atlantic empire; as a diplomat he secured the interests of slaveholders. As a critic of the slave trade and slavery, he was an exception to his section, but he offers a dubious example of antislavery sentiment. With great financial profit to himself, during a time when colonial efforts to restrict the slave trade make crystal clear the contemporary awareness of the trade's social consequences, he helped place white over black in American society and contributed to the American dilemma.

6

Further Light on Archibald Dalzel

Students of the slave trade recognize the name of Archibald Dalzel mainly as author of *The History of Dahomy,* published in 1793. An African country on the Gulf of Guinea, Dahomy, customarily spelled Dahomey, was later taken over by France. Knowledge about Dalzel has long been sparse. Scholars since 1965 have supplied fragments of information. My essay adds to this growing body of knowledge, widening what is known about a man who participated in the trade for four decades. He acted in many roles: historian, slave-ship captain, slave-ship owner, and witness for Liverpool slaving interests before the Privy Council and a committee of the whole house of Parliament. *The Trans-Atlantic Slave Trade: A Database* offers some more information and more accurate dates. It omits some voyages involving Dalzel mentioned in my article. These include the 1778 and 1779 voyages of the *Hannah,* the voyages on behalf of Thomas and William Earle beginning in 1788, and voyages of the *Governor Dalzel* beginning in 1797 and of the *Thames* in 1804.

〰

Scholars of Africa devoted a fair amount of attention to Archibald Dalzel during the years 1965–1967. Interest centered on his *History of Dahomy* and new biographical materials. Trained as a surgeon, Dalzel served as an officer of the Company of Merchants Trading to Africa in 1763–1770 and again in 1791–1802, attempted a career as a slave merchant, and wrote *The History of Dahomy* in 1792.

Observing that "[i]nformation concerning Dalzel's life is scarce," Loren K. Waldman in a 1965 article in the *Journal of African History* asserted that Dalzel's book, relied on by a number of writers,

This chapter first appeared in the *International Journal of African Historical Studies* 17:2 (1984): 317–23.

"is a polemic." Waldman pointed to Dalzel's pro–slave trade activities in 1788, references to him in the controversy over abolition in 1789–1791, and Dalzel's description of Dahomeans as people who went to war by nature and not as a result of the slave trade. Waldman's coverage of Dalzel's pro–slave trade activities is less than complete, and he erroneously dates Dalzel's governorship of Cape Coast Castle as from 1785 to 1790.[1]

In an article published in the same journal the following year, I. A. Akinjogbin exploited Dalzel's correspondence with his younger brother and others, which is in the Edinburgh University Library. With these letters Akinjogbin filled in a good many biographical details, bringing to light some aspects of Dalzel's career as a slave trader. Even so, details were sometimes sparse and there remained great gaps in Dalzel's career. "For the next nine years after 1783," wrote Akinjogbin, "it is not known what was happening to Dalzel or what he was doing for his livelihood. . . . Similarly, Dalzel's activities in the last phase of his life, which was the period between his resignation in 1802 and his death (which probably occurred at an advanced age around 1811), are completely obscure."[2]

J. D. Fage brought out a new edition of *The History of Dahomy* the following year. Noting that "almost the whole of Dalzel's active career of nearly forty years, from 1763 to 1802, was bound up with Britain's trade in African slaves," Fage largely followed Akinjogbin in his biographical account in his introduction and in seeing the book as a polemic. At the same time, he considered the questions of the veracity and usefulness of the book. The gaps remained. "Dalzel's career for the next thirteen years is somewhat obscure," Fage observed for the years after 1778. "From 1783 to 1791, it is not clear, indeed, how he managed to maintain himself at all." As for the years after 1802, Fage, amending Akinjogbin's view that the period is "completely obscure," wrote: "In 1802, Dalzel resigned and returned to Britain, where he lived in straitened circumstances until his death some nine years later." Passing over the years from 1783 to 1788 in Dalzel's life, another historian, F. E. Sanderson,

1. Loren K. Waldman, "An Unnoticed Aspect of Archibald Dalzel's *The History of Dahomey*," *Journal of African History* 6 (1965): 185–92.
2. I. A. Akinjogbin, "Archibald Dalzel: Slave Trader and Historian of Dahomey," *Journal of African History* 7 (1966): 67–78.

found a detail: "[A]fter the war he moved to Liverpool where he sailed in the African trade for John and Thomas Hodgson."[3]

It is the aim of this essay to fill in some of the gaps in Dalzel's life and, in the process, strengthen Fage's assertion that almost the whole of his active career was bound up with Britain's trade in African slaves. Materials making this possible are mainly in the Public Record Office, the British Parliamentary Papers, and Lloyd's *Registry of Shipping*. Helpful as they are, they by no means provide a complete record of Dalzel's activities.

We may begin by supplying further information on Dalzel's slaving career at Dahomey. After a period of service as a surgeon at Anomabo on the Gold Coast, Dalzel became governor of the Company of Merchants' fort at Whydah in Dahomey, where he spent nearly four years. He devoted a good part of his energies to acquiring wealth for himself. Akinjogbin declares that Dalzel was trading with the French and Portuguese, which was prohibited.[4] Beyond this, a contemporary of Dalzel's, Richard Brew, a private trader at Anomabo, asserted that Dalzel imposed heavy charges to insure private traders' goods stored in the publicly maintained company fort and was using his own trade goods—sent him by the company—to buy slaves to be sold by him in the West Indies.

Brew's account, written July 1, 1770, from Castle Brew, Anomabo, to several merchants in Liverpool, relates that as a common practice whenever a governor was preparing to leave the coast he would distribute his goods among the chiefs of the trading posts to buy up the best slaves and make his fortune. Brew wrote:

> A striking instance of which we now have at Whydah, where the governor is realizing his fortune in slaves, and has sent the surgeon of the fort up to Annamaboe to agree with a captain of a ship to go down there and carry him and his slaves to the West Indies; and he has accordingly agreed with Captain Hamilton, of the *Jamaica* storeship, to go down to Whydah the beginning of June, to carry the governor and one hundred

3. J. D. Fage, introduction to *The History of Dahomey*, 2d ed., by Archibald Dalzel (London: Frank Cass, 1967), 8–9; F. E. Sanderson, "The Liverpool Delegates and Sir William Dolben's Bill," *Transactions of the Historic Society of Lancashire and Cheshire* 124 (1974): 65.

4. Akinjogbin, "Archibald Dalzel," 71.

and fifty slaves certain to the West-Indies; so that, till his purchase is made, Captain Norris, of the ship *Unity* of Liverpool, (who is now there) must lie by or take up with such slaves as he can get, as we are to suppose a gentleman will ship none but the primest, when they compose the bulk of his fortune.

Everybody acquainted with this trade must allow, that lodging merchandize of any kind, especially liquor and gunpowder, in a thatched house is attended with a very great risque; so great a one indeed, that I am informed, Governor Dalzel asked Captain Norris of the *Unity* ten per cent to insure his factory during his stay there; how true this is I cannot pretend to say, however Captain Norris will, no doubt, clear up this point on his arrival in England.[5]

Dalzel, Akinjogbin tells us, transported only 104 slaves to the West Indies, where he sold them to a planter named Cuthberts. Making a profit of about £2,000, he accepted a promissory note which was not fully paid, driving him into bankruptcy in 1773.

We may continue offering more information on three slave ships of Dalzel's mentioned by Akinjogbin, showing that Dalzel was more involved in slave trading than has been previously ascertained. Akinjogbin said: "In 1773, he bought a ship entirely on his own, which he named *Little Archie* and sent to West Africa under a captain whom he had engaged." This is Akinjogbin's only reference to the *Little Archie,* but in addition to this voyage of 1773, the *Little Archie* made a second African voyage in 1775.[6]

Writing of Dalzel's plans to operate a number of vessels in the slave trade, Akinjogbin tells us that on his way back from a trip to America, Dalzel bought two ships, the *Nancy* and the *Hannah:* "He sent the *Nancy* off to West Africa on 20 September 1775, and in

5. An African Merchant [Richard Brew], *A Treatise upon the Trade from Great Britain to Africa, humbly recommended to the Attention of Government* (London: R. Baldwin, 1772), 70. A valuable account of Brew and his family is Margaret Priestley, *West African Trade and Coast Society: A Family Study* (London: Oxford University Press, 1969). Captain Robert Norris had a career that paralleled Dalzel's; a slave trader, he became a defender of the trade, giving valuable testimony in the slave trade inquiries at the century's end (together with Dalzel, as we shall see) and writing his anti-African *Memoirs of the Reign of Bossa Ahadee, King of Dahomey* (London, 1789), from which Dalzel borrowed in his *History of Dahomy.*

6. Akinjogbin, "Archibald Dalzel," 71–72; Public Record Office (hereinafter PRO), BT 6/3.

the following November he himself followed in the *Hannah*."[7] To this we may add information about the African destination of these vessels, the character of them, and records of voyages after 1775. The African destination of these two vessels in 1775 appears to have been the Gold Coast. The *Nancy* was classified not as a ship but a schooner, built in New England in 1774; it made not one but three voyages under Dalzel's ownership, in 1775, 1776, and 1778, the last two under Captain A. Anderson. Its tonnage is differently listed for each voyage, respectively 50, 70, and 60 tons.[8]

The ship *Hannah*, consistently listed as 150 tons, formerly the *Liberty*, was built in Bermuda in 1757, sheathed in 1774, and thoroughly repaired in 1775. In addition to the 1775 voyage to the Gold Coast, it made two more slaving voyages under Dalzel's ownership. The *Hannah*, under Captain Dalzel, cleared for Africa in 1776, and again in 1778 under Captain James Gibson. In 1779, now the *Union*, it cleared from Jamaica for London; and later in the same year, now owned by E. Mesnard, it cleared from London for New York.[9] In August of 1778, while returning to England, Dalzel had fallen prey to a privateer and lost everything he had. The sale of the *Hannah* was probably necessitated by this misfortune. After these voyages of the *Little Archie*, the *Nancy*, and the *Hannah*, he again went bankrupt and subsequently became the captain of a privateer.[10]

Further details about Dalzel's African trading in these years appear in the journals of the Board of Trade. In 1775, the board approved "the petition of Archibald Dalzel, for leave to export to the coast of Africa certain military stores on board the ship *Hannah*." In 1777, the board heard the testimony of Captain Thomas Bennett, master of a vessel in the slave trade, that "a ship sailed from the River [Thames] last November belonging to Mr. Dalzel, late Governor of Whydah, who took part of her cargo in Holland." Dalzel's petition, one of many received by the board at this time,

7. Akinjogbin, "Archibald Dalzel," 71.
8. PRO, BT 6/3; *Lloyd's Register of Shipping 1780–* (London, 1973), 1775, 1776, 1778.
9. PRO, BT 6/3; *Lloyd's Register*, 1776, 1778, 1779.
10. After he became a bankrupt in 1778, the spelling of the family name was changed from Dalziel to Dalzel. Nevertheless, the Dalziel spelling frequently appears after 1778 (Akinjogbin, "Archibald Dalzel," 71–72).

was necessitated by the ban on exports of military stores occasioned by the outbreak of fighting in North America. His taking of cargo for Africa in Holland was a more common practice of London slavers in the eighteenth century than historians have appreciated. The practice, among other matters, complicates analysis of the London-African trade relationship.[11]

We need no longer be puzzled as to how Dalzel was maintaining himself from 1783 to 1791. He was commanding vessels in the African trade, notably in the slave trade. In 1783, Dalzel returned to the African trade. The cutter *Europa,* Captain A. Dalzel, cleared London for Africa. Built at Sidmouth in 1779 and raised and equipped with a new deck in the year of the voyage, the *Europa* was owned by James Mather, a London slave merchant who had a large number of vessels in the African trade, dispatching seven in 1783.[12]

The *Europa* apparently was in the direct trade between England and Africa, for later in the year, too soon for a triangular voyage to have been completed, Dalzel was in command of the ship *St. Ann,* which, after giving bond in London on September 13, sailed for Africa. Three hundred twenty tons, a prize taken from the French, with a crew of sixty men and carrying six guns, the *St. Ann* entered Kingston harbor in Jamaica on September 23, 1784, just over one year after she had left London, with a cargo of 330 Negroes from Africa.[13]

The following year Dalzel arrived in London at the command of a new ship, also called the *St. Ann,* 300 tons, thirty-two men, "from or in the African trade," as the record states. This ship was apparently in the direct trade; the record of seamen's sixpences paid (made for the use of the Royal Hospital at Greenwich) shows the first man's entry on July 1, 1785, and the last man's discharge on January 2, 1786.[14]

Later in 1786, Dalzel was in command of the ship *Tartar,* owned by the Backhouses of Liverpool and which left Liverpool for Benin. Built in Liverpool in 1772 and given large repairs in 1781, the *Tar-*

---

11. *Journal of the Commissioners for Trade and Plantations, 1704–1782,* 14 vols. (London: Stationery Office, 1920–1938), *1768–1775,* 138.

12. *Lloyd's Register,* 1783.

13. PRO, CO 142/19.

14. PRO, ADM 68/205.

tar "made a very fatal voyage" in 1786. After being detained a year at the coast of Benin, the *Tartar* lost about one-third of its crew of thirty-seven and about one-third of its cargo of around 360 slaves. There had been a loss of another ten or eleven slaves before leaving the coast. Dalzel explained the long delay in slaving: "I had a badly assorted Cargo; great Competition; few Slaves in the Country; Provisions Scarce in the Country." He arrived, with diminished crew and cargo, at Dominica in the West Indies on March 2, 1787.[15]

Soon after he returned to England he became an active propagandist, defending the slave trade against the rapidly rising agitation to abolish it. Under the pseudonym "Vindex," he contributed letters to the Liverpool press assailing the Society for the Abolition of the Slave Trade. When the Privy Council began to take evidence about the slave trade, Dalzel was deputed by the Liverpool African Merchants, together with John Tarleton, Robert Norris, James Penny, and John Matthews, to testify. Dalzel gave evidence twice, once on the Gold Coast and again on Whydah and Dahomey, and received the thanks of the Liverpool Council and reimbursement for his expenses.[16]

When it became apparent that the slave trade would not be abolished in 1788 but that a bill to regulate the trade might win favor, Dalzel was designated by the African Committee of Liverpool, along with Tarleton, Norris, and Matthews, to oppose the bill sponsored by Sir William Dolben. In giving evidence before a committee of the whole house, Dalzel said he did not believe crowding and stowage of Negroes were the causes of mortality, but thought some regulation, such as provision for distilling sea water, would be in order. William Wilberforce, in introducing his motion in the House of Commons on May 12, 1789, to abolish the African slave trade, referred to Dalzel's views. "It is said," Wilberforce remarked, "that Liverpool will be undone—the trade, says Mr. Dalzel, at this time hangs upon a thread, and the smallest matter will overthrow it." Dalzel was, in 1788, together with Norris and Matthews, in

15. *Lloyd's Register*, 1786; *Parliamentary Papers, Accounts and Papers*, 1789, 24 (633).

16. Sanderson, "Liverpool Delegates," 65, 81 n. 26, 62, 80 n. 14; Elizabeth Donnan, ed., *Documents Illustrative of the History of the Slave Trade to America*, 4 vols. (Washington: Carnegie Institution, 1930–1935), 2:578–79; *Accounts and Papers*, 1789, 26 (646a).

correspondence with Lord Hawkesbury about the wording of the Dolben bill.[17]

By November 1788, Dalzel, according to F. E. Sanderson, "had returned to the slave trade, sailing under Portuguese colours under contract to furnish slaves on the coast on behalf of the ships of Thomas and William Earle." Sanderson leaves the impression that Dalzel continued in this employ until 1791, when on the recommendation of Liverpool merchants he became governor of Cape Coast Castle.[18] His employment by the Liverpool slave merchants could in fact not have lasted long, because in 1789 Dalzel was captain of a London slave vessel. The *Gosport and Havre* packet, built in the River Thames in 1787, 106 tons, carrying a crew of twenty, was owned by William Collow, a leading London slave merchant.[19] The years when Dalzel's career has been said to be unknown or obscure came to an end in late 1791 when he was appointed governor of Cape Coast Castle. Not long after he took up this post, his testimony that wars and kidnapping were not the sources of African slaves was cited with approbation by William Fox in his *Summary of the Evidence Produced before a Committee of the House of Commons,* published in 1793.[20]

Dalzel continued at this post until 1802. It is interesting that during these years and later, from 1797 to 1807, a vessel called the *Governor Dalzel* was a constant trader in the slaving business, carrying Africans to, among other places, St. Vincent's, Demerara, and the Bahamas.[21] The records consulted by this writer do not show whether Dalzel had an interest in this vessel.

Waldman, after referring to Dalzel's *History of Dahomy,* wrote: "At least one other book written by him, *New Sailing Directions for the Coast of Africa* (London, 1799), is known."[22] The statement that Dalzel wrote another book is misleading, as the full title

17. *Accounts and Papers,* 1789, 26 (633); *Cobbett's Parliamentary History of England from the Earliest Period to the Year 1803,* 36 vols. (London: T. Curson Hansard, 1806–1820), 28:5; Donnan, *Documents,* 2:578 n. 1, 586 n. 3.

18. Sanderson, "Liverpool Delegates," 65–66.

19. PRO, Treasury 64/286; *Lloyd's Register,* 1789.

20. William Fox, *Summary of the Evidence Produced before a Committee of the House of Commons* (London, 1792), cited in Donnan, *Documents,* 2:597 n. 4.

21. *Lloyd's Register,* 1797–1807; *British Parliamentary Papers* (Shannon: Irish University Press, 1968), 61:439, 42, 51, 440, 55, 424, 427.

22. Waldman, "Unnoticed Aspect," 185.

makes clear. While he was in Africa for his second tour of duty, his knowledge of navigation of the African coast was incorporated in a volume with the lengthy title *New sailing directions for the coast of Africa, extending from Cape Spartel . . . to the Cape of Good Hope . . . and of the African Islands situated in the Atlantic and Ethiopic Oceans . . . from the journals, manuscripts, remarks, and draughts of Archibald Dalzel . . . Mr. Norris, Mr. Woodville, Captain George Glas, Mr. George Maxwell, Mr. Ralph Fisher . . . and many other navigators . . . adapted to the African pilot, a new collection of charts,* published in London in 1799.

When we come to the years after 1802, which have been said to be "completely obscure," and a period when Dalzel lived in "straitened circumstances," we find that he was living in London, continued to be interested in Africa, and was busily engaged in the slave trade. In 1804, when the African Association—formed to promote the discovery of the interior parts of Africa—was projecting a trip from the coast of Guinea into the interior, it interviewed persons who had resided at Whydah. On August 1, Dalzel met with a committee of the association in the house of a London member. He warned against trying to travel north of Abomey, capital of Dahomey, because the Dahomeans were extremely jealous lest information be carried to the inland Oyo. He advised the prospective traveler to start from Bonny or Old Calabar and keep eastward of Dahomey. The traveler would pass through "countries or tribes of Negroes almost wholly unknown." Dalzel described the slave trade in this dim interior as a chain whose length the African agents of the coastal merchants did not traverse. The slave drivers, he explained, "have regular stages of one or two days journey to which the European assortments are carried progressively, at each stage taken up by merchants who come no further from the interior, than to meet others nearer to the Coast."[23]

For the years after 1802, we also find a record that Dalzel was a persistent slave trader in these last years of the legal trade. By 1804, he had become the owner of the ship *Thames,* 221 tons, built at Southampton in 1791. The *Thames,* under Captain G. Black, who had commanded her under previous owners, cleared London

23. Robin Hallett, ed., *Records of the African Association, 1788–1831* (London: Nelson, 1964), 193–95.

on December 22, 1804, for 250 slaves. The ship was registered again under Dalzel's ownership in 1805, 1806, 1807, and 1808 for London clearances for Africa. In 1809, by which time the slave trade had been outlawed, ownership passed to Miller and Company, which registered her for a voyage from London to Granada.[24]

By 1805 Dalzel had become the owner of a second slaver, the ship *Chalmers*, 271 tons, built at Yarmouth in 1802. The *Chalmers* cleared London for Africa on October 1, 1805, permitted to carry 273 slaves; Dalzel and Co. was registered as the owner. Under the same ownership, it was registered for London-to-Africa voyages in 1806, 1807, and 1808, when it disappeared from the registry.[25]

It is clear that Dalzel was far more active in the African slave trade than has been heretofore known. Beyond the few voyages mentioned by Akinjogbin, he was busily engaged as owner and captain of vessels in the African and slave trades. In the period of his life between 1778 and 1791, described by Akinjogbin and Fage as unknown and obscure, he was also active in the defense of the slave trade; and in a second period of obscurity between 1802 and 1811, he was the owner of at least two vessels engaged in the African trade. His career persisted beyond the forty years from 1763 to 1802 that Fage described. Moreover, his career is a commentary on the notion that the slave trade was very profitable. Twice in his lifetime he went bankrupt, and it is said he died a bankrupt. Yet he persevered in the trade for nearly half a century. It is interesting as well that the vessels in which he was concerned nearly all cleared from the port of London, although historians traditionally have tended to associate him with Liverpool as well as to dismiss London as a port of consequence in the slave trade in the late eighteenth century (see Chapter 2). Further research may indicate that Dalzel may have been even more deeply involved in the African slave trade than we have been able to report here.

24. *Lloyd's Register*, 1804–1809; for earlier voyages under Black, see 1801, 1802, 1803.
25. *Parliamentary Papers, Slave Trade*, 61:450; *Lloyd's Register*, 1806, 1807, 1808.

7

John Newton

AMAZING GRACE

John Newton, composer in the 1760s or 1770s of the enduring hymn "Amazing Grace," had an amazing career.

The sheer length of his life—eighty-two years—is extraordinary for his time. Born of middle-class parents, sparsely educated, he passed through radically diverse phases of experience. The sea called in his youth, at first to sail in the Mediterranean trade and then in the transatlantic slave trade as mate and captain of slave ships. Stricken by an undiagnosed illness, he left that trade.

Religion beckoned, and without formal theological training, but self-taught and a prolific writer, he gained recognition. Wealthy and influential benefactors advanced his priestly career. With some difficulty, because he lacked a divinity school background, he secured a parish in Olney, where he composed "Amazing Grace." Another influential benefactor, John Thornton, said to be the richest man in England, secured a larger parish for him in the heart of London, St. Mary Woolnoth, near the Bank of England. Preaching and writing there, Newton spread his fame.

A new phenomenon, denunciation of the slave trade, tardily appearing in the late eighteenth century, drew the former slave trader into a group of the trade's opponents. He counseled the parliamentary leader of legislation to outlaw the trade. He wrote about his own experience, and twice testified before august government bodies—the Privy Council and the House of Commons. In failing health, he lived to see Parliament ban the trade not long before he died.

This paper was delivered in 2001 to an audience in St. Matthew's Episcopal Church in Lincoln, Nebraska, and has not been previously published.

≈

Amazing grace! How sweet the sound
That saved a wretch like me.
I once was lost, but now am found,
Was blind, but now I see.

'Twas grace that taught my heart to fear,
And grace my fears relieved.
How precious did that grace appear
The hour I first believed!

Through many dangers, toils and snares
I have already come;
'Tis grace that brought me safe thus far
And grace will lead me home.

John Newton, 1725–1807, slave trader, Anglican priest, hymnist, and abolitionist, is perhaps best remembered as composer of the hymn "Amazing Grace." The words are autobiographical in a sense little known.

Newton was born in London, the son of a merchant-ship captain in the Mediterranean trade. His mother was a pious woman who attended a dissenting chapel where the congregation sang hymns in chorus, rather than line by line after the parish clerk as in Anglican churches. In his tender years, John learned a good deal about the Bible and hymns. His mother intended him to study at St. Andrews University in Scotland and then at an academy for clergy. His father intended him to become a sea officer.

Mrs. Newton, a tubercular, died before John was seven. His father remarried and John studied at a boarding school for about two years before leaving school at age eleven. During the years to 1742, he spent much time at sea with his father, a stern disciplinarian. On these voyages, John learned to swear like a sailor, and in the passing of time became a disbeliever, a blasphemer, and sexually promiscuous.

"When I was four years old I could read," he recalled. Through the years, though nearsighted, he taught himself geometry; classics, such as Shaftesbury's influential book *Characteristics* (which asserted that morality is found in a balance between egotism and altruism) and a seventeenth-century paraphrase of Thomas à Kempis' *Imitation of Christ;* some Latin, which he had commenced in school; some French; and enough Hebrew to read the Hebrew Bible.

Late in 1742 on his way to take ship in Liverpool, he stopped at the home of his mother's friend Elizabeth Catlett, where he was smitten by her daughter Mary, called Polly, not yet fourteen. A relationship, discouraged by her father and not encouraged by Polly, resulted in their idyllic marriage in 1750.

Newton, though passionately devoted to Polly, in the years preceding their marriage did not abandon the dissolute life of "a wretch like me." He acknowledged: "I soon lost all sense of religion, and became deaf to the remonstrances of conscience and prudence, but my regard for her was always the same . . . none of the scenes of misery and wickedness I afterwards experienced, ever banished her a single hour together from my waking thoughts for the seven following years."[1]

Captain Newton arranged employment for John on a voyage to Venice and then on another voyage as an officer. But John visited Polly, overstayed the visit, and lost his post. Early in March 1744, while England was anticipating the war with France called the War of the Austrian Succession, John was seized by a government press gang (an event preceding legal impressment). With nine other victims he was placed on the HMS *Harwich,* a fourth-rate—that is, fifty-gun—man-of-war. Before the ship departed England, John deserted at Plymouth, was arrested by a group of marines, and returned to his ship, where, as he wrote, he was "publicly stripped and whipped." Humiliated in front of the crew, he contemplated suicide. At Madeira the *Harwich* impressed two skilled sailors from a ship in the Guinea trade, as the African trade was termed, and John persuaded his captain to give him to the Guineaman as one of two replacements. He rejoiced, not only that he was freed from naval service, but also, as he said, "[t]hat I now might be abandoned as I please."[2]

John Newton in 1745 entered the slave trade, then a respectable business, a kind of lottery that could make a man rich. Only Quak-

1. Richard Cecil, *The Letters of the Rev. John Newton, Containing an Authentic Narrative and Memoirs of His Life by the Rev. Richard Cecil* (New York: Robert Carter, 1845), 7–9.
2. Ibid., 12–13.

ers and a few others condemned the buying and selling of human beings. As Newton said decades later: "I am sure that had I thought of the Slave Trade then as I have thought of it since, no consideration would have induced me to continue . . . I would have been overwhelmed in distress and terror, if I had known or even suspected that I was acting wrongly."[3]

Many of the slaves bought in the next six months were young women and girls, naked and helpless, and Newton joined fellow crewmen in taking advantage of them. Much later, he acknowledged, "I not only sinned with a high hand myself, but made it my study to tempt and seduce others on every occasion," citing 2 Peter 2:14, which begins, "Having eyes full of adultery, and that cannot cease from sin."[4]

A passenger and part owner of the ship, one Clow, was returning to his slave trading business in Africa. Seeing an opportunity to acquire wealth, Newton managed to obtain permission to leave the ship and work for Clow. He neglected to make a contract with his new employer.

Clow conducted his business on three small, uninhabited islands south of Sierra Leone. He had a black mistress, said to be a princess, who was helpful in trading with black rulers. Called P.I., for "Pee-eye," she immediately disliked Newton. When he fell ill and Clow left the island to do business, she badly abused the invalid, withholding adequate water and food from the feverish white man, giving him leavings from her plate. On his return, Clow refused to believe Newton's account of his maltreatment. While the two men were on the trading boat, Newton was required to sleep not in the cabin, but on the deck. During the daytime, Clow chained him to the deck. In the course of time, Clow put Newton in ankle irons while on land and assigned him to help plant lime trees, under supervision of a head slave who worked for Clow. Newton had sunk, as he wrote, to be "a servant of slaves" in Africa.

He had brought only one book with him—Euclid's *Elements of Geometry*. At night he took to going to a remote shore and draw-

3. John Newton, *Thoughts upon the African Slave Trade*, in *The Journal of a Slave Trader (John Newton), 1750–1754*, ed. Bernard Martin and Mark Spurrell (London: Epworth Press, 1962), 99. Originally published as a pamphlet in London, 1788.
4. Cecil, *Letters*, 13.

ing figures in the sand with a stick. In this crude classroom, he mastered the first six books of Euclid. Meanwhile, a second slave trader had set up shop on the island. He managed to persuade Clow to allow Newton to join him. Newton's health and clothing improved, as well as his state of mind, which had been "depressed to a degree beyond common wretchedness."[5] He shared the duties of manager of a trading station, becoming familiar not only with the business, but also gaining respect for the blacks who were being cheated by whites in the exchange of goods for slaves.

Newton had written his father, as well as Polly, about his situation. Captain Newton informed his Liverpool friend Joseph Manesty, a slave merchant and shipowner, about his son's status. Manesty ordered the captain of his ship, the *Greyhound,* which was ready to sail for the Windward Coast of Africa, to find young John and bring him home.

At his African trading post, Newton needed additional goods. Sighting a ship—the *Greyhound*—he sent up a smoke signal, a means of inviting trade. The ship, which was not in the slave trade, took Newton on board for the return journey to England. Sharing the captain's cabin, Newton was a poor passenger, swearing, inventing new oaths, and blaspheming, attacking Jesus, God, and the Bible. It was on the long journey homeward that Newton read *The Imitation of Christ.* At the close of a second reading, the unbeliever had a strange thought: "What if these things should be true?"[6]

Toward the end of the voyage, off the Irish coast, a violent storm struck the *Greyhound,* staving in one side of the ship. Water poured in; someone cried, "The ship is sinking!" A crewman was swept overboard. Newton helped man the pumps.

After four hours of labor he went to the captain with a suggestion about coping with the storm. As he walked away, he said, "If this will not do, the Lord have mercy upon us." His words came as a surprise to him. He next thought, "What mercy can there be for me!" He later said of the experience that it was a "day much to be remembered by me, and I have never suffered it to pass wholly un-

5. Ibid., 91.
6. Ibid., 19.

noticed since the year 1748. On that day the Lord sent from on high, and delivered me out of deep waters."[7]

John Newton had begun an extended, zigzag course to Christian belief. Was the Bible true? Was Christ the Son of God? Had He risen from the dead? Newton began to read the New Testament.

The storm subsided, the pumps kept the *Greyhound* afloat, and she crept into an Irish port. On his return to Liverpool, Manesty offered Newton command of his slave ship *Brownlow*. Believing himself unready to be captain, Newton accepted an offer to be mate. Before departing for Africa, he visited Polly, now twenty. He was still passionately in love with her, in spite of his profligacy; he was tongue-tied and had scant encouragement of a warm relationship until on the eve of sailing he received a cautious but kind letter from her.

The *Brownlow,* 50 tons, Captain Richard Jackson, 20 crewmen, was financed by four investors. She departed Liverpool in 1748 and made her first slave purchase on the Windward Coast, then sailed on to the Gold Coast, where the greatest number of slaves were embarked. Newton suffered a relapse in his religious convictions, saying, "[B]y the time I arrived at Guinea, I seemed to have forgotten all the Lord's mercies, and my own engagements, and was (profaneness excepted) almost as bad as before."[8] When the ship visited the Plantains, his former employer, Clow, made available a black girl for his pleasure—the custom of the coast. The lapse was brief; a violent fever, he said, brought him to himself. During his leisure time he returned to the study of Latin, selecting Horace's odes as his text.

Eight months were spent in slaving before the ship, with 218 slaves on board, sailed for the West Indies. While on the Middle Passage a slave insurrection broke out, leading to the death of one white man and three to four blacks. The first landfall was Antigua before continuing to Charleston, South Carolina. One hundred eighty-nine slaves disembarked, a loss of 28 percent, in addition to the uncounted number who died before the departure from Africa. The venture nevertheless was considered successful, despite the

7. Ibid., 20, 101.
8. Ibid., 101.

long slaving period in Africa and the loss of lives. Long after this voyage, Newton testified that he believed one-quarter of the slaves purchased in the English trade died before disembarkation in the Americas.[9]

Shortly after returning to England on December 1, 1749, Newton was promised a captaincy. An emboldened suitor, he now proposed marriage to Polly. She refused once, twice, thrice, and finally consented. On February 12, 1750, in St. Mary's at Rochester, they married.

Manesty, the principal owner, gave Newton command of the *Duke of Argyle,* an aging vessel of 100 tons and ten guns, built in 1729. The ship sailed from Liverpool on August 11, 1750, with the Windward Coast as its destination. Newton commanded a crew of thirty, a number that shrank to fifteen by the time the voyage ended. On October 23 the slaving commenced at Sierra Leone, before continuing at the Windward Coast. The first mate, the surgeon, and the carpenter died before departure from Africa on May 22, 1751. Newton thwarted an insurrection hours before it was to have been attempted. The vessel survived tornadoes and arrived at Antigua on July 3 with 136 slaves, having embarked with 161. More than a month later, on August 13, the *Duke of Argyle* unmoored and set sail for Liverpool. She arrived October 8, nearly seven weeks later. Newton's journal is blank from July 3 to August 13, leaving unrecorded the contents of the return cargo. From Liverpool and back, the voyage consumed 327 days. From the perspective of the owners, the voyage was a success.[10]

The next slave voyage was on the *African,* built in 1752—a contrast with the decrepit *Duke of Argyle*—and not yet launched when Captain Newton first saw it. A 100-ton vessel, four guns, its principal owner was Manesty; three others shared in the enterprise. With a crew of twenty-two, it sailed from Liverpool June 30, 1752, destined for Sierra Leone, the Windward Coast, and the area from Cape Mesurado to Cape Palmas.

9. Ibid.; Elizabeth Donnan, ed., *Documents Illustrative of the History of the Slave Trade to America,* 4 vols. (Washington: Carnegie Institution, 1930–1935), 4:103.

10. The *Duke of Argyle* in David Eltis, Stephen D. Behrendt, David Richardson, Herbert S. Klein, *The Trans-Atlantic Slave Trade: A Database on CD-ROM* (Cambridge and New York: Cambridge University Press, 1999); Martin and Spurrell, *Journal,* 54, 58.

Slaving began August 12, about six weeks after leaving England. Loading proceeded slowly. In early December, Newton discovered that the slaves he had acquired were plotting an insurrection. Four boys were supplying eight men with knives, a chisel, other stores, and shot. He recorded in his journal: "Put the boys in irons and slightly in the thumbscrews to urge them to a full confession."

With 207 slaves, the *African* on April 26, 1753—nearly ten months after the voyage began—set sail for St. Kitts. During the 36-day Middle Passage, Newton conducted divine services on Sundays and prayed for Polly and the blacks. One hundred sixty-seven slaves, forty fewer than had departed Africa, disembarked at St. Kitts on June 2, and one more at a second port. Sales ended by July 11, and on that day, with a cargo of sugar and cotton, Newton recorded: "At 4 p.m., weighed [anchor], bound by God's permission for Liverpool." The long triangular voyage ended August 29, 1753, and was declared a success with the death of only one crewman.[11]

Newton, after the long separation, had only seven weeks with Polly before he again sailed on the *African* on October 27. Slaving took place on the Windward Coast, from the Sherbro River as far south as Cape Palmas, and extended over a period of more than four months (December 3, 1753, to April 7, 1754).

Slaves were difficult to procure. In contrast to its previous transatlantic voyage with 207 slaves, the ship departed with 87, who miraculously all survived the 44-day voyage to St. Kitts. Sales were completed by June 20 when the *African* sailed for Liverpool. The voyage was a failure from an economic point of view, but a rarity in mortality records.[12]

Manesty did not begrudge Newton his poor business performance, and offered him the choice of another ship. Newton chose the *Bee.* He helped fit out the ship, selected his crew, and loaded his trading cargo. But an event occurred that ended his slaving career. As he related: "I was within two days of sailing and to all appearances in good health as usual; but in the afternoon, as I was sitting with Mrs. N. . . ., by ourselves, drinking tea and talking over past events, I was in a moment seized with a fit, which deprived me

---

11. The *African* in Eltis et al., *Database;* Martin and Spurrell, *Journal,* 71.
12. The *African* in Eltis et al., *Database;* Martin and Spurrell, *Journal,* 82.

of sense and motion, and left no other sign of life than that of breathing—I suppose it was of the apoplectic kind."[13]

The *Bee* sailed under another commander on a disastrous voyage that took the lives of the captain, most of the officers, and numbers of the crew. Newton never returned to the trade, but not out of moral repugnance, for he still believed it legitimate and necessary to the English economy. He later wrote: "I never knew sweeter communion than in my last two voyages to Guinea, when I was either almost secluded from society on shipboard, or when on shore with the natives."[14]

Newton recovered his health and continued his self-education in Latin, French, and mathematics. He became acquainted with the charismatic preacher George Whitefield, who had returned from a dramatically successful visit to the North American colonies and now in England was drawing crowds of a thousand or so. He and John Wesley, who was separating his followers, called Methodists, from the Church of England, were showing that sedate establishment an evangelical vitality that caused bishops to criticize their "Enthusiasm."

Historian D. Bruce Hindmarsh asserts of evangelicalism:

> [T]he first characteristic to emerge and sustain evangelic identity in the popular Protestant movement was an emphasis upon conversion, the belief that the gospel called men and women to a fundamental change of life. . . . This central stress was apparent not only in summaries of theological essentials such as the Methodists' three cardinal doctrines of original sin, justification by faith, and the new birth, with its concomitant holiness of life, but also in the testimony of laymen and clergymen alike, spoken extempore in society meetings or written up for pious edification.[15]

While Newton was experiencing the burst of evangelism and "Enthusiasm" on the English scene, Manesty secured for him the lucrative appointment of tide surveyor in Liverpool. The duties

---

13. Martin and Spurrell, *Journal*, 96.

14. Cecil, *Letters*, 28–29.

15. D. Bruce Hindmarsh, *John Newton and the Evangelical Tradition* (New York: Oxford University Press, 1996), 9, 15.

were to inspect ships and examine imports into England, affording him much leisure time. On a visit to Yorkshire he was repeatedly asked to relate his religious views, and he began to think of becoming a minister.

He applied to the Bishop of Chester to ordain him, but was refused because he lacked a degree from Oxford or Cambridge. An unexpected turn of events occurred when Lord Dartmouth, a pious, wealthy, and influential benefactor (for whom Dartmouth College is named), urged by an intermediary, offered Newton the curacy at Olney in Buckinghamshire. With Dartmouth's help, Newton, now thirty-nine, was ordained by the Bishop of Lincoln.[16]

At Olney, Newton at first drew a large congregation. He published *An Authentic Narrative* (1764), which concerned his religious life and brought him widespread recognition. By the end of the century it had gone through ten British and eight American editions. Three years after its appearance it was published in a Dutch edition. A friend of Dartmouth and Whitefield, John Thornton, who was another figure marked by piety and philanthropy and reputedly the richest man in England, gave Newton an annual allowance of £200 to help the poor and extend hospitality.[17]

The gifted young poet William Cowper, perhaps best known for "John Gilpin's Ride," became acquainted with Newton, who invited him to move to Olney. Cowper, a victim of chronic depression, three times a failed suicide, and twice temporarily insane, had embraced the evangelical outlook, and together with Mary Unwin, a widow with whom he had been living for many years, moved to Olney. While their house was being prepared for their occupation, they lived with the Newtons for five months.

During the next several years Cowper wrote memorable hymns, including "Oh for a Closer Walk with God," and "Jesus, Where'er Thy People Meet." For his part, Newton essayed to compose a hymn each week. In 1779, Newton brought out a collection of their production, *Olney Hymns,* 66 by Cowper and 282 by himself. The popular work included "Amazing Grace," "How Sweet the Name

16. Bernard Martin, *John Newton: A Biography* (London: William Heinemann, 1950), 198–202.

17. Hindmarsh, *Evangelical Tradition,* 15–16; John Pollock, *Amazing Grace: John Newton's Story* (San Francisco: Harper & Row, 1981), 156.

of Jesus Sounds," and "Glorious Things of Thee Are Spoken." As his fame spread, Newton was awarded an honorary degree by the College of New Jersey and offered the presidency of a Georgia college, which he declined.[18]

Newton's congregation and church activities, embracing a weekly lecture and a precursor of Sunday school, expanded his following. He secured from Lord Dartmouth use of the family manor called the Great House. He conducted an enormous correspondence, writing heartfelt letters which he published in 1781 under the title, at Cowper's suggestion, of *Cardiphonia*, the sound of the heart.

In the course of time, Newton's popularity waned with his Olney congregation and with neighboring clergymen as well. Church members divided into factions and attended separate meetings, some rejecting Newton's teaching as well as his influence. Fellow clergymen suspected he was "methodistical" and believed him overly tolerant of other faiths and their feuds. Town riots, in one of which a mob threatened his house, further discomfited him.

A change of scene and widening of influence was made possible in 1779 when John Thornton offered him a London parish, St. Mary Woolnoth on Lombard Street, where the Lord Mayor worshiped. Newton broadened his reach, giving charity to the London poor who came to his house and holding breakfasts that started with prayer.

For fifteen years Newton had been uneasy of mind about the morality of the slave trade. In 1774, John Wesley, with whom he corresponded, published a condemnation of the trade. Others in his circle also wrote in strong disapproval. Cowper published abolitionist poems, including "The Negroe's Complaint," and Hannah More, perhaps the leading literary figure to become an Evangelical and who had come under Newton's influence, in 1788 produced *The Black Slave Trade,* an attack on the institution.

Newton's emergence as an abolitionist began in December 1785 when he opened a letter from William Wilberforce, member of Parliament from Hull and close friend of the prime minister, William Pitt. Recent research has uncovered the fact that Wilberforce, born in 1759, had been in touch with Newton since about 1777. The

18. Pollock, *Amazing Grace,* 166, 173.

letter said, "I wish to have some serious conversation with you," adding, "I must be secret." They became close to one another, conversing and corresponding as Newton deepened the commitment of Wilberforce, once a young man of fashionable society, to Christian doctrines and presumably to abolishing the slave trade. Wilberforce became the leader in the coming twenty-year parliamentary crusade against the trade.[19]

In 1788, Newton published an important pamphlet, *Thoughts upon the African Slave Trade.* It was part confessional: "I hope it will always be a subject of humiliating reflection to me, that I was once an active instrument in a business at which my heart now shudders." He continued: "The slave trade was always unjustifiable; but inattention and interest prevented . . . the evil from being perceived . . . the mischiefs and evils connected with it have been, of late years, represented with . . . undeniable evidence."[20]

That year, Prime Minister Pitt instructed the Privy Council to make a thorough investigation of the slave trade, of which England was a leader. The council summoned Newton, among others, to testify. Alone among abolitionists, Newton himself had been a slave trader.

When he entered the council chamber he saw the prime minister waiting for him. Pitt, who had become prime minister at the age of twenty-four, rose, as did the entire council, and ushered the sixty-three-year-old former slaver and now venerable Anglican priest to a seat.

Newton described the trade, how he had purchased many slaves, two or three at a time, "being sold by the Natives there by Retail." Some were convicts, he said, "but the greater Number are captives made in War." He believed that many came from hundreds of miles in the interior, that some had been kidnapped as they passed through the woods, and that some were born slaves. He did not know whether Africans warred with one another to capture slaves. Though they did not labor as hard as those in the West Indies or suffer such "ill Usage," slaves in Africa were ill fed, eating only bananas and other plants and half a pound of rice twice a day.

19. Robert Isaac Wilberforce and Samuel Wilberforce, *The Life of William Wilberforce,* abridged ed. (London: Seeley, Burnside and Seeley, 1843), 43.
20. Reprinted in Martin and Spurrell, *Journal,* 98–100.

Most slaves were sixteen to thirty years of age, of a standard height about four feet six inches, though some were taller; about two-thirds were male. They were frightened by the sight of the sea and imagined they were to be eaten; the men slaves remained "gloomy" longer than the females and boys. He concluded with the observation that "the Situation of slaves at Home is bad; worse on Board the Ships; and worst of all in our islands."[21]

When parliamentary consideration of abolition commenced, Newton, veteran of five voyages to Africa, was again called to testify. He spoke well of the Africans' abilities, saying, "I always judged that, with equal advantages, they would be equal to our selves." He observed that he had had no scruples about the lawfulness of the trade. He refuted some common beliefs and disclosed surprising details of the trade. Speaking of "the temper and disposition of the Negroes," confining himself to the region he best know, he said, they were "in a degree civilized, often friendly, and may be trusted where they have not been previously deceived by the Europeans." He remarked he had lived in peace and safety among them when he was the only white man for a great distance.

Countering a suggestion that Negroes were lazy, he pointed out that they had few wants. Traders hired them to work on board the slave ships, and they cultivated rice sufficiently to supply themselves as well as the ships. To the defensive claim of Lord Nelson that the slave trade was the nursery of seamen, he replied, "I believe it is a fatal source of mortality of seamen."

When the interrogation continued into the next day, he spoke of white traders who carried away Africans without paying for them and expressed his belief that European traders frequently did this. He declared that male slaves were always fettered during the Middle Passage and that the black cargo in full ships were "uncomfortable, indeed," especially in bad weather when they were "almost destitute of air to breathe." He disclosed that he had experienced two or three plots to revolt, which were frustrated. Punishment of plotters was usually "severe floggings," though some suffered under thumbscrews and he had been told of death as a punishment. The sufferings of Negro women were aggravated, as he deli-

---

21. *British Sessional Papers; Parliamentary Papers, Accounts and Papers*, 1789, 26 (646), part 1, p. 9.

cately phrased it, by "the brutality of the crew" on many ships; he surprisingly added to his account the phrase "if we allow the Negro women to have any degree of sentiment." Children from about eight to sixteen formed about one-fourth of the cargo. In the West Indies market, no effort was made to prevent separation of relatives. "It was never thought of, they were separated as sheep and lambs are separated by the butcher."[22]

Newton's contribution to the attack on the slave trade was substantial, embracing his influence with Wilberforce, Cowper, and More, his pamphlet on the trade, an interview with Thomas Clarkson, who was gathering material for an investigation of the slave trade, and his two testimonies to government inquiries.

His almost-idolized Polly, with whom he was in love for nearly fifty years, was stricken with cancer to which she succumbed in late December 1790, with Newton, as he wrote, "watching over with a candle in my hand." He survived another seventeen years, helping to found the London Missionary Society and the Church Missionary Society.[23]

His health declined; he became deaf, almost blind, needing to be led to his pulpit, confused as he preached. When his young friend and future biographer, Richard Cecil, suggested he abandon preaching, he retorted, "Shall the old African blasphemer stop while he can speak?" Just before Christmas 1807, he breathed his last words: "My memory is nearly gone. But I remember two things: That I am a great sinner . . . and that Christ—is a great Savior."[24]

John Newton spent a dramatic life, a twofold drama—a struggle between sinner and virtual saint, a transformation from slave trader to abolitionist. He was a scantily educated boy who became an Anglican priest without the customary credential of an Oxford or Cambridge degree. As a preacher he lacked eloquence but possessed insight into scriptural interpretation that attracted great numbers who were both humble and influential to him. His fame extended across the Atlantic.

He contributed significantly to the death of the British slave trade, and left a legacy of writings collected in twelve volumes and hymns

---

22. *Accounts and Papers,* 1790, 30 (699).
23. Pollock, *Amazing Grace,* 178–79.
24. Ibid., 181–82.

sung in churches and elsewhere over much of the world. His influence radiated out to parishioners, readers on two continents, men of influence such as Dartmouth, Thornton, and Wilberforce, and figures in the literary world such as Cowper, More, Coleridge, and Wordsworth.

Newton lived to the remarkable age of eighty-two, long enough to see Wilberforce's abolition effort become law. He may have been the inspiration for Coleridge's Ancient Mariner, and part of his *Authentic Narrative* was freely borrowed by Wordsworth in "The Prelude."

8

London's Defense of the Slave Trade, 1787–1807

Approaching the close of the British slave trade, we examine the role of London's representatives in Parliament in the legislative struggle to outlaw the trade. London was the center of the abolitionists, whose network spread out over the kingdom. London was also the center of many business interests involved in and profiting from the trade. The slave trade was flourishing; the historian Seymour Drescher, studying the relationship of abolition and profitability, concluded that abolition connoted economic suicide. To describe the phenomenon, he coined the word *econocide* (see *Econocide: British Slavery in the Era of Abolition* [Pittsburgh: University of Pittsburgh Press, 1977]).

This essay discloses how London, though a center of abolition, stoutly resisted abolition through its elected members of the House of Commons and through the House of Lords and the monarchy.

≈

"The city of London have but one opinion on the Slave Trade, which is, that it should be abolished," intoned the *Times* early in 1788. More than a year later, after parliamentary agitation had begun, the *Times* declared: "[I]f a General Election takes place antecedent to the next Sessions, the abolition of that disgrace to British philanthropy will be one of the chief instructions from the *Constituents* to *the Representatives*."[1]

London's role in defending the Atlantic slave trade while it was being assailed by abolitionists during its final twenty years has been both minimized and ignored by contemporaries and historians.

This chapter first appeared in *Slavery and Abolition* 14:2 (August 1993): 48–69, and is reprinted with the gracious permission of Frank Cass Publishers, London.
1. *Times* (London), March 4, 1788; June 2, 1789.

Historian C. M. MacInness judged that "[a]fter the merchants of London had recovered from the paralyzing astonishment which first affected them when they heard that a movement was afoot to abolish the slave trade, they were active in its defense for a year or so. Gradually, with the development of new trades and problems connected with the French war, London appears to have lost interest in the carriage of negroes." Historian Roger Anstey remarked that Liverpool witnesses favoring the trade "held the floor in the earlier stages of the 1788 Privy Council Inquiry."[2] The abolitionist Thomas Clarkson may have contributed to the diminishing of London's role by his stress on Bristol and Liverpool—the two leading English slave ports at the time he gathered evidence. In general, the well-publicized activity of Liverpool in the trade has tended to obscure London's part in its defense.

Moreover, historians' unawareness until recent years of the continuing and vigorous slave trade from London may have promoted the downplaying of the city as a defender of the trade. England's foremost slaving port in the first three decades of the eighteenth century, London experienced a precipitate drop in clearings in mid-century, only to recover in the trade's final years, becoming the kingdom's second most important slaving port.[3] In addition, London relied less on parliamentary oratory to counter abolition than upon petitions to both houses of Parliament and evidence produced by traders and merchants, often submitted to hearings by counsel. London lacked orators like Sir Banastre Tarleton and Bamber Gascoyne, the Liverpool members of Parliament who in lengthy speeches defended the trade. Even so, London MPs played a significant role in parliamentary resistance to abolition, executing parliamentary maneuvers, and producing witnesses as well as petitions in the great investigations conducted by the Privy Council, the House of Commons, and the House of Lords.

2. C. M. MacInnes, "The Slave Trade," in *The Trade Winds,* ed. C. Northcote Parkinson (London: G. Allen and Unwin, 1948), 256; Roger Anstey, *The Atlantic Slave Trade and British Abolition, 1760–1810* (Atlantic Highlands, N.J.: Humanities Press, 1975), 268.

3. James A. Rawley, "London and the Eighteenth-Century Slave Trade," in *The Transatlantic Slave Trade: A History* (New York: W. W. Norton, 1981), 219–46; David Richardson, "The Eighteenth-Century British Slave Trade: Estimates of Its Volume and Coastal Distribution in Africa," *Research in Economic History* 12 (1989): 151–95. See also chap. 2.

Though Liverpool petitions represented a larger volume of the carrying trade, London petitions probably represented a larger sampling of the overall British economy. Three groups of London-centered interests frequently petitioned Parliament in opposition to anti-slave-trade proposals. London merchants and traders, ship-owners, and manufacturers were the most frequent petitioners. West Indian planters and merchants resident in Great Britain came second, and merchants, mortgagees, annuitants, and other credi-tors stood third. This last group held a special concern for invest-ments made in islands acquired since 1763.

London merchants enjoyed a conspicuous role in the House of Commons. In 1788 more than sixty merchants sat in the Com-mons, the majority of them in business in London. On the eve of the parliamentary election in 1790 the *Public Advertiser* remarked: "Those who are candidates for London should have a thorough knowledge of its extensive trade, qualified to argue with a minister of state on any point relative to commerce." The London-based Society of West India Planters and Merchants kept alert to im-pending abolitionist legislation, and was energetic in organizing opposition.[4] London in fact had much at stake in maintaining the trade in African slaves. In a pioneering and classic article, Richard B. Sheridan, though accepting the view that London virtually aban-doned the trade, brilliantly demonstrated the vital importance of London in the commercial and financial organization of the British slave trade, 1750–1807. Emphasizing the capital invested, the commission agents, the sugar trade, the London-connected slave factors in the West Indies, and the London-centered use of bills of exchange, Sheridan concluded his study with a quotation from the London MP Nathaniel Newnham: "If it [the slave trade] were abol-ished altogether, he was persuaded it 'would render the city of Lon-don one scene of bankruptcy and ruin.'"[5]

---

4. Lewis Namier and John Brooke, *The House of Commons, 1754–1790*, 3 vols. (New York: Oxford University Press, 1964), 1:131–35. The quotation from the *Public Advertiser* is in R. G. Thorne, *The House of Commons, 1700–1820*, 5 vols. (London: Seeker & Warburg, 1986), 2:264.

5. Richard B. Sheridan, "The Commercial and Financial Organization of the British Slave Trade, 1750–1807," *Economic History Review*, 2d ser., 11 (December 1958): 263. See also J. E. Inikori, "The Credit Needs of the African Trade and the Develop-ment of the Credit Economy in England," *Explorations in Economic History* 27 (April 1990): 197–231.

The political, intellectual, and publishing capital of Great Britain, London stood foremost not only in the commercial and financial aspects discussed by Sheridan; it also was an entrepôt of local and regional manufacturing that exported wares to Africa. Midlands wares and Thames-built ships figured importantly in the slave trade. The House of Lords repeatedly called for information about imports of sugar, coffee, and cotton, leading articles of return from the slave-employing colonies. Reports commonly gave aggregate data for Great Britain, but a rare account in the Parliamentary Papers opens a window on the position of London against the other major importing ports for the years 1804–1806. The table discloses that in these years London stood out as the leading importer of sugar into Great Britain. Slave-grown sugar by far figured as the nation's most valuable import.[6]

Table 2
Account of Sugar Imported (cwts.)

	London	Liverpool	Bristol	Glasgow & Greenock
1804	1,972,897	474,265	298,890	251,157
1805	1,965,880	646,460	352,707	309,750
1806	2,344,999	556,470	342,583	356,848

London was the headquarters of the abolitionist movement. Twelve London abolitionists in May 1787 organized the Committee for the Abolition of the Slave Trade. William Wilberforce, MP for Hull, became a supporter and indefatigable proponent of abolition. As the abolitionist force gathered strength, the Society of West India Planters and Merchants formed a subcommittee on

6. *Parliamentary Papers,* 1808, Appendix A, 243–44; B. R. Mitchell and Phyllis Deane, eds., *Abstract of British Historical Statistics* (Cambridge: Cambridge University Press, 1962), 286, 289. See *The Journals of the House of Lords,* 57 vols. (London, n.d.; hereinafter *LJ*), 39:739, for an example of a call for information about imports. Marion Johnson, who provided me with statistics on exports and imports, wrote: "You will note that my tables go only to 1780, after which the existing records cease to make distinction between London and outports" (Marion Johnson, letter to author, July 7, 1983).

February 7, 1788, to oppose the movement. Four days later the prime minister, aware of the flood of petitions instigated by opponents of abolition, instructed a committee of the Privy Council to investigate the slave trade.[7] It was the first of several inquiries made over the next several years. Though expected within a short time, the Privy Council report was not completed until more than a year later.

As the Privy Council made its leisurely inquiry, the king's first minister, William Pitt, unwilling to "broach an opinion" at this time, introduced a bill providing that the House of Commons would consider the slave trade during the next session.[8] Before the bill was enacted, Sir William Dolben, MP for Oxford, executed the first of several flank attacks on the slave trade made over a twenty-year period. Moved by having inspected with his own eyes "the actual state of a slave ship then fitting out in the river Thames," he offered a bill to regulate "that intermediate state of tenfold misery which [they] the slaves suffered in their transport, from the coast of Africa to the West Indies."[9]

As the debate progressed on Dolben's motion, Lord Penrhyn, chairman of the Society of West India Planters and Merchants, MP for Liverpool, and Jamaica planter, offered a petition from Liverpool opposing the measure. William Ewer, London grocer and MP for Dorchester, presented a petition from the merchants, traders, and others of the city of London involved in the trade to Africa. The London petitioners, "seriously alarmed," feared the proposed

7. Thomas Clarkson, *The History of the Abolition of the Slave Trade,* 2 vols. (1808; reprint, London: Frank Cass, 1968), 1:255–58; minutes of the meetings of the West India Planters and Merchants, Library of the West Indies Committee, London, 1785–1792, 71.

8. *Cobbett's Parliamentary History of England from the Earliest Period to the Year 1803,* 36 vols. (London: T. Curson Hansard, 1806–1820), 27:496. Clarkson, *History of the Abolition,* 1:514–18, and James Bandinel, *Some Account of the Trade in Slaves from Africa* (1842; reprint, London: Frank Cass, 1968), 80, assert that Lords Penrhyn and Gascoyne, the two Liverpool MPs, were the only two members who defended the traffic. *Defense* is too strong a word; actually Penrhyn welcomed an inquiry into the slave trade to determine whether charges against it were true or false. Gascoyne said he had no objection to discussion standing over to the next session. Clarkson and Bandinel focus on Liverpool and distort the record. See *Parliamentary History,* 27:495–98.

9. Robert Isaac Wilberforce and Samuel Wilberforce, *The Life of William Wilberforce,* 5 vols. (London: J. Murray, 1838), 1:172; *Parliamentary History,* 27:504.

regulations "may totally ruin the trade to Africa, annihilate the large Property embarked therein, render the Plantations in the Colonies belonging to Great Britain of little Value, and do an irreparable Injury to this Country." The petition thus sketched three main arguments against abolition: the value of the African trade, of the large investment in it, and of plantations in the colonies.[10]

The Commons agreed to hold an inquiry on Dolben's bill. Over a period of a fortnight the House heard testimony for the Liverpool petitions. Though the House declined to hear the London witnesses, believing their interests were the same as Liverpool's, two of the five witnesses designated by Liverpool, Lt. John Matthews and Archibald Dalzel, had close connections with the London trade. The bill passed its second reading on June 17 on a 56–5 vote, passed its third reading the next day, and went to the Lords for consideration.[11]

London opposition to regulation now mounted; its merchants and others trading to the coast of Africa petitioned the Lords the day after the overwhelming Commons vote. The Society of West India Planters and Merchants and others met at the London Tavern in Bishopsgate Street and resolved to petition the Lords.[12]

As the Lords were considering the bill, John Tarleton, a major Liverpool slave trader, read to them letters from Le Havre and Bordeaux offering advantageous terms to put English ships in the French African slave trade. The French houses offered to remit good bills on London; if the offers were accepted, the Bordeaux letter continued, "a principal House in London will likewise give you the strongest assurances of the Solidarity of our Bordeaux friends." The correspondence sharply pointed to what became a standard argument of the trade's defenders: if Great Britain regulated or abolished the trade, foreign flags would assume larger shares, to the detriment of British trade and without benefit to humanitarian concern for Africa. The correspondence also pointed to the importance of London in the remittance of bills of exchange in the slave trade.

10. *The Journals of the House of Commons* (London, 1547-) (hereinafter *CJ*), 43:515. Wilberforce and Wilberforce, *Life*, 1:172–73, mentions only Liverpool in protesting Dolben's bill.

11. *Parliamentary Papers, Accounts and Papers*, 1789, 24 (633); *Parliamentary History*, 27:599.

12. *LJ*, 38:240; minutes of the West India Planters, 1785–1792, 73–74.

When the two houses of Parliament disagreed over some lords' amendments that were "thought to trench on the privileges of the House of Commons," the bill was discarded in favor of a new one that passed both houses, but not before the London opponents had again petitioned the Lords in protest. In the Lords the weight of the government tipped the scale as Pitt exerted his influence; a crucial compensation clause passed by a margin of two votes, 14–12. A circular letter from the Treasury several weeks earlier to leading African merchants, saying that the government would not agitate abolition in this session, doubtless promoted passage.[13]

As the year 1789 began, with anticipation of both the Privy Council report and action on Pitt's motion that the Commons in this session take up the question of the slave trade, London defenders organized their opposition. The Society of West India Planters and Merchants called a meeting to consider "proper Measures . . . on the present alarming Crisis." That the Bristol West-Indies Society relied heavily on the Londoners became plain in a letter from the Society that warned: "If the Gentlemen in London should decline any interference in the business, it is much to be feared that an application from hence will have very little effect." The London meeting adopted four resolutions describing how abolition would injure sugar cultivation and diminish the navigation, manufactures, trade, and revenue of Great Britain.[14]

Giving weight to the meeting, a fifth resolution provided that the resolution be communicated "to all the great trading Towns throughout Great Britain." The *Times* declared: "The Meeting, in point of respectability and commercial consequence, was extremely important: we may say, the whole of the West-India and African consequence were there, as well as our Manufacturers, who are interested in this question." At a meeting on April 24 the Planters and Merchants prepared a petition to the Commons and created a fund to finance opposition to abolition in both houses of Parliament.[15]

The following day the Lords received the long-anticipated report

13. *LJ*, 38:251, 261; *Parliamentary History*, 27:652; Nathaniel William Wraxall, *Memoirs*, 5 vols. (London: Bickers & Son, 1884), 5:139.
14. *Times* (London), March 26, 1789; minutes of the West India Planters, 1785–1792, 78–81.
15. *Times* (London), April 11, 1789; minutes of the West India Planters, 1785–1792, 85, 90–99.

of the Privy Council. In massive detail, the report gave the testimony of witnesses for both sides. Several acknowledged they had been encouraged by Clarkson to testify and expected to have their expenses paid by the abolitionists. A number of anti-abolitionists were identified with London, including Lt. John Matthews and Archibald Dalzel.[16]

Half a month later, on May 12, 1789, in a masterly display of rhetorical power and eloquence, William Wilberforce opened what turned out to be the long war against the slave trade. He described the trade's evil effects on Africa, the notorious Middle Passage, the cruel state of Negroes in the West Indies, the high mortality of seamen in the trade, and the hope to establish a legitimate trade with Africa. When, at a late hour, Wilberforce concluded, Lord Penrhyn rose to declare the abolitionist had misrepresented much concerning the West Indies. Alderman Newnham, MP for London, partner in a banking firm, former head of a grocery business and sugar merchant, though willing to sanction "wise regulation" at this time, said that abolition "would render the city of London one scene of bankruptcy and ruin." Another London MP, Alderman John Sawbridge, distiller and hop merchant, spoke in the same vein; he was "not ready to say that it was expedient for the country to abolish the slave trade altogether," but wise regulation might be beneficial. Charles Spooner, a London merchant "of considerable respectability" and agent for St. Kitts, presented a petition against abolition on behalf of Grenada and the Grenadines.[17]

London slave-trade defenders were bestirring themselves. On May 20 Newnham offered a petition of the London merchants, shipowners, manufacturers, tradesmen, and others interested in the African slave trade. The petitioners, many of whom "employed the whole of their own Capital," spoke of the "fatal Consequences" of abolition to the nation at large, the merchants adventuring to Africa, and "many thousands" who lived by the African trade.[18]

16. *Accounts and Papers*, 1789 (646a). Londoners included John Barnes, Richard Miles, Jerome Bernard Weuves, Captain Robert Heatley, and John Shoolbred.

17. *Parliamentary History*, 28:42–67, 76; *Times* (London), April 11, 1789, p. 4; *CJ*, 44:356, 358. For more on Sawbridge, see Carla Hay, "John Sawbridge and 'Popular Politics' in Late Eighteenth-Century Britain," *Historian* 52 (August 1990): 551–65.

18. *CJ*, 44:380.

Brook Watson, MP for London, a founder of Lloyd's, and director of the Bank of England, who conducted his mercantile business on Thames Street, introduced a petition representing a different constituency: "the Merchants, Mortgagees, Annuitants, and other Creditors of the Sugar Colonies," who, with parliamentary encouragement, had "advanced, from time to time, many Millions." Unwilling to oppose some regulation of trade, Watson declaimed that "speedy abolition of it" was "repugnant to every principle of humanity, of justice, of common sense, and of reason." The following day he questioned Dolben's claims that he could prove the cruelty of the trade and that the West Indies could be cultivated without Negroes. "Justice and policy," Watson insisted, were "deeply interested in not abolishing the slave trade immediately." Samuel Smith, who had stood for a London seat in 1784 and then abandoned his quest in favor of a seat for Worcester, countered various abolitionist arguments and declared that in event of abolition, slave owners should be compensated.[19]

The *Times* remarked: "The slave bill will be fought hard by those Members who are deeply involved as merchants in that trade, backed as they are by a powerful phalanx of men of the first consequence in the West-India trade." The anti-abolition petitions from London and elsewhere, combined with the unwillingness of some MPs to accept evidence taken by the Privy Council, led to a decision that the Commons would make its own inquiry.[20]

On Tuesday, May 26, 1789, the Commons resolved itself into the Committee of the Whole on the slave trade. With Dolben in the chair and London slave trade interests represented by counselors Pigot and Trowers, the committee took testimony about the trade over nine specified days. If, as Roger Anstey observed, Liverpool witnesses held the floor during the earlier stages of the Privy Council inquiry, London witnesses dominated this one. Of eleven witnesses examined, eight were London merchants, shipowners, slave ship captains, and former employees of the Company of Merchants Trading to Africa. On June 23, when defenders of the trade said

19. *CJ*, 44:383–84; Watson quoted by Namier and Brooke, *House of Commons*, 3:612, from *The Parliamentary Register* (London: John Stockdale, 1802), 17:237, 250–51; Smith quoted in Namier and Brooke, *House of Commons*, 3:451–52.
20. *Times* (London), May 23, 1789, p. 3.

they still had many witnesses to introduce, Newnham, with Wilberforce's consent, successfully moved to discharge the committee until the following session. Defenders of the trade had stopped Wilberforce's assault.[21]

The defenders maintained their vigorous resistance the next year. Despite opposition from Newnham, Sawbridge, and Sir Watkin Lewes, a London MP who had sat quiet in 1789, the Commons resolved to form a select committee, rather than the Committee of the Whole, to hear evidence. With Lewes's adherence, all four London MPs sided against the abolitionists.[22]

Londoners figured prominently in opposing further legislative inquiry into the trade. A general meeting of Merchants, Mortgagees, Annuitants and Others, in response to "the present very alarming occasion," attracted eighty-eight persons and established a fund to fight abolition. A meeting of the West India Planters and Merchants heard a report that "no further evidence should be produced . . . in order that the question may be brought to a decision as speedily as possible." An array of London opponents embraced merchants, discounters, creditors, insurers, and owners of West Indies estates, especially in the islands ceded to Great Britain after the Seven Years' War. James Baillie, owner of estates in Grenada and St. Vincent for which he had paid £33,000, testified to the need for slave imports to cultivate undeveloped lands. Head of the London firm James Baillie & Company, which accepted bills of exchange in the slave trade, and a cousin of George Baillie, a large-scale West Indian slave factor, he estimated from his vantage point that "the gross value of the West India and African trades together exceeds seven millions sterling per annum."[23]

George Hibbert, London sugar merchant and member of a family prominent in Jamaica and Manchester, testified that his house had made considerable advances to Jamaican planters for whom it served as factor. The Hibbert firm annually imported five to six thousand hogsheads of sugar and other articles with a gross value

21. *Accounts and Papers*, 1789, 25 (635) (this document, stating that the witnesses were called in support of Liverpool petitions, reflects the tendency to neglect London's defense of the trade); *CJ*, 44:485.

22. *Parliamentary Register*, 27:17.

23. *Accounts and Papers*, 1790, 29 (698), 181–206; Sheridan, "Commercial and Financial Organization," 255–56.

of between £200,000 and £300,000. Hibbert estimated the debt of the sugar islands to be not less than £20 million—perhaps one-third the value of the colonies. He enumerated the classes of creditors, beginning with the largest class—the merchants—and continuing with mortgagees, annuitants, legatees, and consignors of goods. The creditors' security, he emphasized, "rests intirely [sic] on the produce of estates cultivated by negroes." So far as the London merchant was concerned, he collected a "two and one-half per cent commission on the gross sales of produce, the same on amount of supplies shipped, and one-half per cent on making insurance of each." Insurance outward and inward was underwritten not by the firm but by the merchant as an individual. The West India merchant further participated in the system as ships' husbands (organizers of voyages) and holders of shares in ships.[24]

Wilberforce did not introduce an abolition bill in 1790, saying he wished to accommodate other gentlemen and expedite examination of witnesses by naming a select committee that might proceed without distraction. Debate in Parliament raged over establishing the select committee and revising Dolben's slave-carrying act. On this matter Sawbridge, Newnham, and Lewes raised procedural questions, Sawbridge seeing a bad precedent and fearing the Commons "would lose the habit of doing business as a House of Parliament." Lewes pointed out that "in the House, the parties could have the benefit of counsel, whereas above stairs [that is, in a select committee] they could not." Newnham declared that a select committee made the matter a private business, whereas "it was a public business, and the crowded gallery proved how much the public were interested in it." In the end, the speaker of the house intervened and the select committee was named.[25]

Debate on revising Dolben's act centered on Gascoyne's motion to allow vessels above 200 tons to carry slaves in the same proportion as smaller vessels. Newnham, sniffing "a side wind" to abolish the slave trade, supported the attempt, which succeeded one day and failed the next, Newnham strenuously objecting. Watson, declaring himself "an enemy to the abolition," favored "wise and humane regulations" and said he would vote for the restric-

24. *Accounts and Papers,* 1790, 29 (698), 385–403.
25. *Parliamentary History,* 28:307–9, 311, 313.

tion, which passed, 95–69. Watson was named a commissioner "to enquire into losses sustained by merchants" as a result of Dolben's act.[26]

When on February 4, 1791, in the following session Wilberforce moved "for a committee to sit above stairs on the Slave Trade," Fenton Cawthorne, a member of the Society of Planters and Merchants and possible holder of "commercial interests in the slaving port of Lancaster," complained of the "great mischief" done to merchants and planters by the prolonged inquiry. When the committee was appointed, West India MPs withdrew from it.[27]

In April Wilberforce moved to bring in a bill to prohibit importation of slaves into the British West Indies. Taking strong exception, Sir William Young, member of the Society of West India Planters and Merchants, friend of London merchants, proprietor of 1,300 acres in the West Indies, and agent for St. Vincent, made a lengthy reply. He argued that abandonment by Great Britain would not effect abolition of the Atlantic slave trade. He pointed to the fact that in 1788 Spanish merchants and planters had come to London and Manchester to inquire about how to carry on the trade; that in 1790 Londoners were insuring slave ships from Boston, Virginia, and Charleston; and that London witnesses had testified that abolition would cause creditors to press the planters, whose slaves were liable to seizure for debts. He further declared that in 1787 the total value of exports from Great Britain to the British West Indies was £1,638,702 and of imports not less than £3,749,447, paying £1,614,689 in excise and customs. Abolition, he asserted, would be a blow to British commerce, shipping, and capital, and ultimately lead to a surrender of the colonies.[28]

Watson, maintaining the defenders' onslaught against Wilberforce's motion, claimed that the Africans "were taken from a worse state of slavery in their own country, to one more mild," and contended that abolition "would ruin the West Indies, destroy our Newfoundland fishery," which, he callously continued, "[t]he slaves in the West Indies supported, by consuming that part of the fish which

26. *Parliamentary Register,* 27:676–79; Stephen D. Behrendt, "A Commercial History of the British Slave Trade, 1785–1806" (M.A. thesis, University of Wisconsin, 1988), 52.
27. Thorne, *House of Commons,* 3:737–38; *Parliamentary History,* 29:1207.
28. *Parliamentary History,* 29:278, 294–314.

was fit for no other consumption, and consequently by cutting off the great source of seamen, annihilate our marine."

Debate extended over two days; at half past three on the morning of April 21 the Commons adjourned, having taken measure of rival strength by a vote of 88 for the motion, 163 against. The defenders of the trade had won again.[29]

Wilberforce's motions for abolition were becoming an annual affair; in preparation for the year 1792 the Society of West Indian Planters and Merchants enlarged its subcommittee to oppose abolition and assigned it a new task to circulate publications defending "the Cause of the Colonies." The preceding August, slaves in St. Domingue had risen in bloody revolt, wreaking widespread damage. The Society subsidized the publication of speeches made in the French National Assembly by deputies from the island, under the editorship of George Hibbert. A pamphlet entitled "A Summary of the Evidence Produced before the Committee of the Privy Council, and before the Committee of the House of Commons; Relating to the Slave Trade" was published under the editorship of Gilbert Francklyn, Londoner and partner of the late Anthony Bacon, who had engaged in the African trade and supplied slaves for the West Indies. In testimony given in 1790, Francklyn had described his residence in Antigua for nearly twenty-one years, largely superintending Negroes "let by contract to government by himself" and Bacon. Together the partners owned about four hundred Negroes. The Society distributed eight thousand copies of an anti-abolition tract among the aldermen and common council of London and others.[30]

Learning that the question of the slave trade was again about to be deliberated, the planters and merchants, mortgagees, annuitants, and others petitioned the Commons in strenuous objection. The petitioners pointed out, among other matters, that the ceded islands did not have at that time a sufficient number of Negroes to cultivate them. The land had been bought from the government not only "upon the Faith of Liberty and Encouragement given to pur-

29. Ibid., 343, 359.

30. Namier and Brooke, *House of Commons*, 2:35; *Accounts and Papers*, 1790, 29 (698), 78–79; Lowell J. Ragatz, *The Fall of the Planter Class in the British Caribbean, 1763–1833* (New York: Century Co., 1928), 269. See *Times Literary Supplement*, January 30, 1976, p. 113, on authorship of the pamphlet.

chase Negroes," but also with a forfeiture clause in the event cultivation was not completed within a certain period.[31]

In early April, Wilberforce asked leave to introduce a resolution that the African slave trade be abolished. James Baillie, the London sugar merchant, now also agent for Grenada and MP for Horsham, holding in his hand the Society of West India Planters and Merchants pamphlet concerning the "destruction" of St. Domingue, promptly rose to demand "the principles of good policy and faith" inherent in parliamentary acts. He, a nearby MP, and a third person had purchased the lands in St. Vincent granted in 1773 or 1774 by the Crown to General Monckton. Fifteen hundred acres remained unsold and would be valueless if the slave trade were abolished, Baillie lamented, in a speech he subsequently published.[32]

The debate progressed to a great length; Henry Dundas proposed that Wilberforce's motion to abolish be amended to include the word *gradually*. By an overwhelming vote of 230 to 85, "The question, 'That the abolition of the slave trade ought to be gradually abolished'" passed. The Commons wearily adjourned at 6:30 A.M. on April 3. It was a famous victory; after four years, stoutly fought by a complex of interests, abolition—albeit gradual—had decisively won approval in the lower chamber. Wilberforce subsequently would often refer to the victory of 1792.[33]

But how gradually should the trade be abolished? Three weeks later Dundas submitted proposals for contraction of the trade culminating in total abolition on January 1, 1800. He begged the House "not to insist upon too short a period," but to be mindful of two classes of interest: the mortgagees, annuitants, or trustees for the estates of infants with property in the West Indies; and "[t]he persons engaged in the trade itself, owners of vessels belonging to the ports of London, Liverpool, and Bristol."[34]

As debaters parried over policy and time, Watson remarked that nothing had been said on behalf of the city of London: "With regard to the city that he had the honour to represent, their shipping was numerous, and he was persuaded that if the slave trade were to be

31. CJ, 47:632–33.
32. Parliamentary History, 29:1073–81.
33. Ibid., 1158.
34. Ibid., 1203–18; Dundas quoted, 1205.

speedily abolished, the capital of the merchants of Great Britain would go into the hands of foreign countries," its benefits lost. Immediate abolition was impracticable, and abolition in 1796, as was now proposed by Charles James Fox, was "tantamount to an immediate abolition." The Commons divided, 151 members voting for abolition to take place on January 1, 1796, and 132 voting against. A bill was ordered, approved, and sent to the Lords on May 3.[35]

Anti-abolitionists in the Lords at once assailed the measure. The Duke of Clarence (the future William IV), closely associated with London interests, made his maiden speech. Reflecting royal disapproval of abolition, he questioned the evidence taken by the lower chamber and invoked the constitutional privilege of the House of Peers to make its own investigation. He believed that "the moment this trade was lopped off from this country, there were [sic] a junto from other countries at this time in London, to close an agreement with the merchants and planters for the same." Other influential lords, including the bishop of London, favored an independent investigation, and in the end the House decided to make its own inquiry.[36]

Seizing the opportunity, planters, merchants, mortgagees, annuitants, and others petitioned the Lords, asserting that both regulation of shipping and abolition endangered the very foundation of "the whole System of Colonial Laws respecting Property, the Provisions of Families, and the Security of Creditors." Another constituency, the merchants, traders, and shipowners concerned in the African slave trade, made apprehensive by the Commons vote, petitioned that the action threatened not only private property invested under parliamentary sanction, but also that "many thousand Manufacturers and Families dependant [sic] thereon would be deprived of the Means of Subsistence, to the great Detriment of the Commerce, Revenue and Navigation of this Country." The Lords began their inquiry and resolved to continue it the following year. More conservative than the Commons, the Lords had snatched defeat from the jaws of victory. Fifteen years would pass before abolitionists would prevail.[37]

35. Ibid., 1293.
36. Ibid., 1349–50.
37. *LJ*, 39:415, 461.

In February 1793 England declared war on revolutionary France, whose excesses, combined with those in St. Domingue, tended to discredit reform and abolition. Besides addressing these effects, the war with France had two other major results. One was to expand the British slave empire through conquests in the West Indies, widening the market for slaves and investment. The other was to absorb British energies during most of the long years of abolitionist agitation. When, a fortnight after the declaration of war, Wilberforce proposed that the Commons go into a Committee of the Whole on the slave trade, the House voted him down.[38]

In late March the Lords received two anti-abolitionist petitions presented by the Duke of Clarence, one from West India planters, the other from Liverpool shipowners. Taking up the abolition of the slave trade the following month, the Lords listened to a diatribe against the "evil" philosophy of the French Revolution and to an intemperate attack on Wilberforce by the duke, for which he quickly apologized. Wilberforce now undertook a flank attack on the slave trade, bringing in a bill to prohibit trade with foreign territories—a substantial portion of the British involvement. In alarm, the West India Planters and Merchants gathered at London Tavern and asked Lord Carhampton to wait on Pitt to inquire whether the bill had his support. His lordship reported that Pitt did not intend anything prejudicial to the British West Indies. The bill failed to pass the Commons and the Lords voted to postpone consideration of the slave trade until the next session. The action of 1793 had reversed the work of 1792.[39]

The spread of warfare at sea endangered British slave ships through depredations of the French navy and at the same time encouraged the prospect of weakening the enemy by cutting off the slave supply to foreign territories. In 1794, Wilberforce's renewed effort to prohibit the foreign slave trade won favor in the Commons. Alderman Newnham, now MP for Ludgershall, spoke determinedly against the effort, fearing it would ruin individuals, diminish government resources, and end in emancipation of slaves. "Immense property" was embarked in the West India trade, he said, and if

38. *Parliamentary History*, 30:513–20.
39. *Parliamentary Register*, 36:141; *Parliamentary History*, 30:652–60; *CJ*, 48:780–924 passim.

Great Britain gave up the trade, others would carry it on—"the cause of humanity would not be served." A petition from the planters of the West India colonies resident in Great Britain and of the merchants trading to the colonies underscored the same points.[40]

After gaining approval in the Commons, the bill moved forward in the Lords until British conquests of French islands in the West Indies opened up new markets under the British flag. The Lords, rejecting a motion intended to expedite the bill, examined witnesses, all of whom opposed abolition. In early May the Lords defeated the measure, 44–5.[41]

During the next three years Wilberforce annually moved to abolish the slave trade, only to find his effort in 1795 postponed by a majority of 17, in 1796 lost by a margin of 4, and in 1797 lost by a margin of 8. In the latter year, a stratagem sponsored by two MPs with large holdings in the British West Indies aimed at delaying action against the trade indefinitely. Parliament approved an address (not a law) to the colonial legislatures urging on them a voluntary amelioration of the slaves' conditions. In the same year a law repealed the section of the Credit Act of 1732 that made Negroes chattel for payment of debts. Both measures looked to soften humanitarian concerns.[42]

After a decade of agitation, abolitionists had secured only regulation of shipping and the two measures described above. Wilberforce's efforts for abolition again failed, 83–87, in 1798 after extended debate. A proposal that year to increase the space in ships allotted to each slave provoked strenuous controversy. The slave merchants of London and Liverpool joined to protest that the measure would "entirely ruin the trade." Planters, merchants, and others interested in the West Indies also petitioned against the change. Many merchants had altered their vessels to conform to the previous year's legislation; these vessels would be useless in the slave trade if the measure passed. Moreover, reduction in the number of slaves that could be carried in large ships would drive those vessels from the trade.[43]

40. *Parliamentary History*, 30:1441–42.
41. Ibid., 31:470.
42. *CJ*, 50:179; 51:425: 52:577; *Parliamentary History*, 33:831–34.
43. *Parliamentary History*, 33:831–34; *CJ*, 53:569, 614; Behrendt, "Commercial History," 52.

A second attempt in the same year to reduce the scope of slaving found expression in a bill to prohibit the trade on a thousand-mile strip of the African coast, from the Gambia River to Cape Palmas. Merchants of London trading to Africa complained the prohibition would not only injure them but also "give a complete Monopoly of the Whole to Foreigners." John and Alexander Anderson of Philpot Lane, London, proprietors of Bance Island in the Sierra Leone River, where they had "established a great Trade," protested that the bill would destroy their investment. John Anderson had sat as MP for London since 1793. Liverpool merchants complained equally vociferously, and the bill, though it passed 59–23 in the Commons, failed 63–68 in the Lords.[44]

In the decade's final year Wilberforce once again introduced an abolition bill, which was decisively struck down by a vote of 54 to 84. The project to increase deck space in slave ships now passed its third reading in the Commons without a vote. London merchants and traders concerned in the African trade as well as planters and merchants interested in the West Indies turned to the Lords with a petition against the bill. The Duke of Clarence spoke against it, but when it came to a vote he failed to frustrate passage. John and Alexander Anderson unsuccessfully petitioned the Lords to allow their ship the *Concord,* put out of the trade by the previous regulating act, to clear after the new law's deadline of August 1.[45]

The measure to prohibit slave trading on a long stretch of the African coast, introduced afresh, met vigorous opposition. Planters, merchants, and others interested in the British West Indies, alluding to the recent defeat of Wilberforce's abolition bill, quickly branded the measure as an effort to thwart in part that determination. John and Alexander Anderson once more petitioned the Commons against the bill. Liverpool interests offered three petitions in protest. Despite this opposition, the Commons passed the bill 59–23 and sent it to the Lords. There the Duke of Clarence, joined in opposition by three other royal dukes, spoke lengthily and vehemently against the restrictive bill. When the Lords heard witnesses, John Anderson gave evidence against the bill. Opponents had

44. *CJ,* 53:636, 624.
45. *Parliamentary History,* 34:565; *LJ,* 42:222, 242, 295.

the satisfaction of witnessing defeat of the bill, 25–32, with 36 proxies on each side.[46]

A bill to restrict the carrying trade to only three British ports— Liverpool, Bristol, and London—proposed in 1799, incurred the objections of planters, merchants, and others interested in the British West Indies. Several merchants of London and others petitioned the Lords to permit ships from the British West Indies to sail for Africa with rum and other articles—a "very profitable branch of commerce." The opposition failed and the bill became law.[47]

After the failure of his abolition bill in 1799, Wilberforce did not try again until 1804. War, peace, and war again intervened; Pitt, friend of Wilberforce and abolition, resigned the prime ministry in 1801 and was succeeded by Henry Addington, who believed in gradual abolition. Parliament ignored the question; the index to the *Journals of the House of Commons* does not list the slave trade from 1800 to 1803.

Early in 1804 Wilberforce gave notice he would bring in a new motion to end the trade. Parliament soon received correspondence disclosing the failure of the attempt to urge the colonial legislatures to work toward gradual abolition. The Society of West India Planters and Merchants rejected both abolition and suspension of the trade, which Pitt had contemplated in 1800. When the bill was introduced and had its first reading, the Society approved a petition to the Commons and named a committee to oppose the bill, including three members of the Hibbert family and James Baillie. John Anderson, the MP, presented the petition on June 6; it pointed to the "savage anarchy" in St. Domingue resulting from abolitionist doctrines, the previous legislative encouragement of the trade, and the great importance of the trade to British manufacturers, agriculture, commerce, navigation, revenue, and capital investment. The Commons agreed to a third reading by the substantial majority of 69 to 33 and sent the bill to the other house.[48]

---

46. *CJ*, 54:382–83, 403; *Parliamentary History*, 34:1092–105, 1139; House of Lords Record Office, Slave Trade, May 28, 1799. Dale H. Porter, *The Abolition of the Slave Trade in England, 1784–1807* (Hamden, Conn.: Archon Books, 1970), 102, mentions only the Liverpool objections.

47. *LJ*, 42:322–24. This branch of slave commerce has been neglected by historians.

48. *CJ*, 59:303–4; Porter, *Abolition of the Slave Trade*, 124; minutes of the West

In the Lords the Duke of Clarence actively resisted the bill. He presented petitions in opposition from Liverpool and certain merchants and mortgagees interested in the West Indies. He spoke against the bill and was gratified to see the Lords postpone action until the next session. At a meeting of the Planters and Merchants in mid-February 1805, attended by the duke, the members observed "with the deepest sorrow & alarm that the Question of an Abolition of the Slave Trade will soon be received in Parliament."[49]

Not long after Wilberforce's bill had passed its first reading, a petition, together with those from Liverpool and Birmingham, appeared in the Commons, stressing the need for laborers to settle the interior of the islands. The Commons gave short shrift to the bill, and with a vote of 70–77 defeated it by the parliamentary tactic of postponing it for six months. Haunted by two successive years of failure to legislate abolition and aware of the drive to increase the trade, Wilberforce turned to Pitt, again prime minister after Addington's abdication. Heading a precarious government, Pitt responded to Wilberforce's threat to bring in a bill for partial abolition with the device of an order-in-council that in general prohibited importation of slaves into colonies captured since 1802. The order sharply curtailed the British slave trade, reducing it by one-half or more and making a long stride toward abolition.[50]

The following year the government introduced a bill to confirm the order and extend it by law. The attorney general, in presenting the bill, underplayed its humanitarian benefits and argued his case on the grounds that the law would weaken the enemy during the war and reduce the labor force in colonies restored after the war. The historian Dale H. Porter has written that the order "attracted little notice from defenders of the slave trade. . . . As in 1788, the defense of the trade was left to the Liverpool representatives and to the champions of the trade in any form like George Rose" (a Treasury official and husband of an heiress to Antigua sugar es-

Indies Planters, 1793–1801, 316–22, and 1801–1804, 73–78; *CJ*, 59:321; *Parliamentary Debates*, 2:871 (from 1803 the title is no longer *Parliamentary History* but *Parliamentary Debates*).

49. *Parliamentary Debates*, 2:889–90, 932–33; *LJ*, 44:638–88; minutes of the West Indies Planters, 1805–1822, 1 ff.

50. *CJ*, 60:90; Wilberforce and Wilberforce, *Life*, 3:183–84; House of Commons, *Sessional Papers*, 1806 (124), 1:289.

tates). In actuality London interests vigorously and repeatedly protested the bill and sounded an alarm over the order-in-council. Sir William Young's claim in a Commons speech that "at a numerous meeting of London merchants . . . a majority had agreed" the bill would be "a boon to the West India merchants" is without a record in the archives of the Society of West India Planters and Merchants.[51]

London merchants, in fact, with remarkable perseverance and zeal, petitioned the Commons three times and the Lords once in opposition. Each of the Commons petitions pertained to a different aspect of the African slave trade. Several merchants, ship owners, and manufacturers of London who had "embarked a considerable part of their properties" in the colonies before the order-in-council was issued now protested the bill, saying they would apply for a repeal. Sir William Curtis, MP for London, who presented the protest, declared slavery to be "an evil that could not be remedied."[52]

Another body of London merchants, who traded with South Carolina and Georgia, denounced the projected prohibition on fitting out and dispatching any foreign ship in the African slave trade from any part of the British Empire. The petitioners had been serving as agents for Americans in fitting out American vessels from British ports with cargoes of British manufactures and East India goods. The law, they apprehended, would inflict a "great loss and probable ruin of many of the Petitioners."[53]

A third petition described a heretofore little-noticed sector of the trade. London merchants and manufacturers who were engaged in the manufacture and export of British piece goods and other goods suitable for consumption in Africa and Spanish America spoke of "a treble operation to distress the petitioners." A prohibition on foreign ships from obtaining cargoes in Great Britain was one source of distress. A second source was the ban on British merchants from carrying on the slave trade with the conquered territories, exchanging British manufactures for slaves. The third blow leveled by the bill was its prevention of exports both from Great

51. Porter, *Abolition of the Slave Trade*, 132–33.
52. CJ, 61:226.
53. CJ, 61:154–55.

Britain and the Free Ports of the West Indies into the Spanish Main, and particularly the River Plate. The Free Port Act had made it lawful for foreign, single-decked vessels to transport from designated ports slaves who had been imported in British ships. The Spanish government would allow no vessel to enter any port unless it carried slaves. British vessels regularly carried no more than ten to fifty slaves to the Plate "by way of passport." The Londoners said: "The real object is to bring to sale a cargo of British goods, of the value of from 15,000 to 20,000 for each ship." They estimated the total value of British manufactures involved to be not less than £3,500,000. Passage of the bill, they concluded, "would be of great detriment to the resources and welfare of the Nation."[54]

The petitions augmented those from owners of estates in conquered territories, Jamaica, and Liverpool. Sir Charles Price, MP from London, "at the instance of several very respectable merchants of the City of London," opposed the law, declaring it "would be injurious to the country in general and to London in particular. This was not a time to shut a door by which we were enabled to export Manufactures to the annual amount of £2,800,000."[55]

On the day of the third London petition and Sir Charles's plea, the bill, moving expeditiously through Parliament, passed its third reading by a vote of 35 to 13. It now went to the Lords, where the same London interests submitted three petitions. The Duke of Clarence, who presented one of the petitions after "a long conversation" in the chamber, won the right to have all petitioners heard by counsel. Six of George III's sons "threw their weight against abolition," but the combined forces failed to defeat passage. By a vote of 43 to 18, the Lords approved the decisions taken by the Commons and the imperious order-in-council of 1805.[56]

With the same expedition and less protest, both houses approved a resolution introduced by Charles James Fox, long a foe of the slave trade, to abolish the trade at such time as should be thought advisable. It was in fact a commitment to abolish the trade the fol-

54. CJ, 61:269–70.
55. *Parliamentary Debates*, 6:1023.
56. LJ, 45:609; *Parliamentary Debates*, 7:1023; Sir Samuel Romilly, *Memoirs of the Life of Sir Samuel Romilly*, 3 vols., 2d ed. (London: J. Murray, 1840), 2:146.

lowing year. Within days, not only had the Commons overwhelmingly approved the resolution by a vote of 114 to 15, but the more conservative Lords also agreed by a vote of 41 to 20. In this heightened abolitionist temper of mind, the decision having been taken to destroy the foreign slave trade, Parliament passed a bill limiting the African slave trade to those ships already engaged in it.[57]

The year 1806 marked the turning point in the protracted struggle to abolish the British slave trade. Parliament by substantial and consistent votes had rebuffed defenders of the trade. It had taken three long steps toward abolition, passing the foreign slave-trade bill, Fox's resolution to abolish the trade, and the ship restriction bill. The succeeding parliamentary elections witnessed a victory for the abolitionists.[58]

On January 2, 1807, heartened by the successes of 1806 and the parliamentary elections, Lord Grenville initiated an abolition bill in the Lords. It was a calculated switch; historically the Lords had stood as an obstruction. The West India Planters and Merchants, meeting at the London Tavern, voted to entrust the standing committee with full powers to take such steps as should be necessary. Petitions from this committee, Jamaica, Trinidad, Liverpool, and London poured in on the Lords. The London interests embraced merchants, shipowners, ship builders, artificers, and manufacturers, who asked their lordships not to assent to an abolition bill, or to give adequate compensation. On the vital second reading, the Lords approved the bill 100 to 36, and on February 10—only five weeks after Grenville had introduced the bill—the Lords passed it.[59]

In the Commons the same set of London interests "with profound alarm" reminded the House of the long legislative sanction of the trade and of the pursuit of the trade until about 1786 without the stigmatization of those involved—conduct of the trade being considered among "the natural rights of man"—and warned that the bill endangered "the prosperity, nay almost ensures the ruin of thousands." The Londoners prayed that the House would either not assent to the bill or provide adequate compensation.[60]

57. *Parliamentary Debates*, 7:603, 8:801–9; *LJ*, 45:730; *Parliamentary Debates*, 7:1145.
58. Porter, *Abolition of the Slave Trade*, 136.
59. Minutes of the West India Planters, 1805–1822, 114–21; *LJ*, 46:49, 53.
60. *CJ*, 62:129.

Other London interests joined in strident protest. Planters, merchants, mortgagees, annuitants, and others feared "the worst consequences," not alone to themselves, "but also deeply injurious to the interest of the British empire at large." John and Alexander Anderson, as proprietors of Bance Island, spoke of their "very great capital" invested and "a great trade at the said island." The bill would serve both to render their property of no value and make impossible their collection of debts from Africans who had no other way of repayment except by slaves, they complained.[61]

If heretofore London MPs had been less vocal in the Commons than Liverpudlians, London now found a knowledgeable and indefatigable spokesman in the person of George Hibbert. The Mincing Lane merchant, head of the "first house" in the Jamaica trade, had given important evidence to the Commons in 1790. Elected alderman in 1798, he later failed to win a seat in the Commons for the City, and in 1806 was returned for Seaford. In his maiden speech, asserting that the West India merchants needed time to meet in opposition to the abolition bill, Hibbert succeeded in postponing the second reading for a fortnight. When the bill did come up for debate, at a "late hour," he invoked "more than 25 years extensive connection with the island of Jamaica" and about sixty estates there to speak at length in opposition. He favored continuance of a limited trade, anticipating an annual importation into "our old colonies" of about seven thousand slaves. Portraying Africa as long prey to wars among its own sovereigns, he described the continent as from an early date "inviting the slave trade, not the slave trade seducing Africa." Abolition would open the door to France to extend its slave empire and to take over the slave trade to Spanish America. He made a special plea in behalf of "minors, of lessors, and all proprietors of estates under trust." His eloquence was in vain; the House passed the second reading 283 to 16.[62]

Hibbert presented a petition from the planters, merchants, mortgagees, annuitants, and others interested in the British West Indies that described distress in the islands. Two weeks later he had it read

61. CJ, 62:146, 148.

62. Sidney Lee, ed., Dictionary of National Biography, 22 vols. (London: Oxford University Press, 1921–1922), 9:794; Thorne, House of Commons, 4:193–94; A. E. Furness, "George Hibbert and the Defence of Slavery in the West Indies," Jamaican Historical Review 6:1 (1965): 56 ff.; Parliamentary Debates, 8:717–22; 981–93, 995.

to the Commons and delivered an extended speech detailing the need for relief of the economically depressed sugar industry. The abolition bill came up for its third reading on March 16. Hibbert took the floor, knowing he could not change the course of the measure, and spoke at length: "Sir, twenty-five or thirty years ago, when I commenced merchant, had I canvassed both houses of parliament for an opinion how a mercantile capital could be adventured in foreign commerce the most advantageously to the public, nine out of every ten would have advised me to embark it upon the cultivation of the colonies." He adverted to past legislative support of the trade. "What have merchant adventurers to trust to but written laws?" he cried. Denouncing "delusive theories" of abolitionists, "popular clamour . . . artificially and enthusiastically excited," he remained convinced that abolition would be destructive to a main source of national prosperity.[63]

An amended bill passed without a division and returned to the Lords for approval. In desperation, certain planters, mortgagees, merchants, and others petitioned against a clause added to the Commons bill freeing Negroes seized as a result of illicit trade. The Lords approved an amended bill and returned it to the Commons, which agreed. On March 24 the historic—and long sought and resisted—abolition bill won the royal assent.[64]

For two decades London slave trade interests successfully resisted zealous attempts to abolish the trade. London resistance has been misjudged. From the foregoing account it should be plain that London slave merchants were active in defense of the trade not merely for a year or so but for twenty years. It should also be clear that London's defense did not rest solely on commercial and financial aspects of the trade. A significant volume of the trade cleared for Africa from London throughout these years. Further, as if impressed by the greater volume of the Liverpool trade, contemporaries and historians have tended to concentrate on Liverpool's defense to the neglect and misunderstanding of London's role.

A congeries of interests centering in London persistently opposed abolition, contributing to the long delay in accomplishing what the *Times* thought imminent in 1788. In spite of the *Times*'s

63. *Parliamentary Debates*, 9:85–101, 130, 132.
64. Ibid., 9:168–70, 176; 47 Geo. III, p. 36.

estimate of unanimous abolitionist sentiment in London and the presence of the headquarters of the abolition committee, London voters repeatedly returned pro-slave-trade members to the Commons. These lawmakers were men of impressive status—former aldermen, lord mayors, and leading merchants—who gave strength to the defense. No London MP spoke out against the trade. Over a score of years London MPs presented pro-slave-trade petitions revealing a variety of interests at stake, and gave speeches and employed tactics designed to frustrate abolition.

Almost to the end, London defenders enjoyed the support of the voters, the House of Lords, and the monarchy. Defeat came with a shift of government leadership and shrewd abolitionist employment of parliamentary tactics, crippling the trade in 1806 as a matter of national interest and capturing the Lords in 1807. The Crown acquiesced to abolition and London capitalists redeployed their fleets and their capital.

9

Captain Nathaniel Gordon, the Only American Executed for Violating the Slave Trade Laws

The Atlantic slave trade, with its notorious cruelty, fell prey to abolitionists more readily than domestic slavery, which involved an entrenched population, the recognition of slaves as property, and a large labor force. We saw in the chapter on Henry Laurens that John Jay, shortly after the Peace of Independence in 1783, said it was "the intention of the . . . States entirely to prohibit the importation" of slaves. Laurens, the southern slave merchant, said that "true policy lies on the side of the abolition of slavery." Actually both prohibition of importation and abolition of domestic slavery lay years in the future.

The framers of the Constitution bowed to slave-state interests and deferred the prohibition of slave importation for twenty years. In 1807 the United States enacted a law to ban importation. Three weeks later the British Parliament passed a similar act.

Illegal importation persisted. Congress in 1820 decreed the death penalty for offenders. The illegal trade continued, a good part of it centered in New York and reported in the New York press. Though offenders were captured, none were executed.

England, with its vaunted naval superiority, had taken the responsibility for exterminating the trade, winning support from foreign countries but failing to secure the cooperation of the United States. Southern interests strongly influenced national policy, southerners ironically enjoying representation in the House of Representatives for three-fifths of its slave population, making slaves an unwitting influence in national policy. Moreover, presidents were often from the South or needed southern votes to get elected and enact laws.

This chapter first appeared in *Civil War History* 39:3 (1993): 216–24, and is reprinted with the permission of the Kent State University Press.

The election in 1860 of the northerner Abraham Lincoln, who had denounced the immorality of slavery and stood on a party platform of banning its expansion into the territories, opened the possibility of enforcing the death penalty. Captain Nathaniel Gordon became the first and sole American to he executed under a decades-old law. In the same year as his execution—1862—the United States signed a treaty with Great Britain to cooperate in exterminating the now-nefarious trade.

≈

Early on an August morning in 1862, the lookouts on the USS *Mohican*, a member of the African Squadron, sang out, "Full-rigged ship off the port bow." Steaming across the broad entrance to the Congo River, intent on apprehending violators of American slave-trade laws, the *Mohican,* Comdr. Sylvanus W. Godon, signaled the *Erie* to show its colors. The *Erie* responded by raising the American flag and shortening sail. Godon dispatched an armed boat, and, on boarding the 500-ton ship, his party discovered 897 Africans concealed below the deck, tightly packed together. Godon directed his capture to the port of Monrovia, Liberia, where the hapless Africans were handed over to an American agent. He sent the *Erie*'s captain, Nathaniel Gordon, to New York for trial in a federal court.[1]

The United States had prohibited importation of slaves in 1807, as did Great Britain three weeks later. Increasingly condemned by the Western world, the transatlantic slave trade—with its uprooting of peoples, brutal transport to the Americas, and consignment of its victims to perpetual slavery—bore a more serious aspect than domestic slavery, which continued in the British Empire until 1834 and in the United States until 1865. Broadening its legislative attack, in 1800 the United States prohibited American participation in the foreign trade, which had continued to Brazil and Cuba as well as to some extent to the United States. In 1820 Congress took the extraordinary step of declaring the slave trade to be piracy and

1. Warren S. Howard, *American Slavers and the Federal Law, 1837–1862* (Berkeley and Los Angeles: University of California Press, 1963), 137; U.S. Congress, *Senate Executive Documents* (hereinafter *SED*), 35th Cong., 2d sess., 1861, 3, pt. 1: 8–9. Apparently no scholarly history of Captain Gordon and his trial exists, but a good popular account is William S. Fitzgerald, "Make Him an Example," *American History Illustrated* 17:9 (1983): 40–45.

prescribing the death penalty for persons found guilty of violating the laws. The United States at this time stood alone among nations in branding participants in the black traffic as pirates.[2]

Assigned to enforce this draconian measure was the United States Navy. Congress found it easy to legislate against the trade but hard to appropriate funds to enforce the laws. A cluster of factors worked mischief in efforts at enforcement. Southern slaveholders were sensitive to a vigorous assault by the national government on the trade. Great Britain had become the self-appointed constable of the seas in stanching the trade, and patriotic Americans resisted British zeal in boarding suspect American vessels, remembering British impressment of American sailors before the War of 1812. A spirit of diplomatic independence and frugality characterized Congress. It appropriated meager amounts, sometimes as little as $5,000 per year, to enforce its policy. Naval action in these circumstances could only be minimal. A House of Representatives report to the Seventeenth Congress revealed that the first U.S. cruiser reached Africa in March 1820 and remained only "a few weeks." Since that display of the flag, only four other vessels in two years had made visits. But "since the middle of last November . . . no vessel has been, nor, as your committee is informed, is, under orders for that service." Similarly, the courts were lax in efforts to convict persons accused of violating the slave trade laws. Until 1862 no American suffered the mandatory capital punishment.[3]

International denunciation of the trade mounted in the second third of the nineteenth century. Pope Gregory XVI in 1839 declared the traffic "utterly unworthy of the Christian name." European nations prohibited the trade, and a five-power treaty—the United States conspicuously absent—stigmatized the trade as piracy and agreed that the signatories might search one another's suspected vessels. Conscious of international pressures, the United States in an 1842 agreement with Great Britain—the world's leading maritime power as well as enemy of the traffic—undertook to maintain

2. W. E. B. Du Bois, *The Suppression of the African Slave-Trade to the United States of America, 1638–1870* (1896; reprint, New York: Schocken Books, 1969), 245, 121–22, 253; U.S. Congress, *Statutes at Large* (Boston: Little, Brown, 1861), 3:600–601; Howard, *American Slavers,* 192–93. See also chap. 1.

3. Du Bois, *Suppression,* 122, 125.

a squadron of at least eighty guns to patrol the West African coast, the center of slave embarkations.[4]

The African Squadron thus created, with its distinctive provision for guns, not ships, fared no better for several years than had previous naval assignments. Matthew C. Perry served as the first commander, but he apprehended no prizes. He and his successors commanded squadrons of three to six vessels—most commonly four—some of which often were not on station. Apathy on the part of the public and officials goes far to explain the failure to stop the trade. An economical Congress, the sparsity of cruisers for African stations, and leniency and difficulty in prosecution reflected this apathy. Moreover, most of the slave trade flowed to Brazil and Cuba and not to American shores.[5]

Still it is untrue what historian John R. Spears wrote in 1900, that enforcement was a "sham" until "the advent of Abraham Lincoln." Lincoln's Democratic predecessor, James Buchanan, perhaps spurred to action by southern efforts to legalize and revive the trade as well as by the raging domestic controversy over slavery, began an assault on the foreign trade. Congress increased its enforcement appropriations, raising the amount from $8,000 in 1857 to $75,000 in 1859 and to $900,000 in early 1861. Secretary of the Navy Isaac Toucey, though sympathetic to the South, expanded the African Squadron from three vessels in 1857 to eight in 1859. He appointed William Inman, captain of the first-class sloop *Constellation,* to command the squadron. Toucey's instructions warned about slave traders: "Nothing but the utmost vigilance and caution will enable you to detect them." Under Inman the squadron captured fourteen slavers; under Inman's predecessor, Thomas A. Conover, four; and under Conover's predecessor, Thomas Crabbe, none. To increase efficiency in patrolling the West African coast, Toucey moved the squadron's base from Porto Praya in the Cape Verde Islands (15 de-

---

4. Ibid., 145–46; Howard Jones, *To the Webster-Ashburton Treaty: A Study in Anglo-American Relations, 1783–1843* (Chapel Hill: University of North Carolina Press, 1977), 144–45; William M. Malloy, ed., *Treaties, Conventions, International Acts, Protocols, and Agreements between the United States and Other Powers,* 2 vols. (Washington: Government Printing Office, 1910), 1:650–56.

5. Alan R. Booth, "The United States African Squadron, 1844–1861," in *Boston University Papers in African History,* ed. Jeffrey Butler (Boston: Boston University Press, 1964), 1:100 ff.

grees north latitude) to Loanda in Portuguese Angola (8 degrees south latitude), near the heart of embarkations.[6]

The *Mohican,* a new, second-class, steam screw sloop-of-war, formed a part of the enlarged, modernized squadron, which for the first time included steam-propelled vessels. Sylvanus W. Godon, the sloop's commander, had been born in Philadelphia in 1809 and entered the navy at the age of ten. He had seen service in East India, the Mediterranean, the Pacific, and in the Mexican War, where he took part in the capture of Vera Cruz. Made commander in 1858, he was assigned to the *Mohican* when it was part of the Pacific Squadron.[7]

Nathaniel Gordon, born in 1826, master of the slaver *Erie,* hailed from a Maine family often referred to by the newspapers as "respectable." However, a Nathaniel Gordon, perhaps father of the above, was master of the brig *Dunlap* of Portland, Maine, and was brought into the Circuit Court of the Southern District of New York in 1838. The U.S. district attorney, William M. Price, charged Gordon with importing "with force and arms" a Negro slave from Guadeloupe to be held as a slave in the United States. The criminal case filed in the National Archives does not disclose the outcome of the jury trials.[8]

Most Americans involved in the slave trade sold their victims in the voracious markets of Brazil and Cuba. The U.S. market absorbed an estimated average of only one thousand per year. A decade after the New York episode, Nathaniel Gordon, whether the older or the younger is unknown, fell under suspicion as a slaver in Rio de Janeiro. Lt. Comdr. William W. Hunter of the USS *Al-*

6. John R. Spears, *The American Slave-Trade; an Account of its Origin, Growth, and Suppression* (1900; reprint, Port Washington, N.Y.: Kennikat Press, 1967), 215; Du Bois, *Suppression,* 122; "Toucey, Isaac," in *Dictionary of American Biography;* Earl E. McNeilly, "The United States Navy and the Suppression of the West African Slave Trade, 1819–1862" (Ph.D. diss., Case Western Reserve University, 1973), 261–62; Howard, *American Slavers,* 240; "Inman, William," in *The National Cyclopedia of American Biography,* vol. 9; U.S. Congress, *House Executive Documents* (hereinafter *HED*), 36th Cong., 2d sess., 1861, 578.

7. Howard, *American Slavers,* 240; *SED,* 36th Cong., 1st sess., 1139; "Godon, Sylvanus," in *National Cyclopedia,* vol. 9.

8. U.S. Circuit Court for the Southern District of New York, *United States v. Nathaniel Gordon,* Indictment G. 14, filed August 1, 1838. I am indebted to Anthony Fantozzi of the National Archives, New York Branch, for bringing this indictment and that of 1860 to my attention.

leghany, assigned to stop participation in the slave trade, held Navy Department instructions that described how to identify a slave ship—among the signs to look for were an unusual number of water casks and special fittings. His superior, Commodore Storer, gave him orders to watch Capt. Nathaniel Gordon's *Juliet,* a 138-ton schooner from Portland, Maine. Consul Gorham Parks of Rio had alerted Storer to local gossip that the *Juliet* was a slaver.

When Gordon put out to sea on June 10, 1848, Hunter followed. Five miles out, Gordon's huge iron-hulled steam vessel hailed the small sailing vessel. Hunter sent aboard a boarding party that spent eleven and a half hours searching the *Juliet.* No incriminating evidence could be found, and the *Juliet* continued on its course. Weeks later, Rio again buzzed with rumors: the *Juliet,* under Brazilian management, had returned to Brazil carrying a cargo of slaves.[9]

Three years later Capt. Nathaniel Gordon again turned up in Rio, commanding the *Camargo.* After remaining in port for several months, the *Camargo* sailed for the Cape of Good Hope under circumstances that aroused the consul's suspicions that the vessel was a slaver. Brazilian authorities later arrested and imprisoned crew members and charged them with having engaged in the slave trade. The authorities also arrested and held an American citizen, resident in Rio for many years, on suspicion of a connection with the *Camargo* and its voyage.

Edward Kent, the consul, talked with two of the detained sailors. They informed him that the *Juliet* had indeed touched at the Cape of Good Hope and then, in an unusual voyage pattern for the transatlantic slave trade, sailed to the east coast of Africa, evading the African Squadron. In the consul's words: "[A]t an unoccupied spot . . . she took on board about five hundred negroes, with water, Etc., and . . . succeeded in reaching the Brazilian coast about two hundred miles south of this port . . . and the negroes were there landed safely, and . . . soon after all hands left the vessel, which was set on fire and burned." He continued: "[I]t is now reported that Captain Gordon has gone to the United States, but this fact is not certain."[10]

9. Philip D. Curtin, *The Atlantic Slave Trade: A Census* (Madison: University of Wisconsin Press, 1969); Howard, *American Slavers,* 85–90; HED, 35th Cong., 2d sess., 9, 1861, 5–6, 10, 19.

10. *HED,* 34th Cong., 1st sess., 56–57.

Early in 1860 Capt. Nathaniel Gordon, commanding the *Erie* of New York, fell under the suspicious eye of the U.S. consul in Havana. When Gordon applied for his clearance papers, the consul, C. H. Helm, detained the *Erie* for two days. But having no clear evidence that the vessel was a slaver, though bound for Africa and laden with a cargo that could be used in the slave trade, he accepted Gordon's affidavit that "my said ship is chartered for a legal voyage to the coast of Africa." Nevertheless, Helm advised U.S. Secretary of State Edward Everett, "I am morally convinced this vessel, if not taken, will bring a cargo of African negroes to Cuba."[11]

The *Erie* cleared Havana harbor in April 1860, and a month out some seamen began to suspect they had signed onto a slaving voyage. The cargo included 150 or more hogsheads of liquor, a number of barrels of pork and beef, bags of beans, barrels of bread and rice, 250 bundles of staves, and many hoops for making barrels or casks. These crewmen went aft, confronted the captain, and demanded to know where the *Erie* was going. Gordon curtly replied that the vessel was on a legal voyage; he reminded the sailors that he was the captain and that they had no business asking such a question.[12]

The *Erie* entered the Congo River, dropping anchor about forty-five miles upriver, above Shark's Point. Carpenters converted the staves and hoops into casks, which were filled with water from the river. On the night of August 6, 1860, Captain Gordon called crew members aft. In the presence of the mate and several Spaniards, Gordon announced that he was taking on a cargo of blacks and that the sailors would receive one dollar per head for every black landed on the Cuban coast. When one sailor asked whether they could get more, Gordon answered no. The next day Spaniards brought aboard 897 Africans, some in rags, from barracoons on the mainland, transporting them by launches in about three-quarters of an hour. The transaction demonstrated that slave trading was a well-planned business.

The next morning, between seven and eight o'clock, Captain Gordon stood on the forecastle peering through his glasses when the USS *Mohican* came in view. He had stowed the Africans under hatches, the men in one section and the women in another. The

11. *HED,* 36th Cong., 2d sess., 596–97.
12. *New York Daily Tribune,* November 10, 1861, p. 3, col. 6.

naval boarding party discovered the concealed, illicit cargo, and Lieutenant Todd of the *Mohican* took charge of the *Erie* and proceeded to Monrovia. He found that the Africans had been packed so tightly that his officers, after bringing the victims on deck for water, could not fit them back into their places. He appealed to Captain Gordon, who showed the officers "the manner of doing it, which was by spreading the limbs of the creatures apart and sitting them so close together that even a foot could not be put upon the deck." Gordon was made prisoner and taken to New York City, where he was incarcerated in the City Prison—the infamous Tombs—without bail. The *Erie* was condemned and sold on October 4, 1860, for $7,823.25.[13]

What was in store for Gordon? Forty years had passed since the law declared the slave trade piracy, and though many persons had engaged in the trade, no one had suffered the death penalty provided by the law. Gordon could take heart from the recent case of Capt. James Smith, the first man found guilty of being a slave trade pirate and therefore subject to execution. Though convicted by a jury, Smith, represented by a wily lawyer, subsequently heard the judge declare a mistrial. Rather than undertake a second trial, the district attorney and Smith's attorney arranged for Smith to accept a sentence of two years in jail and a fine of two hundred dollars. After a time, President Buchanan gave him a full pardon.[14]

New York City, where Gordon was to be tried, was perhaps the leading U.S. port for fitting out slavers. The British consul at New York estimated that "[o]f 170 slave-trading expeditions fitted out in little more than three years preceding 1862, no fewer than 74 were known or believed to have sailed from New York, 43 from other American ports, 40 from ports in Cuba, and the rest from European ports." The city had a well-established reputation for profiting from the trade as well as a close commercial connection with the prewar South. Gordon was indicted "for piratically detaining negroes with intent to make them slaves," a capital offense under the law of 1820. The government was overconfident that it could obtain a conviction. The Republican victory of 1860 had resulted

13. Ibid., November 8, and June 21, 1861, p. 9, col. 6; *SED*, 37th Cong., 2d sess., 2.

14. Howard, *American Slavers*, 194–95.

in the replacement of a Democratic district attorney by a zealous Republican, E. Delafield Smith. The trial was conducted June 18–21, 1861, in the United States Circuit Court for the Southern District of New York. Some essential witnesses had not been found, thus weakening the prosecution's case. The jury was out all night, and on coming into court the next morning it informed District Judge William D. Shipman that it had been unable to agree: seven jurors favored conviction, five acquittal. District Attorney Smith gave notice that he would file for a new trial.[15]

Judge Shipman and an associate justice of the United States Supreme Court, Samuel Nelson, the latter sitting as circuit judge, presided over the second trial, which began November 6. Smith now produced witnesses who had not testified at the first trial. They told of their confrontation with Gordon over the voyage's purpose, of the offer to the crew to be paid one dollar for every Negro landed in Cuba, and, contrary to the defense's claim, of Gordon remaining in charge of the *Erie* after the Spaniards came aboard in Africa.[16]

After the summing up by counsel, Judge Nelson charged the jury. He disposed of the defendant's claims that Gordon was not a citizen of the United States because he may have been born on a foreign voyage and that the *Erie* was not an American vessel because it had been sold to foreigners. Arriving at "the merits of the case— and the question is," Nelson stated, "is the prisoner guilty or not of forcibly confining or detaining the negroes on board of this vessel in the Congo River, with the intent of making them slaves." The jurors retired at about seven in the evening of November 8; in contrast to the first trial, they returned in twenty minutes with a verdict of guilty.[17]

Gordon's counsel made a motion for an arrest of judgment and a motion for a new trial. Justice Nelson and Judge Shipman denied

15. William Law Mathiesen, *Great Britain and the Slave Trade, 1819–1865* (1929; reprint, New York: Octagon Books, 1967), 165; U.S. Circuit Court for the Southern District of New York, *United States v. Nathaniel Gordon,* filed October 29, 1860, National Archives; *New York Daily Tribune,* June 18, 1861, p. 7, col. 5; "Delafield Smith, E.," in *National Cyclopedia,* vol. 11.

16. *New York Daily Tribune,* November 9, 1861, p. 8, col. 1.

17. *New York Times,* November 9, 1861, p. 3, col. 3, and November 10, 1861, p. 3, cols. 5–6; *United States v. Gordon,* in *Federal Cases,* 30 vols. (St. Paul: West, 1894–1897), 25:1364–67.

the motions, and Shipman, speaking for both, passed a sentence of death on Captain Gordon to be carried out February 7, 1862. Gordon's counsel, Gilbert Dean, a resourceful man and a former judge, next hastened to Washington and presented all the evidence he had in favor of Gordon, urging a pardon or commutation of the death penalty. President Lincoln asked the advice of his cabinet, which agreed to a short respite but not a pardon. Attorney General Edward Bates told the president that he saw no reason for him to interfere but advised Lincoln that he had the power to grant a reprieve. Three days before the scheduled execution, Lincoln, by proclamation, reprieved Gordon for two weeks, in order to make "the necessary preparation for the awful change which awaits him."[18]

Dean asked the two judges to certify a difference of opinion between them, enabling him to bring the case before the United States Supreme Court for a writ of prohibition restraining the circuit court from further proceedings and a writ of certiorari commanding the circuit judges to send all papers, process, and proceedings to the Supreme Court. Three days later, on February 17, the high court, Chief Justice Roger B. Taney—notorious author of the pro-slavery Dred Scott decision—presiding, refused Dean's motion, declaring the court had no jurisdiction.[19]

The next day Dean again went to Washington to appeal to the president for a commutation of the death sentence. Gordon's wife, his mother, and Rhoda E. White, a New York civic activist and wife of a New York judge, also went to Washington with a petition signed by eleven thousand New Yorkers urging the president to

18. *Federal Cases*, 1367–68; Spears, *American Slave-Trade*, 220 (Spears erroneously says that Nelson passed sentence); *New York Daily Tribune*, December 2, 1861, p. 7, cols. 3–4; *New York Times*, February 21, 1861, p. 5, col. 2; Howard K. Beale, ed., *The Diary of Edward Bates, 1859–1866* (Washington: Government Printing Office, 1933), 229–30; Edward Bates to Abraham Lincoln, February 4, 1862, Robert Todd Lincoln Papers, Library of Congress, Washington, D.C.; Roy P. Basler, ed., *The Collected Works of Abraham Lincoln*, 9 vols. (New Brunswick, N.J.: Rutgers University Press, 1953), 5:128–29.

19. Carl B. Swisher, *The Taney Period, 1836–1864*, vol. 5 of *History of the Supreme Court of the United States* (New York: Macmillan, 1974), 706; *New York Times*, February 19, 1862, p. 5, col. 3; J. S. Black, *Reports of Cases Argued and Determined in the Supreme Court of the United States at December Term, 1861*, 2 vols. (Washington, D.C.: W. H. & O. H. Morrison, 1862), 1:503–6.

commute the sentence. Lincoln refused to see them; backed by Bates as well as by his long-standing opposition to the foreign slave trade, he held firm.[20]

On the following day Dean appeared in the United States Circuit Court for the Southern District of New York where Judge Shipman heard an appeal for a writ of habeas corpus. Dean argued that the City Prison where Gordon was due to be executed was city, not federal, property and under New York law could not be used. "This man," he declared, "should not be executed under a judgment perhaps irregular." Shipman, after consulting with another judge, denied the application for a writ. Gov. Edwin D. Morgan of New York made a last-minute appeal to Lincoln to grant a respite.[21]

On February 21 about two hundred authorized persons—city and county officials, members of the state legislature, and the press—crowded into the grand central square of the City Prison. Hundreds of others found places high on neighboring buildings to witness the public execution. Rumors that a rescue would be attempted led the U.S. marshal to request a guard from the Navy Yard. Under Captain Cohen, about eighty men with rifles loaded and bayonets fixed faced the gallows in double file. Local police maintained guard outside.

At noon the marshal and his deputies escorted Gordon to the gallows. During the night he had unsuccessfully attempted suicide by taking strychnine; now, supported by his escorts, he was placed "beneath the fatal beam." Soon he was "a lump of dishonored clay."[22]

The execution of Captain Gordon preceded by only a few months ratification of a treaty negotiated by Secretary of State William H. Seward and the British minister to the United States, Lord Lyons. War against the slaveholding Confederacy, the need to recall the African Squadron for service against the enemy, and the rise of antislavery sentiment all combined to make possible concessions to Great Britain that would have been impossible in earlier years. The two nations agreed that vessels of either party might visit and search

20. Beale, *Diary of Edward Bates,* 233; Rhoda E. White to Abraham Lincoln, February 17, 1862, Robert Todd Lincoln Papers.

21. *New York Times,* February 21, 1862; *New York Daily Tribune,* February 22, 1862.

22. *New York Daily Tribune,* February 22, 1862.

suspicious vessels of the other's flag. The treaty provided for three mixed courts—at New York, Sierra Leone, and Cape Town—composed of an equal number of judges from each nation to try suspects. The mutual cruising area lay within two hundred miles of the African coast in specified latitudes and within thirty miles of Cuba. The United States Senate unanimously ratified the treaty on April 25, 1862.[23]

Secretary of the Navy Gideon Welles had ordered the African Squadron home. The *Mohican,* described by Welles as a steam sloop with six guns, arrived September 27, 1861, in ample time to see service in the Civil War. Reporting to Congress in December 1862, Welles declared that only the USS *Saratoga* remained on the African station. The last anti-slave-trade cruiser, the sloop had transported the first commander of the squadron, Matthew C. Perry, to the station. Sylvanus Godon served with distinction in Civil War naval operations at Port Royal and Fort Fisher. Promoted to captain in 1861 and commodore in 1863, he was commissioned rear admiral in 1866, and from 1868 to 1870 was commandant of the New York Navy Yard.[24]

The year 1862, with the first execution of a slaver and the negotiation of the Lyons-Seward treaty, marked a turning point in the history of the transatlantic slave trade. British naval vessels promptly went to work visiting and searching suspected vessels heretofore protected by the Stars and Stripes. Slave traffic to Cuba dramatically dropped from 30,473 in the year ending September 30, 1860, to 143 in the year ending September 30, 1865. Abuse of the American flag in order to carry on the slave trade between Africa and the Americas ended. New York ceased to be a center for outfitting slave vessels. The British consul in New York reported: "It would be perilous to attempt such an adventure in the face of the recent convictions, the vigilance of the police, and the change in public sentiment, in reference to the execution of the laws for the suppression of slave trading."[25] The interplay of naval, political, judicial, diplomatic, and humanitarian forces had terminated a centuries-old infamous traffic.

23. Malloy, *Treaties,* 674–87.
24. *SED,* 37th Cong., 2d sess. 2, 3:11; McNeilly, "United States Navy," 244; *SED,* 37th Cong., 3d sess., 23.
25. A. Taylor Milne, "The Lyons-Seward Treaty of 1862," *American Historical Review* 38 (April 1933): 511–25.

10

A Summing Up

The trade helped form an Atlantic community, involving western Europe from Denmark and a German state to the Iberian Peninsula; western Africa, mainly between the Senegal and Congo Rivers, with some participation by Atlantic islands and southeastern Africa; and nearly all of the Americas, mainland and Caribbean.

The slave trade formed one of the greatest migrations in history, moving approximately ten million people to the New World. Strikingly, all were enslaved and all black. They shaped the history of their new homeland, as well as the racial mix.

It may astonish some readers that the United States, where blacks today form about one-eighth of the population, received a very small proportion of Africans, less than 6 percent, and Brazil a very large proportion, varying over periods of time. Readers may also be astonished to learn that, though the United States banned the trade relatively early, an illicit trade persisted for more than half a century, with New York City, the major port in a free state, actively participating in the illicit and immoral traffic.

The firmness of President Abraham Lincoln, known for his clemency, in refusing appeals for pardon effected the execution of a condemned slave-ship captain in New York City, and signaled the close of a sorry chapter in American history.

≈

The Atlantic slave trade is a significant theme in the history of the modern world. Beginning in the early fifteenth century, it endured until the second half of the nineteenth. The trade formed a part of Europe's transition to capitalism, the nation-state, and imperialism. An expression of the Commercial as well as the Industrial Rev-

This is the final chapter of my book *The Transatlantic Slave Trade: A History* (New York: W. W. Norton, 1981).

olution, it fumbled its way through state-conferred monopoly and mercantilism and early went over to free trade. Fostered by crowns and parliaments, it nourished the growth of western European nations and empires. Solving an acute labor problem, it made possible the development of tropical and semitropical America. It was the most important link between Europe and America, on the one hand, and Africa on the other. It enhanced the standard of living for many Europeans and Americans, while degrading the lives of many enslaved blacks.

In this concluding chapter we shall examine the progress of the movement to abolish the trade, make a new estimate of American slave imports, and suggest a legacy of the trade.

When Denmark in 1792 decreed an end to the slave trade, the act was influenced by new currents of thought and belief that Great Britain, foremost slaving power, was about to abolish the trade. The history of the abolition of the slave trade has been well told and is outside the scope of this book, but it is necessary for us, if only in a few brief strokes, to observe how the trade at last came to a close.

The movement to abolish the trade arose as a major concern not only late but quickly. On both sides of the Atlantic one notes the dramatic contrast, within a short space of years, between the roles played by Thomas Jefferson in 1776 and 1806 and the British prime ministers in 1783 and 1792. Jefferson, draftsman of the Declaration of Independence in 1776, as the price of South Carolina and Georgia support of his document, had expunged his excoriation of George III's sanction of the slave trade; thirty years later, as president of the United States, he readily won approval of a constitutional amendment outlawing the American slave trade. In 1783 Lord North, the British prime minister, rejected a Quaker petition to end the slave trade, asserting that the trade was in some measure necessary to all stations in Europe and that it would be almost impossible to persuade them to abandon it. In 1792 William Pitt, occupying the same post, urged immediate and total abolition by Britain, looking forward to the day when Europe would participate in a "just and legitimate commerce" with Africa.[1]

1. *Cobbett's Parliamentary History of England from the Earliest Period to the Year*

The movement against the Atlantic slave trade drew its strength from idealistic and realistic sources alike. Primarily an idealistic phenomenon, the movement sprang from religious, philosophical, and humanitarian thought. Quakers, with their concern for brotherly love; Evangelicals, with their belief in conversion and sanctification; men of the Enlightenment, with their faith in natural rights; and humanitarians, with their compassion for sufferers—all combined to spread in the Atlantic world the new view that the slave trade was contrary to religion, philosophy, and humanity.

Side by side with these motives to abolish the slave trade ran less lofty ones. The realization that the trade had been unprofitable contributed to the Danish decision to relinquish it. In the United States idealism was joined by apprehensions of servile insurrection and racial amalgamation, prospects of a rise in slave values if importation ended, and Northern hostility toward the South.

Like the slave trade itself, abolition was an Atlantic-wide phenomenon. Its origin was in America, its center came to be Great Britain. Rapid in emergence, it was long in fulfillment, in part because the United States for two generations ironically refused the cooperation necessary to suppress the traffic. The Philadelphia Quaker Anthony Benezet, through his writings, was an early advocate of abolition. The Anglican clergyman Thomas Clarkson, through his investigation of the slave trade, was an early activist in the movement. Abolition societies in Philadelphia, London, and Paris corresponded with one another in an international network of opponents of the traffic.

American colonies and states took an early lead in legislating against the importation of slaves, and in 1787 the framers of the United States Constitution devised a compromise by which the authority of the new government to abolish the trade was acknowledged, but exercise of that authority was prohibited for twenty years. In 1788 the Privy Council made the first of several British governmental inquiries into the slave trade and Parliament enacted a law regulating the trade. Whereas in the United States a law ending the trade was accomplished easily, in the United Kingdom attempts to end the trade encountered vigorous resistance. In 1807

1803, 36 vols. (London: T. Curson Hansard, 1806–1820), 23:1026–27; *The Parliamentary Register* (London: John Stockdale, 1802), 32:405–8.

the two English-speaking nations outlawed the importation of African slaves.

In 1815 the Atlantic slave trade seemed on the verge of extinction. Spanish American colonies in South America had erupted in revolt against the mother country, and in the process of liberating themselves they outlawed the slave trade. The Dutch banned the trade in 1814. France during the Revolution and the Napoleonic regime had ended the trade, resumed it, and ended it again; the restored Bourbon government enacted an abolition law. In the treaties of 1814–1815 terminating the long struggle against France, Great Britain secured a general condemnation of the slave trade by European powers and the United States.[2]

But "that execrable sum of all villainies commonly called A Slave Trade," as John Wesley branded it, persisted for nearly half a century.[3] Slave ships in this period transported from Africa to America perhaps two million blacks, about one-fifth of the immense, involuntary migration that had begun three centuries earlier. Much of this trade was illegal, contrary both to national law and international agreement, and in defiance of Great Britain, which had constituted itself constable of the seas.

Virtually all the traditional carriers took part in the illicit trade. The insistent demands of tropical agriculture, sharpened by heavy mortality, offered an inviting market for slaves. Great Britain, now morally committed to extirpating the trade which it once had led, employed diplomacy, high-handed laws of Parliament, and the Royal Navy in measures that were long only partly effective. David Eltis has estimated that without British suppression policies, Brazil and Cuba between 1821 and 1865 would have imported half again as many slaves as they did.[4]

2. David Brion Davis's *Problem of Slavery in Western Culture* (Ithaca: Cornell University Press, 1966) and *Problem of Slavery in the Age of Revolution, 1770–1823* (Ithaca: Cornell University Press, 1975) form a superb study.

3. John Wesley, *The journal of the Rev^d. John Wesley . . .* (London, 1836), 656.

4. David Eltis, "The British Contribution to the Nineteenth-Century Transatlantic Slave Trade," *Economic History Review,* 2d ser., 32 (1979). Philip D. Curtin, *The Atlantic Slave Trade: A Census* (Madison: University of Wisconsin Press, 1969), 234, estimated slave imports for the period 1811–1870 at about 1,900,000. The subsequent research of Eltis, Serge Daget, and others, as we have seen, indicates this figure is too low. E. Phillip Leveen, "A Quantitative Analysis of the Impact of British Suppression

Deeply determined to suppress the slave trade, Lord Palmerston, British foreign secretary in the 1830s, negotiated treaties with France and Spain allowing Britain to capture and break up vessels equipped to conduct the trade. Recent scholarship has shown that Frenchmen continued to be involved in the slave trade until mid-century; as late as 1862 Palmerston, now prime minister, lamented that the slave-trade treaty with Spain "does not prevent some 15 or 20,000 Negroes and perhaps more from being every year imported into Cuba."[5]

Believing that the means justified the end, Great Britain invaded the sovereignty of Portugal and Brazil. Parliament in 1839 authorized the British navy to capture slave ships flying the Portuguese flag as if they were British. Six years later Parliament authorized British admiralty courts to adjudicate cases of slave vessels operating contrary to an Anglo-Brazilian treaty of 1826. When Brazilian imports of slaves actually rose after passage of this British law, Great Britain instituted a thoroughgoing search and seizure of suspected vessels, bringing the Brazilian trade to a close in the mid-fifties. Toward the end of his long crusade against the traffic, Palmerston declared, "The achievement which I look back to with the greatest and purest pleasure was the forcing of the Brazilians to give up their slave trade."[6]

One large American market remained—Cuba. The chief obstacle to suppression was the United States of America, under whose flag much of the trade was conducted. The United States on two scores was hypersensitive to cooperating with the British. One was the bitter memory of British visit and search of American vessels leading to the outbreak of war between the two countries in 1812. Combined with this was the powerful presence of Negro slavery in the United States, inhibiting the government in both national and international efforts to stop the trade. Opportunity presented itself during the American Civil War, when the government, for the first

Policies on the Volume of the Nineteenth-Century Atlantic Slave Trade," in *Race and Slavery*, ed. Engerman and Genovese, 51–81.

5. Harold Temperley and Lillian M. Penson, eds., *Foundations of British Foreign Policy from Pitt (1782) to Salisbury (1902)* (Cambridge: Cambridge University Press, 1938), 303.

6. Ibid.

time under an antislavery administration, negotiated an Anglo-American treaty that allowed British vessels the right to search and arrest suspected slavers flying the United States flag off the coasts of West Africa and Cuba. This treaty of 1862 was the coup de grâce to the Atlantic slave trade. A long, dark chapter in modern history had ended.

In retrospect, the Atlantic slave trade may appear an anomaly in modern history, more appropriate perhaps to the ancient and medieval worlds with their acquiescence to forms of servitude. The trade began at the dawn of modern history and lasted for over four centuries while Europeans were striving for greater economic opportunity and aspiring for rights and liberty. At the same time that millions of blacks were being transported across the Atlantic into slavery, millions of whites were migrating from Europe to America in search of greater independence in religion, work, and politics. The Atlantic frontier offered opportunity for whites only.

Part of the explanation of this anomaly is the discovery of the New World, whose warm climate could produce in abundance commodities, often luxuries, much wanted by Europeans. Sugar was crucial to the institutionalization and spread of slavery. Sugar and other tropical and semitropical products, mainly consumer articles, account for the major employment of slave labor.

The commodities produced by slave labor helped to define a new style of life and contributed to a rising standard of living for the middle as well as the upper classes. The slave trade was also the product of the new economic forces of the modern era. It was part of the Commercial Revolution with its exchange of commodities in long-distance trade. It was made possible by the growth of raw capitalism with its values of investment, risk, and profit, and exploitation of labor. The trade illustrates various stages in the history of capitalism, moving from mercantilism and state-conferred monopoly to free trade and individual enterprise to concentration, and from royal to bourgeois direction.

The New World provided the land, Europe the capital and entrepreneurs, leaving the problem of finding labor for the numerous manual tasks of staple agriculture. Experiments in free and unfree labor, red and white, ended in resort to unfree black labor. Relative immunity to certain killer diseases was important in making this decision. The availability of a large pool of labor was indispensable. Skin color was also significant, making possible, within the framework of European thought, the placing of blacks, and blacks only, in permanent slavery.

The transportation of labor from Africa to America was in some measure both inconvenient and expensive. Why did Europe not use the land in Africa and eliminate these disadvantages? Europeans in fact did attempt to grow sugar in West Africa for export. Each attempt failed and authorities have assigned a number of reasons in explanation of this failure. West Africa was different from the West Indies; its climate was more deadly for the white man; it did not have the tradewinds to power windmills; and unlike the islands, it made escape relatively easy.

When in 1752 the Company of Merchants Trading to Africa attempted to foster sugar growing in Africa, the Board of Trade countered with a series of objections. "There was no saying where this might stop," it said. "The Africans who now support themselves by war would become planters & their slaves be employed in the culture of these articles in Africa which they are now employed in in America." The Board further expostulated that "our possessions in America were firmly secured to us, whereas those in Africa were open to the invasion of an enemy, and besides that in Africa we were only tenants in the soil which we held at the good will of the natives."[7]

Each of these factors helps in understanding why Europeans did not cultivate sugar in West Africa and why they carried labor thousands of miles to land in America. In addition to all these factors, it may be pointed out, West African soil was unsuitable to sugar growing. It differed from West Indian soil; it posed difficulties of drainage and salinity, which appeared insuperable. Even today, very little sugar is grown in West Africa.

The Atlantic slave trade was a great migration long ignored by historians. Euro-centered, historians have lavished attention upon the transplanting of Europeans. Every European ethnic group has

7. Henry A. Gernery and Jan S. Hogendorn, "Comparative Disadvantage: The Case of Sugar Cultivation in West Africa," *Journal of Interdisciplinary History* 9 (1979): 437.

had an abundance of historians investigating its roots and manner of migration. The transplanting of Africans is another matter, and investigation of the roots and transit of the millions of Afro-Americans largely belongs to the future. Historians have given much attention to the political and intellectual history of abolishing the trade, to the diplomatic and naval history of suppressing it, and to all aspects of domestic slavery.

Though the trade was an integral part of empire, it is instructive to read conventional histories of empire and consult their indexes, noting how little heed is given to the slave trade. In the era of the trade, empire in America was important to Europe by virtue of the slave-grown commodities the colonies could produce. Contemporaries, though not without bias and hyperbole, were somewhat closer to the mark than conventional historians. In his work *A Survey of Trade,* William Wood in 1718 declared the slave trade was "the spring and parent whence the others flow." Over half a century later the author of *A Treatise upon the Trade from Great Britain to Africa* asserted, "[T]he African trade is so very beneficial to Great Britain, so essentially necessary to the very being of her colonies, that without it neither could we flourish nor they long subsist."[8]

The effects of the Atlantic slave trade upon Africa are not easy to ascertain. The depopulation of the Dark Continent was large. Upwards of twelve million Africans were exported, many of whom died before arriving in America. An inestimable number perished before departing from Africa. However, over much of the same time Europe was being depopulated without apparent deleterious effects upon its polity. What would have been the level of African population without the slave trade? The eighteenth-century student of population, Thomas R. Malthus, examining the African pattern of emigration, mortality, and checks upon population growth, believed that the peoples of Africa were "continually pressing against the limits of the means of subsistence." The level of population was doubtless influenced as an incident of the slave trade through the introduction of two important new food crops—maize and

8. Wood quoted in Eric E. Williams, *Capitalism and Slavery,* 51; an African Merchant [Richard Brew], *A Treatise upon the Trade from Great Britain to Africa,* (London: R. Baldwin, 1772), 5.

manioc. Also known as Indian corn and cassava, these plants were widely grown beginning as early as the sixteenth century, significantly sustaining and possibly increasing the African population.[9]

The size of the population of Africa in the era of the slave trade is unknown; nor is there information about the rate of natural increase. Therefore it is impossible to ascertain the rate of population loss or the numerical severity of its impact. It may be recognized, though, that slave traders carried away some of the healthiest members of the population, persons in their prime, and favored males over females in a ratio of about two to one. The demographic effects of such losses are incalculable.

Beyond all this, it seems plain that the impact of the trade upon the African population was uneven, both in respect to time and place. The impact was obviously lighter when the export of slaves was relatively light. In the early years natural increase probably exceeded loss; in the later years it perhaps equaled loss.[10]

The slave trade made whatever impact it had mainly upon West and Central Africa, and to a lesser extent upon Southeast Africa. Large parts of Africa were not involved. Within this localized, if yet large, area, the trade shifted, starting in Upper Guinea and moving at various times to Lower Guinea and within Lower Guinea, to Central Africa and Mozambique. It seems probable that African societies differed in their proportion of losses, given the differences existing between coastal and inland societies, between societies that sold slaves and those that were the sources of slave supply, and between exploiters and exploited. At the same time the impact upon each of these variables was doubtless not uniform.

Nor was the political impact uniform or unrelieved of benefit. Some political entities grew in wealth, size, and authority; others suffered disruption and even near-dissolution. The slave trade fostered tensions among Africans and promoted power politics. It may

9. J. D. Fage, "Slavery and the Slave Trade in the Context of West African History," *Journal of African History* 10 (1969): 393–403, and a response by C. C. Wrigley, "Historicism in Africa: Slavery and State Formation," *African Affairs* 70 (1971): 113–24. Fage returned to the argument in "The Effect of the Export Slave Trade on African Populations," in *The Population Factor in African Studies,* ed. R. P. Moss and R. J. A. R. Rathbone (London: University of London Press, 1975), 15–23. Malthus quoted in Richard B. Sheridan, "Africa and the Caribbean in the Atlantic Slave Trade," *American Historical Review* 77 (1972): 33.

10. J. D. Fage, *A History of Africa* (New York: Random House, 1978), 254.

have developed some communities, damaged others, and left others little touched. Political unity and effective government existed along with anarchy and disorder.

The effects of the slave trade upon African society are also mixed. The importation of brandy, rum, and other spirits may have made little difference, because the Africans had their own liquors. The introduction of firearms fostered warfare and augmented the power of victorious users, but these results were in a measure offset by occasional effective use of bowmen, by the poor quality of guns, and by the expense of getting and maintaining firearms and ammunition. African spending of slave-trade profits in luxuries and consumer goods had its analogies in European tastes and practices; slave labor in America produced sugar, tobacco, and coffee for Europeans. The stratification of society was most apparent in the ruling class, which sold Africans into American slavery, and in the rise of a new class of merchant princes.

The economic impact was not clear-cut. Plainly a large supply of labor—characteristically young, male, and healthy, as we have said—was taken away from Africa. A vigorous, continuous commerce in slaves throve in Africa; slaves were the major export. Alongside this commerce, and stimulated by it, was a diverse trading in gold, ivory, hides, wood, gum, and palm oil in exchange for European and American imports. Africans in all this activity were required to carry on the functions of production, procurement, transport, and marketing of these wares. It is not easy to answer the question whether the slave trade impeded the development of "legitimate" trade and of natural resources in Africa.

What seems more plain is that international trade did not become the instrument of economic growth in Africa. Diversification, modernization, importation of technology, control of commerce beyond the ocean's edge, retention of earnings in Africa, and dispersal of economic benefits among a substantial sector of the population did not characterize the African economy.[11]

To sum up, any generalization about the impact of the slave trade upon Africa is difficult to make. The matter is complex, with

---

11. A. G. Hopkins, *An Economic History of West Africa* (London: Longmans, 1973); Walter Rodney, *How Europe Underdeveloped Africa* (Washington: Howard University Press, 1974), 95–103.

many variables. There are offsets to the obvious debits. Historians divide in their judgments. Few would accept the indictment made in the nineteenth century by the black writer who said the slave trade was "purely destructive." A number of scholars minimize the impact, pointing to some of the considerations we have seen. Others attribute Africa's woes to the European and American slave trader. It is to be held in mind that the colonial subordination of Africa came after the slave trade era. In the earlier period the African retained his independence, acting as sovereign, warrior, and merchant. The European conquest of Africa, with its system of imperial overlordship and economic exploitation, occurred in the last quarter of the nineteenth century.

Change marked the Atlantic slave trade, change in national carriers, volume, place of export and of import, conduct of business, mortality and medical care, and public attitude.

The dimensions of the transatlantic slave trade are an indispensable base for the history of the trade. Knowledge of the dimensions leads not solely to the moralists' question of guilt but to the question of historical fact—the historians' concern to learn what actually happened.

The "numbers game" has preoccupied scholars for decades of fruitful research. Philip D. Curtin, in *The Atlantic Slave Trade: A Census* (1969), gave the game new rules as well as a new reckoning. We have carefully considered his findings, while at the same time presented subsequent research.

The large outline offered by Curtin remains intact but in many particulars it has been changed. The changes spring from research in unpublished sources, which he did not endeavor to conduct. They show the volume carried by five of the six major carriers was larger than he had estimated. Only the number assigned to the Dutch remains unchanged, and this coincidence is a fluke because the bases of his estimate have been altered. The result is an overall sharp rise in the volume of the transatlantic slave trade though still just within the generous 20 percent range of error Curtin set for himself.

Research in this important matter of the trade's volume is not yet complete. More work is still to be done. Not all scholars accept the revisions we have recorded here. In a history of the African slave

Table 3
Estimated Slave Imports into the Americas by Importing Region,
1451–1870

Region & Country	Curtin	New Estimate (round numbers)
British North America[1]	399,000	523,000
Spanish America[2]	1,552,100	1,687,000
British Caribbean[3]	1,665,000	2,443,000
French Caribbean[4]	1,600,200	1,655,000
Dutch Caribbean[5]	500,000	500,000
Danish Caribbean[6]	28,000	50,000
Brazil[7]	3,646,800	4,190,000
Old World[8]	175,000	297,000
	9,566,000	11,345,000

Sources:

1. James A. Rawley, *The Transatlantic Slave Trade: A History* (New York: W. W. Norton, 1981), Table 14.1.

2. Ibid., Table 3.1.

3. Before 1673, my estimate; for 1673–1690, Curtin, *Atlantic Slave Trade,* 122; for 1690–1807, Table 7.1 in Rawley, *Transatlantic Slave Trade,* plus my estimate of additional an 75,000 carried by London vessels; after 1810, Eltis, "British Contribution," 226.

4. To 1700, Curtin, *Atlantic Slave Trade,* 121; for the eighteenth century I have accepted Curtin's estimate of imports, but I believe a larger share of these was carried in French ships; for the nineteenth century I have added to Curtin 55,000 slaves as suggested by David Eltis, "The Direction and Fluctuation of the Transatlantic Slave Trade, 1821–1843: A Revision of the 1845 Parliamentary Paper," in *The Uncommon Market: Essays in the Economic History of the Atlantic Slave Trade,* ed. Henry A. Gemery and Jan S. Hogendorn (New York: Academic Press, 1979), 288.

5. Rawley, *Transatlantic Slave Trade,* Table 4.1.

6. Ibid., chap. 4.

7. Ibid., Table 2.1.

8. Curtin, *Atlantic Slave Trade,* 268. Curtin estimates no imports into the Atlantic islands after 1600. Thomas Bentley Duncan, *Atlantic Islands: Madeira, the Azores, and the Cape Verdes in Seventeenth-Century Commerce and Navigation* (Chicago: University of Chicago Press, 1972), 210, estimates 150,000 imported of whom 28,000 were transshipped to Spanish America.

I should add that I have made no estimate of imports into Europe after 1700, nor of the bilateral trade between the Caribbean and Africa.

trade published by UNESCO in 1979, J. F. Ade Ajayi and J. E. Inikori state: "[O]n present evidence it would seem that Curtin's global estimate for the Atlantic trade may be at least 10 per cent too low. We think therefore that it would be more realistic for the moment to raise Curtin's figures for the Atlantic trade by 40 per cent, making total exports from Africa by way of that trade 15.4 million."[12]

It is therefore with great diffidence that a tentative revision of the vexed question of numbers is here presented. The new total exceeds Curtin's 1969 estimate (to which he has accepted numerous changes) by about 1,779,000 Africans imported, or nearly 19 percent.

The Portuguese were the inaugurators of the trade and almost throughout the trade's long, tragic history continued to be important carriers. The monopoly they held for a century and a half was broken by the Dutch, who for a brief while in the seventeenth century may have been the foremost slave traders. The incursion of the French and the English marks the late seventeenth century; in the succeeding century these two nations carried just under half of all slaves transported across the Atlantic. The English, however, in the competition for empire and the slave trade, won ascendancy in the second half of the century, and, rather astonishingly, at a high point of activity in the first decade of the nineteenth century voluntarily relinquished the trade. The Americans entered the trade late, not significantly until the middle of the eighteenth century, and never gained a share comparable with the European giants. Spain, holder of the largest American empire, was a buyer of slaves from other carriers until the nineteenth century when it became a significant carrier to Cuba. In the last half-century of the trade, before its suppression in the 1860s, Spanish, French, Brazilian, and American ships were important carriers.

The flow had a distinctive chronological shape, forming, as it were, a huge bubble in the eighteenth century. Of the whole volume, only about 3 percent moved before 1600, and only about 14

---

12. J. F. Ade Ajayi and J. E. Inikori, "An Account of Research on the Slave Trade in Nigeria," in *The African Slave Trade from the Fifteenth to the Nineteenth Century* (Paris: UNESCO, 1979), 248.

percent moved in the seventeenth century. Over three-fifths of the traffic swelled across the Atlantic in the years 1701–1810, billowing to an annual average of nearly 100,000 in the decade of the eighties, thereafter waning; but leaving to the period 1810–1870 a greater bulk of the trade than for the entire seventeenth century.

The pattern of exports begins, understandably enough, with that part of sub-Saharan Africa closest to Europe. The Portuguese vanguard in the fifteenth and sixteenth centuries took slaves primarily from Upper Guinea; starting in the early seventeenth century Angola became an important source for the Portuguese trade. The English in the seventeenth century drew heavily from Lower Guinea, especially from the Gold and Windward Coasts. Similarly, the Dutch concentrated their trading in this century upon the lower Guinea Coast, notably the Gold Coast, although about one-third of Dutch exports derived from the Loango-Angola region. The Spanish and the French in this early period depended very heavily upon other flags.[13]

In the long sweep of years from 1701 to 1810, West Africa exported nearly three-fifths of all slaves. Four regions accounted for nine-tenths of this total; in descending order of importance, they were: the Bight of Benin, which alone exported 30 percent of the total, the Bight of Biafra, the Gold Coast, and the Windward Coast. Exports from central and eastern Africa jumped in the 1730s, and surpassed those from West Africa in the last three decades of the period. The general pattern shows a shift eastward in lower Guinea and a shift southward and eastward toward central and eastern Africa.[14]

In the period from 1811 to 1870 the exports were principally to Brazil and Cuba. Portuguese and Brazilian slavers drew very heavily upon Angola and the Congo, with an increased reliance upon the region of the Congo. From the late eighteenth century Southeast Africa exported large numbers of slaves to Brazil. Proximity to market influenced both the Brazilian and Cuban trades. The bulk of Spanish exports cleared from West Africa, where Sierra

13. Curtin, *Atlantic Slave Trade*, 110, 112, 123.

14. Philip D. Curtin, "Measuring the Atlantic Slave Trade," in *Race and Slavery in the Western Hemisphere: Quantitative Studies*, Stanley L. Engerman and Eugene D. Genovese, eds. (Princeton: Princeton University Press, 1975), 112; Curtin, *Atlantic Slave Trade*, 211.

Leone and the Bights of Benin and Biafra were the large suppliers. Exportation in this period was complicated by efforts to suppress the trade, as the African coast, largely north of the equator, was rather uncertainly patrolled by British and American naval vessels.

The pattern of imports into the Americas begins with Spanish America, which in the period to 1600 absorbed three-fifths of the American total. In this same period the eastern Atlantic island of São Tomé took off more African slaves than Spanish America, and the Old World in all imported more slaves than the New. In the seventeenth century Brazil established its place as the foremost importer of slaves—a place it held during the remainder of the slaving era. Brazil in this century obtained 40 percent of the whole American import, its total of 560,000 slaves representing an elevenfold increase over the previous period. Spanish America, the British Caribbean, and the French Caribbean followed in rank, Spanish America receiving nearly twice as many slaves as the French Caribbean.

In the span of years from 1701 to 1810 the Brazilian proportion of the trade diminished, the ranking of receiving regions altered, and new regions significantly appeared. Brazil's share dropped to 31 percent, the British Caribbean with 23 percent of the total took second place, the French Caribbean third, and Spanish America fourth. The Dutch Caribbean became an important importing region, increasing its imports almost twelvefold over the seventeenth century. British North America (after 1776, the United States), whose imports had been minute before 1700, became a large importing region. The Old World was importing slaves in negligible numbers.[15]

In the period from 1811 to 1870 Brazil conspicuously was the dominant American market, taking three-fifths of all imports; the British, Dutch, and Danish Caribbean had stopped importing; and Spanish America, now chiefly Cuba and Puerto Rico, imported a larger number of slaves than it had in the 110 years of the preced-

15. Curtin, *Atlantic Slave Trade*, 268, lists no imports into the Old World after 1700. The matter is little explored, but in the papers of the Duke of Chandos there is the astonishing record of English importation, through the South Sea Company, of about 150 African boys and girls into Lisbon, "where we are given to understand they'll come to a good Market." Chandos Letterbook, 1721–1722, Henry E. Huntington Library, MS film 417.

ing period. Much reduced in extent, the French Caribbean was third in importance; and the United States was fourth. Throughout the long slaving era, within these changing, broad contours of importing as well as exporting regions, there were shifts of American and African markets.

In the conduct of the trade there was a tendency for some merchants in the major ports to specialize in slaving. Early in the trade's history merchants engaged in a general trade, and slaves were one of many commodities. Many merchants engaged in only one slave venture. By the middle of the eighteenth century communities of merchants who specialized in slaving, though not to the exclusion of other trades, existed. They habitually sent out slave vessels. Often the sons or grandsons of slave-ship captains and merchants, they reveal a familial pattern, which took form in partnerships of fathers and sons and brothers. Possessing accumulated knowledge of the trade, they were quick to adapt, searching out new sources of slaves in Africa, the best markets in America, the consumer demands of Africans, and ever bargaining on such matters as insurance and bills of exchange. Innovators, they copper-bottomed their ships and availed themselves of advances in tropical medicines.

The profits derived from the slave trade are no longer looked upon by historians as princely. It is recognized that the business was intricate, comprehending the formation of the venture in Europe or America, the buying of slaves from autonomous Africans, the selling of slaves to often indebted Americans, and uncertainty of outcome. Average profits were perhaps no more than 10 percent, and investors could readily have done as well in a host of other enterprises. The trade was marked by hazard, and it is perhaps the speculative trait, with an occasional chance for large profits, that explains the persistence of the trade. Moreover, there were national differences in profit margins. The Danes and the Dutch did not fare well, the former finding it "a losing trade" and the latter making a meager return of just over 2 percent for the one hundred voyages of the Middleburgh Company. The merchants of Nantes, subsidized by the Crown, earned only 6 percent; it was the English merchants, with a return of 8 to 10 percent, who were probably the most successful. The returns were not impressive, and they serve to discount claims that the slave trade financed the Industrial Revolution in England and France.

It is true, as A. G. Hopkins has observed, that some persons—such as merchants and captains—did become rich through the trade in slaves. It is also true that some industries profited from the trade; these included sugar refining and the making of textiles, hardware, and guns. But the trade's contribution to industrialization, as these cases suggest, was specific and limited. Supply and demand in the domestic market was more important to industrialization than supply and demand in the African market. The bulk of England's foreign trade was not with Africa or the Americas but with Europe. Moreover, the capital flowed in both directions, and if traders financed industrialists, so too did industrialists finance traders. The formation of industrial capital was more complex than the working of the Atlantic slave trade.[16]

The notion that the business was enormously profitable is but one of many myths that have clustered about the trade. A major myth has concerned its size, exaggerated to as high as 50 million slaves transported, and commonly and carelessly stated to be about 15 million. The systematic and careful estimates of Curtin and others have trimmed the American importation to about 11 million.

Another popular misconception has been about the African transaction. It has been widely believed that slaves were procured through kidnapping by white men or unequal bartering between cunning whites and naive blacks. Historical research indicates that slaves were supplied to white traders by Africans, who procured their supplies through making war, consigning unfortunates for sale, and condemning criminals. Research further indicates that black traders had a high degree of sophistication, retaining sovereignty over forts and factories, collecting customs duties and business fees, organizing systems of supply and marketing, and showing discrimination in the commodities they would accept for slaves.

The most familiar misconception is of the Middle Passage, an unrelieved horror of suffering, brutality, and death. Outrage against the Middle Passage is surely not misplaced, but outrage alone does

16. Hopkins, *Economic History of West Africa*, 117 ff. For evidence of wealth among slave merchants and captains, see Robert Louis Stein, *The French Slave Trade in the Eighteenth Century: An Old Regime Business* (Madison: University of Wisconsin Press, 1979), 180–87, and Jay Coughtry, "The Notorious Triangle: Rhode Island and the African Slave Trade, 1700–1807" (Ph.D. diss., University of Wisconsin, 1978), 48–51.

not conduce to an understanding of the Atlantic crossing. The theme is intricate, and indubitably overcrowding, shackles, inadequate diet, epidemics, and high mortality were tragic elements. At the same time, economic self-interest fostered delivery of cargoes alive and well. Historical documents abound with proof of precautions taken to maintain the health of slaves. The death rate decreased in the eighteenth century. Historians now point to the slaves' health at the time of embarkation as a significant factor in explaining mortality at sea. Moreover, they have placed this mortality in a comparative context, showing the fearful tolls of white lives taken by the Atlantic and the tropics. Finally, they have assessed the state of tropical medical knowledge in the era of the slave trade.

The large number of blacks in twentieth-century America has seemed self-evident proof that a considerable portion of the enforced migration landed in North America. Historical investigation shows the contrary. North America was a late customer and a minor purchaser. The Atlantic slave trade was nearly three centuries old before it found a significant market in North America. By the date of abolition of the trade in 1808, the United States had received less than 6 percent of the whole migration. What is equally surprising, perhaps, in this misunderstood situation, is the predominance of Brazil, an early and persisting market that absorbed two-fifths of the entire trade. A corollary of these functions as markets is the realization that the United States was a minor carrier of slaves, Portugal a major one. Portugal, Great Britain, and France were the principal villains of the tragic drama, a fact often left out of the history books.

The legacy of the slave trade may be found on both sides of the Atlantic. As an outcome of the trade, the peopling of the Americas was vastly different from what it would have been had only Europeans migrated to the New World. The Americas are distinctive, in part because of the large African element in their population. Beyond this, the Americas grew more rapidly than they otherwise could have done because of black labor. The course of U.S. history has been continuously affected by the presence of blacks; the American Civil War is but the most dramatic illustration of this home truth.

Historians err in portraying the legislation prohibiting the slave trade as a final moral triumph. The slave trade continued following enactment of prohibitory laws. It continued often because nations closed their eyes to the clandestine traffic. It continued because the moral triumph was not sufficiently complete to dissuade individuals from taking part in the trade.

The slave trade was an aspect of labor exploitation that did not end with either abolition of the trade or even emancipation of the slaves. Systems of semiservitude such as apprenticeship, peonage, and contract supplanted the older system of slavery. As the demands for cheap labor persisted, new sources of labor that could be oppressed, that is, Asian, were sought. In the United States, black labor, agricultural and industrial, notoriously suffered exploitation long after freedom had been attained.

Racism alone cannot explain the exploitation of blacks by the Atlantic slave trade. But racism, described as white belief in the inferiority of blacks, permeated the policy of the carrying nations. Though it was once believed that racism was virtually nonexistent in the Iberian experience, historians in recent years have demonstrated that both the Portuguese and the Spanish looked upon blacks as unequals. The French, for all the fame of the *Code Noir,* kept Negroes a people apart, for example in 1777 prohibiting any black or mulatto, free or slave, from entering the kingdom of France. Racial prejudice on the part of Englishmen has recently been studied, and the phenomenon in U.S. history is a matter of global disrepute.[17]

In some measure a conventional Eurocentric view of history, shutting out racism, blacks, and Africa, has diverted attention from the Atlantic slave trade. With the more abundant knowledge now available, the time has come to acknowledge the Atlantic slave trade as a vital part of the history of the Western world.

17. C. R. Boxer, *Race Relations in the Portuguese Colonial Empire, 1415–1825* (Oxford: Clarendon Press, 1963); Emeka P. Abanime, "The Anti-Negro French Law of 1777," *Journal of Negro History* 64 (1979): 21–29; Winthrop D. Jordan, *White over Black* (Baltimore: Penguin Books, 1969).

Suggested Reading

Basic to the study of the Atlantic slave trade is Elizabeth Donnan, ed., *Documents Illustrative of the History of the Slave Trade to America,* 4 vols. (Washington: Carnegie Institution, 1930–1935).

Aiming to document every slave ship voyage is David Eltis, Stephen D. Behrendt, David Richardson, and Herbert S. Klein, *The Trans-Atlantic Slave Trade: A Database on CD-ROM* (Cambridge and New York: Cambridge University Press, 1999). The scholars unearthed material on more than 26,000 voyages.

Madeleine Burnside, *Spirits of the Passage* (New York: Simon & Schuster, 1997).

Michael H. Cottman, *The Wreck of the Henrietta Marie* (New York: Harmony Books, 1999).

Philip D. Curtin, *The Atlantic Slave Trade: A Census* (Madison: University of Wisconsin Press, 1969).

Bernard Martin and Mark Spurrell, eds., *The Journal of a Slave Trader (John Newton), 1750–1754* (London: Epworth Press, 1962). The Newton literature is large; his own writings run to twelve volumes, and biographies and studies abound.

James A. Rawley, *The Transatlantic Slave Trade: A History* (New York: W. W. Norton, 1981).

David Richardson, "The Eighteenth-Century British Slave Trade: Estimates of Its Volume and Coastal Distribution in Africa," *Research in Economic History* 12 (1989): 151–95.

David D. Wallace, *The Life of Henry Laurens* (New York: G. P. Putnam's Sons, 1915).

Index

Abolition, of slave trade, 168, 178–79; debate over timetable for, 136–37; efforts toward, 104–5, 163–64; by European countries, 151, 162–64; London as center of, 123–24, 126; opponents' projected results of, 129–31; opposition to, 124–28, 130–36; Parliament abolishing, 147–48; Parliament's debate over, 133–37, 141–48; Parliament's steps toward, 136–37, 144–45; vs. regulation, 133–34; Wilberforce's proposals for, 130, 135–36, 138–40

Act of 1698, regulating slave trade, 12–13

Adams, John, 94

Addington, Henry, 141

Africa, 3, 5, 76, 132; bilateral vs. triangular trade with, 16, 29, 48, 56, 103; coast patrols to prohibit slave trade, 151–53, 160, 175; company vs. separate traders in, 11–14; competition for trade with, 6–8, 79; effects of slave trade on, 2, 168–71; England's nonslave trade with, 16, 34–36; English forts/castles in, 62–70, 100, 105; English in, 13, 70, 106; English trading strategies in, 46–50, 90–91; Europeans in, 6–7, 167, 171; introduction of new crops to, 17, 168–69; London in trade with, 29–30, 126; navigation along western coast, 3, 105–6; population of, 168–69; proposal to limit slaving in, 140–

41; responsibility for slave trade, 145; ships clearing London for, 20–21, 24–28, 31–35, 41; slavery in, 119–20, 134–35; slaves from, 174–75; slave trade within, 48, 106, 155, 169. *See also* Trade goods, for Africa

African (slave ship), 114–15

African Association, 106

African Committee of Liverpool, 104

Africans, 4–5, 120, 178; European trade with, 6, 177; relations with white slavers, 111–12, 120. *See also* Race/racism; Slaves

African Squadron, 151–54, 159–60

Agriculture: need for slave labor, 135–36; new crops introduced to Africa, 17, 168–69. *See also* Sugar cultivation

Ajayi, J. F. Ade, 173

Akinjogbin, I. A., 99–101, 107

Albion, 14

Alcohol, as trade goods, 16, 170

Alexander VI, 6–7

Alleghany, USS, 153–54

"Amazing Grace" (Newton), 108–9, 117

Amelia, 92

American Revolution, 25, 34–35, 94, 103

Americas, 17, 58, 162; black vs. white migrations to, 166–68; given to Spain by papal bull, 6–7; Morice's trade with, 48, 51, 54. *See also* North America; specific countries

Anderson, A., 102

147–48; demographics of, 5, 40, 51, 121, 169; effects of, 17, 161–62, 168–71, 176; enforcement of ban on, 149–54, 156, 158–60, 163–65; English role in development of, 58, 83–85, 96; English wanting protection for, 12, 75–77; extent of, 19, 87, 171–73; histories of, 83, 168; illegal, 164, 179; import duties in, 61, 70–75, 88–89; individuals participating in, 52, 57, 153–55; influences on, 34–35, 92, 138, 166; Laurens in, 88–91, 93; legacy of, 178–79; limits on, 142–44; London's importance in, 10, 18–30, 32, 41, 125; management/organization of, 14–15, 60–61, 106, 176; Morice in, 41–42, 54–55; New York in, 149, 161; Newton in, 108, 110–16, 119; opposition to, 108, 118, 150–51, 163–64; persistence of, 164, 176; profitability of, 17, 21, 24–25, 85, 89–90, 96, 107, 163, 176–77; projected effects of ending, 125, 127–28, 134, 147; regulation of, 85–86, 93, 104, 127, 130–31, 133, 139–41; relative importance of London, Bristol, and Liverpool in, 32–38, 39 table 1, 58. See also Abolition, of slave trade; Parliament; Slaves

Sloane, Hans, 61
Smith, Adam, 11
Smith, E. Delafield, 157
Smith, James, 156
Smith, Samuel, 131
Smith, Thomas, 63–64
Smith, William, 46, 56
Snelgrave, William, 42–43, 44, 47, 50, 52
Society for the Abolition of the Slave Trade, 104
Society of West Indian Planters and Merchants, 125–29, 134–36; on attempts to limit slave trade, 138, 143; rejecting attempts to abolish slave trade, 141–42, 145
South America, 3–4. See also Brazil

South Carolina, 72, 91; opposition to limits on slave trade, 85, 143; preferences in slaves' origins, 87–88; slavery in, 84, 96, 162; trade through Charleston, 82–83, 87–88. See also Colonies; United States
South Sea Company, 75; and London's role in slave trade, 20–21, 32, 41; supplying slaves, 58, 72–74, 85
Spain, 179; and British slave trade, 76–77, 79, 134, 144; slaves taken to colonies of, 73–74, 145, 172, 174–76; in slave trade, 43, 155, 157, 173–74; and slave trade ban, 164–65; territories of, 4, 6–8, 143; trade competition by, 6–7, 86. See also Asiento
Spears, John R., 152
Spooner, Charles, 130
Squirrel, 50
St. Ann, 103
Standard of living, relation to slavery, 162, 166
Starke, Thomas, 1
St. Domingue, 79; French control of, 7, 77, 138; slave revolt on, 135, 141
St. Eustatius, 7
St. Kitts, 115
St. Mary Woolnoth, 108, 118
Storer, Commodore, 154
St. Paul (slave ship), 92
St. Vincent, 132, 136
Sugar: in Atlantic system, 1, 4; consumption of, 2–3, 9, 17; prices of, 13, 16, 79–80
Sugar cultivation, 3–4, 77, 166–67
Sugar industry, 80; and abolition of slave trade, 129, 146–47; in colonial empires, 7–10; credit given to planters, 132–33; London's importance in, 10, 126; refining in, 10, 177; relation to slave trade, 79, 115, 166, 177; shipping in, 55, 79, 115; wealth from, 9–10
Survey of Trade, A (Wood), 168
Sweden, 8